D0881238

SHAKESPEARE

SHAKESPEARE

Poet and Citizen

———————◆———————

VICTOR KIERNAN

VERSO

London · New York

First published by Verso 1993
© Verso 1993
All rights reserved

Verso
UK: 6 Meard Street, London W1V 3HR
USA: 29 West 35th Street, New York, NY 10001-2291

Verso is the imprint of New Left Books

ISBN 0-86091-392-9

British Library Cataloguing in Publication Data
A catalogue record for this book is available from the British Library

Library of Congress Cataloging-in-Publication Data
A catalogue record for this book is available from the Library of Congress

Typeset by Leaper & Gard Ltd, Bristol
Printed in Great Britain by Bookcraft (Bath) Ltd

Contents

Foreword

The first of various drafts of this book (and of its intended sequel, concerned with the later half of Shakespeare's work) was written more than forty years ago. An author with such a confession to make must fear, like Mark Antony, that it can be taken only in 'one of two bad ways': either he has been deplorably sluggish, or he is offering his work as guaranteed by its age, like a cobwebbed bottle of port, to be much better than it really is. And during so unconscionably long a time he must have had many uneasy thoughts as to whether there is anything left to be said about a dramatist already so often – like Jehovah's name in *Doctor Faustus* – 'Forward and backward anagrammatized'; or whether he is not merely exposing himself to Swinburne's censure on the rash newcomer who seeks to 'append his name to the long scroll of Shakespearian parasites' (25). During these years critical opinion has undergone various shifts. Commentators of many persuasions seem, as Levin remarks in his survey of three recent decades, to feel bound to offer novel 'readings' of any play they discuss, each a 'complete interpretation' with its own 'thematic' key (*New Readings*, pref.; ch. 1). In the course of the hunt for buried treasures, some of the progress has been of a retrograde sort. Half a century ago it had come to be more or less recognized that Shakespeare, like every other artist, was a child of his times. Since then some 'New Critics' have appeared to 'see literature as non-referential, as having no connection with a world outside' (Rabkin 32). This is to turn Shakespeare into a solipsist.

Fortunately there has also been much writing of a more fertile kind; and meanwhile knowledge of Shakespeare's background has greatly expanded. Understanding of the professional conditions under which he worked has grown. Investigation of the condition of England in his lifetime, and its European setting, has gone much further. Thanks in good part to Marxist scholarship, what Rabkin calls 'the inscrutability of history' (61) has been a good deal diminished. It is the possible connecting threads between what Shakespeare wrote and the environment whose air he breathed that are the subject of this study.

We know little more than before, it is true, about his own life; his inner life must remain a mystery. Still, there is plentiful evidence of links between art and society in other times and places. By thinking about the grand problem of Shakespeare, we may hope to learn a little more. We have a secure starting point in the fact – daunting as it may be – that in one brief time and one small place it was possible for a poet to compose both the greatest tragedies and the finest comedies ever written. What is attempted here is a survey of the picture of human life in its social or collective aspects, and their sway over the individual, that can be derived from Shakespeare's writings; with the caveat that his impressions of life cannot be separated from the growth of his powers of expression as a poet.

Part I sketches his historical setting, and some guidelines for a search for meanings in the plays. There is no ideal order of reading for these. In the decade roughly of the 1590s Shakespeare was writing, side by side, two very different groups of plays: the English Histories, and the farces and romantic Comedies – testimony to the extraordinary diversity of his genius and the contradictory impulses, from a country in the turmoil of change, that nourished it. He must have found it refreshing to possess two such territories, and come and go between them. Here the two are looked at separately, beginning with the Histories; each play by itself, and then the contribution of all of them to specific leading themes. Nearly all the plays offer difficulties over dates of writing or production, which I have not tried to delve into. But the Histories, except for *King John*, clearly fall into two sequences, the historically later one written first. Together they cover the years from 1398 to 1485, ending on the threshold of the Tudor period. With the Comedies there are more uncertainties, and no arrangement yields a consistent line of development. But there are evidently early, middle and later stages, and within these what seems the least unlikely order has been chosen. It is to be remembered that Shakespeare was not a freelance writer but one of a theatre partnership, and cannot always have been free to follow his own bent.

In between the two main groups have been placed the miscellaneous set of other compositions. There are two early tragedies; and two long narrative poems, published in 1593 and 1594, which occupied an interval when the theatres were closed because of plague. The Sonnets were probably beginning to be written – not for publication – about the same time, and may have gone on down to any date before 1609, when they (or all of them that we have) appeared in print. All or some of them are, or may be, the only utterances we possess of Shakespeare speaking directly for himself. Finally, in Part V some general reflections are gathered together about what appears to be his unfolding outlook on life; his sense of how the happenings that affect mankind come about, and the direction of his thinking or feeling towards the work of his later career, with Tragedy predominant.

It would be an advantage to be able to include quotations liberally; but in a study seeking to cover so much ground there is room only for very brief ones. Readers, it may be hoped, will have copies of Shakespeare at hand, and look up some of the references supplied in the text. These are to the Cambridge edition edited by Quiller-Couch and Dover Wilson. (Line numbers are omitted when the scenes they belong to are brief.) References to books and articles also are given in brackets in the text, by the author's name and a brief title if more than one work of his or hers has been cited. The Bibliography contains details of all writers and works quoted, but of no others.

The date or approximate time of writing of each play is taken from the latest (1989) edition of Harbage's catalogue; the order in which the plays have been arranged is in not quite exact conformity with this.

Over the years I have benefited by profitable discussions with more people than can be recorded here. One who cannot be omitted is my wife, a memorizer of Shakespeare from childhood and still an infallible remembrancer and an ardent disputant. A second is my friend Sydney Bolt, himself a writer on Shakespeare and the donor of a number of helpful volumes from his collection.

PART I

A Time Out of Joint

1

Late Tudor England

If there was ever a Merrie England, it was not in William Shakespeare's time. During the sixteenth century population levels in Europe were rising; between 1500 and 1650 England's may have risen from about two to five million. This put heavy strains on inelastic societies and economies. One effect, emphasized recently by J.A. Goldstone, was to increase the number of younger people, always likely to be the most restless; and the fact that most property – in land especially – went to eldest sons, added to the number of discontented juniors. Massive unemployment, homelessness, vagrancy, were evidence of how gravely England's social framework was being dislocated. There was much migration, chiefly from the countryside into the towns; above all into London, whose population, further swollen by foreigners, by 1600 was approaching 200,000, immensely greater than that of any other English town. Within the limits of the medieval 'City' the capital was self-governing, with an elaborate oligarchical constitution; its wealth made it a political factor that no government could ignore. Outside the walls were suburbs and dismal slums.

Too many commentaries on Shakespeare's background have been concerned with Elizabethan society as a whole, Krieger observes in his Marxist study, whereas it is often necessary to think of discordant social classes (66). England had a nobility of great landowners, few in numbers but powerful in their own provinces and influential nationally. Under it was a large and growing gentry-class, whose support – or at least assent – was indispensable to the government. There was more social mobility in the later sixteenth century than before or after, particularly in terms of landownership. Many were rising into the gentry; others were sinking out of it. These were fewer, but there were loud laments over the ruination of old families, weighed down by debts or dissipation, which could be viewed as an index of national decay. On the land, where most people lived, semi-capitalist relations were spreading most quickly. Landlords rented out their estates to substantial farmers, who worked the soil with the help of hired labour – a hybrid system never so widespread anywhere else as it came to be in England. Population growth was accompanied by rising food prices, which benefited landowners and yeomen-farmers but depressed real wages, while more and more smallholders were sinking to the degraded status of farm labourers. Those who were doing well were prospering more at the expense of the poor than by virtue of any productive improvements. Hardships of poverty were augmented by a prolonged climatic down-turn, at its worst during Shakespeare's lifetime; bad harvest years were recurrent, a series of them occurring in the later 1590s.

Penury and misery threw a heavy shadow over the scene Shakespeare was born into. 'Sturdy beggars', or tramps, inspired alarm, and were brutally treated by way of reprisal. But there were always some writers ready to protest, even if ineffectively, against rampant social injustice. In a play by Robert Wilson the clown reproached the greedy rich and prophesied that oppressors would end in hell (Bradbrook, *Player* 189). In 1608 a pamphlet by Thomas Dekker expressed a Londoner's disillusion with ideas of rural felicity, on finding 'the poore husbandman made a slave to the riche farmour; the farmour racked by his landlord ...' (*Belman* 109). Excessive profiteering might be condemned by the government itself, because liable to provoke disorders. A Privy Council circular to Justices of the Peace on 22 September 1597 denounced 'engrossers' who were trying to corner food supplies, as miscreants 'more lyke to wolves or cormorants than to naturall men'. Such sermonizing was unlikely to soften hard hearts. Next year the major of Dartmouth was accused of embezzling part of a grain supply intended for the hungry poor (J.T. Kelly 126).

For its favourites life held new comforts. Multitudes of families of all ranks from yeoman upward were building themselves new houses, with chimneys and glass windows. Women of the better-off classes seemed to foreign visitors surprisingly free, though they were always being reproved from the pulpit for wanting more freedom than could be good for them. The 'middle classes' were multifarious, ranging from very rich to very modestly furnished. There were families and groups that can be labelled 'bourgeois', but there was scarcely as yet a 'bourgeoisie', with a collective line of development and ambition. Capitalism was forging ahead amid a complex of other impulses, material or moral, at work in early modern Europe, which may be summed up as 'individualistic'.

Many self-made men were eager to become *bourgeois gentilhommes*, while those above them who were shrewd enough to keep up with the times were now *gentilhommes bourgeois*, esteeming profits as highly as pedigrees. Competition was in many ways the keynote of the age. Each man must push himself to the front, without too much scruple about means, or be elbowed aside. A highly litigious spirit was stirring; lawyers were in great demand. It was a society that could breed all kinds of morbidities (Stafford-Clark 29), an age of anxiety. Madmen thronged the drama. But it was equally an age of opportunity and progress. Hardships and tensions do not by themselves engender literature; they can help to do so when they are interacting with opposite factors, fresh inspiration, new ideals. Individualism separates, but can also recombine, by amplifying men's ability to respond to other personalities. No era before that of Bacon and Shakespeare had felt so deeply the truth that 'No man is an island'.

Social individualism in the western Europe of the sixteenth and seventeenth centuries had its opposite pole in authoritarian government. It was the age of the 'New' or 'Absolute' monarchies. In England the Tudor dynasty seized power and ended the Wars of the Roses in 1485; it lasted until the death of Elizabeth in 1603. It was often arbitrary enough in its methods; but it differed from the Continental model in being less despotic, less well equipped with authority to levy taxes, and therefore less able to build up a standing army to enforce its will. It depended for supplementary revenues on Parliament; this institution therefore stayed alive, when most of the many similar ones on the Continent were dying out. It met only at irregular intervals, when the government wanted it; but little by little its importance was growing. There was an increasing appetite for seats in the House of Commons, where the gentry were heavily overrepresented. A bulky bureaucracy like the French was as much out of the Tudors' reach as a regular army, and local adminis-tration had to be left, under loose government supervision, to town councils, reliably undemocratic, and landowners, still half-feudal, acting as Justices of the Peace.

Nationalism was a buttress to authority; it was growing, along with individualism and conscious class division, in a union of contraries. As everywhere it was a product of changing forces, economic and cultural, and had close links with religion in a Europe now bitterly divided over the control of routes to Heaven, as well as to the Indies. In England it could be identified with a Tudor mystique and a 'cult of personality' on which Elizabeth depended heavily. She was easy to idealize, as England's preserver through long years; but ordinary Englishmen seem to have had very mixed feelings about the regime they lived under. Her court was a synonym for depravity and arrogance; there must have been a strong admixture here of middle-class feeling against a luxurious aristocracy and its pretensions. Among the noble families, old and new, civil wars had been exchanged for a more modern form of power struggle, with the court as an arena for intrigues and feuds. Politics was still a danger-ous game, and through the Tudor epoch a long line of ambitious men followed one another to the block, ending with the Earl of Essex, Elizabeth's erratic favourite, in 1601.

From Mary Tudor's death in 1558, a Church of England was being pushed or pulled together. In the earlier years it was very much a makeshift: conservatively episcopalian in structure, partly Calvinist in theology. Church attendance was compulsory (though this was impossible to enforce in full); the main Sunday business was the reading out of Homilies which expounded the duty of unquestioning obedience to government and law, under penalty of hell fire. But repeated official changes of religion in mid century had made for indifference. There was a large, only slowly dwindling number of Catholics, or half-Catholics; but war with Spain, at first undeclared, intensified patriotic feelings and helped to merge them with radical Protestantism, or Puritanism, and its Calvinistic creed. 1588, the Armada year of triumph, was the high-water mark of Puritan influence before the 1630s, and brought on a premature attempt to rid the Church of bishops which suffered a sharp check from authority.

During and after the 1590s, as a result – fortunately for the drama then reaching its heights – Puritanism was on the defensive, obliged to content itself with quieter activities. Its strength was among the middling classes, including sections of the gentry. It was growing from below – among urban artisans, small traders and the like, compelled to practise thrift, sobriety and prudence in order to survive; and from above – sponsored by bigger businessmen and serious-minded magistrates, in whose eyes its virtues were needed to form good citizens and zealous employees. Economic progress, increasingly on capitalist lines, could not go on without reliable, conscientious workmen (Collinson, ch. 5). Drunkenness, vice, time-wasting frivolities like the theatre, were to be condemned because they made workers – London 'prentices, for instance – less industrious, and might make them unruly. Most of the poor, all the same, continued to prefer ale, when they could get it, to prayer.

A rough balance of forces prevailed, at any rate in London, between aristocracy, headed by the Court, and middle classes, led by the City; each camp with many dividing-lines of its own. This, and a government not much interested in theology so long as it did not disturb the political order, gave England an invaluable interval during which the pressure of religion on minds open to ideas was greatly relaxed. There was air for breathing by men, Shakespeare among them, ready to profit by this degree of freedom – very exceptional in Europe then and long after – and think for themselves. They might take religious ethics seriously, while troubling themselves very little about dogmas. As users of the English language they benefited from the various translations available of the Bible, much of whose phraseology was passing into common speech. They could not be unaffected by the misgivings about the state of the human soul that were spreading and deepening along with social tensions, and were at last to break out in the 'Puritan revolution'. In a wider view these uneasy, even morbid sensations were part of a general expansion of human consciousness. Self-examination stimulated curiosity about both depths and heights of the human personality, and accompanied questioning of the world and all its laws.

It was a maxim of statesmanship, warranted by Machiavelli, that the best – if not the only – way to avert strife at home was to engage in wars abroad (Hale; Kiernan, 'War'). The New Monarchies were habitually at war. Victories and conquests were their most potent means of impressing their subjects. England was involving itself in the affairs of western Europe, as well as pushing on the conquest of Ireland. English forces assisted the Revolt of the Netherlands against Spanish rule; in France they gave aid to the Protestant leader Henry of Navarre, who inherited the throne (as Henri IV) and made sure of it by turning Catholic in 1598 but granting religious toleration. To fill the English ranks, conscription often had to be relied on; the system, cheap but inefficient, pressed heavily on the poor, and war was popular chiefly among those who did not have to fight. By some moralists it was condemned, and middle-class attitudes – except to defensive action, as against the Armada – were often ambivalent. Puritan influence could favour continuance of the Spanish war; Spain was the champion of popery, and also represented Empire and its gold, which some of the merchantry were eager for a share in.

Shakespeare belonged to a period of half-dawn, when an old order and its panorama of life were fading or crumbling and a new one was only fitfully taking shape. History and mythology jostled together, magic and science, theology and reason. Such a situation might well be ideal for stirring poetic impulses. Although in early modern times the higher classes in western Europe were drawing apart, in social habits and cultural tastes, from the mass of the people, there was still much common ground. Well into the seventeenth century there was a reading public avid for stories borrowed from or imitating old romances of chivalry, or tales of fairyland (Wright, esp. ch. 11). They could blend well enough with classical literature. Ovid's storehouse of mythology was being translated after 1560 and won many hearts, Shakespeare's among them.

In his far-off corner of Europe, and with a brief working life of barely more than two decades, Shakespeare might seem as if bounded into a nutshell. That he could nevertheless become king of infinite space owed much to the fact that English culture was not suffering from insularity, but in many ways was part of a cosmopolitan whole. He read Montaigne, took plots from Italian novels; he was very English, but was also a European phenomenon: his later universal appeal is a confirmation of this. Well-off families were sending their sons abroad to learn. Publishing was enjoying vigorous growth. Literacy was keeping pace with it, in London spreading down to all but the lowest levels (Stone 68, 79), and with it a remarkable degree of interest in words, idioms, the capacities of the English language. For an increasing variety of employments, education was a necessary passport (Trevor-Roper 27). For the intellectual cream, whose members might be also men of affairs, the times could hold incitements to immense undertakings. Bush cites Bacon's *Instauratio Magna*, Spenser's *Faerie Queene*, Raleigh's *History of the World*, as each 'the partial accomplishment of an impossibly vast design' (262). Rowse writes of Dr Dee and his circle as examples of an 'insatiable passion to know about the unknown and unknowable' (*Renaissance* 285). Marlowe's Tamburlaine could talk of 'climbing after knowledge infinite' (Part I.ii.7); words highly inappropriate in so barbaric a mouth, but perfectly characteristic of his creator's era.

2

Society and Art

In a lecture in 1949 R.H. Tawney maintained that nothing is known – and implied that nothing can be known – about links between the art of an age and its economy; our business is to admire genius, not to try to explain it (33–4). Turgenev showed more insight when he praised his admired philosopher Belinsky for recognizing that 'in the development of every people a new literary epoch comes before every other, that without experiencing and going beyond it, it is impossible to move forward' (115). Lukács credited art with a still more direct contribution when he wrote that the more intricate the problems of a changing society, 'the greater the part literature can play in social evolution, in the ideological preparations for some great crisis in social relations' (*Realism* 107).

Since the late eighteenth century this has been the task especially of the novel, with its power of exploring situations whose facts are becoming comprehensible; for an era like Shakespeare's, with charts still mostly guesswork, the poetic drama offered a uniquely fitting means of expression, on a plane less realistic but more highly imaginative. Hazlitt contrasted Chaucer's thoughts, each 'separate, labelled, ticketed', with the 'sociability' of Shakespeare's, all tumbling into one another (*Characters* 71). It was partly a difference between narrative and drama, but akin also to that between dry land and sea; Shakespeare's endlessly combining images have an effect of light reflected from rippling waves, as in Impressionist painting. They mirrored an England in a state of fluid change, as Shakespeare's own art always was. Poetic drama has a universalizing nature; the changeful times it has accompanied have lifted men, by accentuating their consciousness, to heightened awareness of elemental things shared by all.

It may be conceivable, but is extremely unlikely, that Shakespeare could have written as he did about war, death, property, all the while contemplating their grimness from an Olympian peak of detachment. Joseph Conrad disclaimed any moralizing intention in one of his novels, but added that 'even the most artful of writers will give himself (and his

morality) away in about every third sentence'. Shakespeare grew up in
the tradition of the old 'morality' plays, Fripp writes: 'The ancient
didactic clings to him, and he has no wish to cast it away' (66–70). It was
part of a general consensus that literature can be justified only by a
serious purpose. It was conventional wisdom with Elizabethan men of
letters, as with Hamlet, that Art should hold a mirror up to Nature, or
social reality; and the mirror of Art is a magic one which does not merely
photograph but selects, magnifies, colours, shows things unseen. A poet's
mind is 'a mirror by which the soul receives visions', in a modern critic's
words (Beckerman 28). It seems misconceived of another critic to assert
of Shakespeare that 'there is never anything outside his plays that he
wanted to "say"' (Frye, *Shakespeare* 2). On the contrary, they are full of
notions, interpolations, of his own that may have little or nothing to do
with their plots.

His English Histories, the most substantial part of his output before
about 1600, raise the essential problems of human nature and society
which underlie his later, greatest writing. In his time there was no
political activity going on that might have attracted him. He could not
be, whether he would have wished it or not, a political citizen like his
great successor Milton; but he was more – at least more directly – a
political poet. With few forerunners, he was more strongly drawn to
national history-writing than any of his fellow-playwrights; this is
enough to prove his strong concern with affairs of state. That he wrote
unmatched political plays can only appear 'a strange paradox' to a reader
bent, like Palmer, on convincing himself that Shakespeare's sole interest
was in 'the private mind and heart of the individual' (vi). Pope found it
'perfectly amazing' that he should display such skill at presenting 'great
and public scenes of life', as he so often did, and could only suppose that
the poet knew his world 'by Intuition' (Smith 49). It is more natural to
suppose an affinity between his temperament and interests, and the
spectacle of public affairs, men in action. As Dover Wilson said, his
numerous topical allusions show him brimming with interest in current
events and personalities, 'the real background of his plays' (*Shakespeare*
13). (With this may be coupled Saintsbury's warning that as evidence for
dating they are 'open to the gravest suspicions' ['Life and Plays' 175–6]).

Kenneth Muir could descry no philosophy in the plays beyond 'a
blend of medieval morality, pious platitudes, and stoical consolation'
(*Singularity* 135). Coleridge took an ampler view, and pronounced
Shakespeare 'not only a great poet, but a great philosopher' (*Shakespeare*
58). As regards politics, while some have denied him any interest in
men's collective life, others have attributed to him strenuous political
convictions of a sort better suited to the most philistine of petty
functionaries. L.B. Campbell discovered in the Histories 'a dominant

political pattern characteristic of the political philosophy of his age' (6) –
of the official Church and its Homilies, that is. Caroline Spurgeon found
in his imagery a deep-seated fear of social disruption, an almost mystical
attachment to social harmony (75). For all conservative students the key-
word has been Order.

It is easy enough to quote passages embodying this message –
utterances of an archbishop in *Henry V* or a merry old *bon vivant* in
Coriolanus – and to conclude that 'Shakespeare's thought was in fundamental agreement with the prevalent views of his day' (Phillips 4, 94).
But Shakespeare was a dramatist, and had to make such characters talk as
they would in life. It is by no means so easy to believe that England's
foremost poet, in a time of profound social disturbance and distress, was
a conservative to the backbone. He was on his way to becoming a man of
property, it is true; but property was of many kinds, and was to be ranged
before long in very different political camps. As to principles, we may
recall Prince Hal's ironical remark to Poins: 'thou art a blessèd fellow to
think as every man thinks' (*2H.IV* II.ii). This is surely Shakespeare
speaking, and disclaiming in advance the average-man opinions so often
ascribed to him.

It may often be a safe rule that what his characters say when playing
an active part in the story belongs to them: when they turn away to
generalities, the ideas are likely to be his. We are best served when the
two things converge. We sometimes hear him speaking through the
mouths of his villains. Shylock, not Portia, denounces the cruelties and
injustices of Venice. Richard Crookback's soliloquies are not self-
disclosure alone, but a running commentary on the follies and vices of
his feudal world. The final test of when Shakespeare believed, or took
seriously, what his men and women were saying must always be his
language, and how much conviction it carries.

It must no doubt be true that he, like any other sensible person,
disliked the thought of anarchic disorder. It is about the *causes* of disorder
that he must have differed from many others. Evidently he had a vivid
sense of the fragility of civilization, and the chaos it might fall into. He
was willing on occasion to join in preaching nationalism of the most
aggressive sort, as a prophylactic. A better, more permanent security, a
new equilibrium of individual and society, was harder to find. Shakespeare was exploring confusion, instability, within human beings, as well
as in the State ruling over them by the grace of God. Like the more clear-
sighted of the Romantics of later days, he was deploring not the passing
away of a rigid feudal order but the loss of genuine human ties supposed
to have once existed. His ideal (as we may at least glimpse it) was not the
Order of a Metternichian police state but a community with a natural
harmony of its own, growing out of men's feelings for one another and

for their common tasks. It was a dream or fantasy of a future more than of the past; it could be transposed most persuasively into the mythic imagery of the 'music of the spheres', in the idyllic garden scene at the close of *The Merchant of Venice*, following the anger and hatred of the courtroom.

An orderly – or order-worshipping – society, like the France of Louis XIV, can be expected to have its reflection in a formal, well-disciplined type of art. Elizabethan drama combined energy and imagination with a striking indifference to form. Intensity of feeling – immediate, consuming – was its soul. England combined, like its drama, 'immortal longings' and much dislocation, a turmoil of contrary impulses. Shakespeare's plays were no exception. And in recent years, 'Order' has been losing ground as an answer to all his social questionings; more note has been taken of the 'scepticism, tensions, and equivocations' of political thinking in his time' (Berry 231; Kettle), as well as of his own in-dependence of judgement.

He may fairly be called a 'progressive': a man, that is, dissatisfied in many ways with things as they were, and wanting to see changes for the betterment of the human lot. He can be called so only with due caution, because in his day no clear lines of division had been drawn, or programmes advanced, except over some matters of the Church and foreign policy. There were no two 'sides', one recognizably more forward-looking than the other. Instead there was a rising hubbub of controversy over miscellaneous contentious issues. We cannot enrol him as an adherent of a defined class, a trumpeter of its views. There were no 'parties' for him to join; though by the time of his death or soon after, the beginnings of a nationwide split were to become visible. Meanwhile, instead of consistent attitudes there were 'irreducible contradictions within outlooks and codes' (Heinemann, 'Drama' 162).

In a 1938 Shakespearian controversy among Soviet scholars, the most helpful view (not the most favoured) was that of I.M. Lifshitz, who explained the gropings and uncertainties of great writers of the past in terms of 'objective class confusion', absence of distinct class conscious-ness (11). It may be that the same factor helps to explain their greatness: they had no shibboleths, coined by others, to fall back on, no band-wagons to tie themselves to. Brecht adopted a similar view of Shake-speare and his fellow-writers: as men living in an uncharted space between declining feudalism and nascent capitalism, and echoing the clash of values between them (Heinemann, 'Brecht' 206–7). An example of the blurring of social horizons can be seen in the readiness of London 'prentices and civic patriots to enjoy tales where great city merchants and benefactors of past times were extolled as patricians, as well able as any belted earl to display warlike prowess when need arose (Stevenson 6, etc.).

Even on the battlefields of the 1640s the issues men were fighting over look far less clear to the historian than they did to the combatants, who thought – or talked – in the kind of abstractions habitual to men in action all through history. The civil war was a 'bourgeois revolution' in the sense that it brought the bourgeoisie a bigger share of power. But the bourgeoisie was seldom seen on those battlefields; and it is the same in Shakespeare's plays. There is 'not a single bourgeois character of significance' there, it has been said, except Shylock (Sinsheimer 84). Somehow one cannot imagine a businessman talking in verse. Noblemen have never declaimed metrically either, but we swallow the fiction of their doing so because we think of them as a small, remote, powerful race, and because their lives were passed under the towering banners of conflict and death.

The sources Shakespeare took his plots from – annals, legends, folk-tales – had nothing to tell him about rising middle classes. He belonged to these himself; but it was a truthful enough instinct that kept them out of his Histories. The doings of money-men, entrepreneurs, have been of vast historical importance, but not often heroic. When swords were out they were usually in the background, ready to pick up lost property, like the traders who followed Roman armies and the rest and bought up the soldiers' plunder cheap. In Shakespeare's time there was a bourgeoisie ruling Holland, but the fight for freedom was mostly left to foreign mercenaries led by the great feudal house of Orange, which was not even Dutch. England's bourgeoisie has always been typical of its species in wanting to enter the aristocracy, not to overthrow it. Among Shakespeare's contemporaries admiration of commerce, or capitalism, was shared by only a few, 'whereas his suspicion of it was shared by nearly all' (McVeagh 52).

It is easier in some ways to see what Shakespeare was against than what he was for. There were social types for which he had a special distaste, like the boorish landowner Thurio in *Two Gentlemen*, or the foppish courtier in *Henry IV Part 1* – both of whom would have followed the standard of Charles I. But besides Cavaliers and Roundheads there was a third camp, of the common people, in the 1640s a mostly silent majority, with little liking for either idle rich or busy moneygrubbers. Shakespeare could sympathize with the hardships that sometimes goaded them into revolt. His rebel leader Jack Cade, with a rough-and-ready mission of putting down kings and grandees and setting a new nap on the commonwealth (*2H.IV* IV.ii.5), may not have dropped out of his mind, any more than out of English history. In the 1640s the Levellers were to put it into more modern guise.

Shakespeare could draw at least on a reservoir of the fantasy-life of common people, and an oral record of their experience of reality.

Elizabethans were heirs to a treasury of folk-tale and myth, enshrining fears, dreams, legends of centuries, waiting to be turned to account as it could only be through an art form like Shakespearian drama. Another medium in which wisdom or feeling of the past was preserved was the proverb. Shakespeare cited an astonishing range of proverbial sayings, far more than any other English poet except Chaucer (Obelkevich 56). We can hardly think it beyond him to realize at times that what was disagreeable in the plebs, from volatile thinking down to garlic breath and sweaty caps, was not born with them but brought about by the degradation to which class society condemned them.

Writers and artists have been more eloquent in denial or protest than in affirmation. Evils they attack are known, tangible; improvements they hope for are only floating in the air. But the old has to be undermined before it can be demolished and something better put in its place. Meanwhile the mouldering away of the old, morally if not physically, is more apparent than any budding of the new; hence the marked vein of deteriorationist thinking in Shakespeare's time, which found a way into some of his plays, along with the idea that the end of the world was at hand. Good things as well as bad were decaying, and he was clearly sensitive to the weakening of old social relationships, which must have been more obvious in London than anywhere. Yet somehow the climate of his plays, compared with that of any of the other playwrights, seems far more fully suffused with the warmth and pulse of life. His people show more interest in one another as human beings, more mutual awareness. They seem real to us because of the images they build up in other minds, and through this in our own.

He belonged by birth – and maybe by lifelong preference – not to London, where aggressive individualism was pushing hardest, but to Stratford, one of those many modest-sized towns that offered microcosms of a way of life destined to decay. With all its crudities and inequalities, the old order had linked folk together in a pattern smoothed and softened by use and wont, which had a place and a function, however humble, for all. Still, it was in many ways inert, dull-witted, stuck in the mud; the new order now forcing its way in was mentally far more alert. It could awaken some at least to the wants and concerns of others, more clearly than of old, even if its tendency was atomistic and might often encourage the selfish separation of man from man. We are free to read into Shakespeare's thinking a desire to preserve the best of the old world for the benefit of the new, by adapting its virtues to a changed setting.

We can see him, in other words, as far less a conservative than a 'conservator', a cherisher of civilized values deriving from all classes and from generations past and present. Between aristocracy and the moneyed strata lines of social distinction were clear, but they had not yet hardened

into political lines, and in fact never fully did so; this made it easier to
contemplate a blending of the better qualities prized by each. In the
heyday of fascism a socialist writer could feel that he was defending,
besides socialism, the best of a liberal tradition on which the heirs of its
bourgeois founders were turning their backs; Shakespeare might feel that
in drawing some of his portraits he was restoring what was worthy in an
old feudal–chivalrous tradition, debased now by courtiers and parasites.
In one way or another he was struggling all his life with the knightly
concept of Honour, a kind of honour not to be plucked from the moon,
like Hotspur's, but with a vital place in a real world. It was a problem of
rescuing men from a drift into moral scepticism or nihilism; part of a
'transvaluation of values', itself part of a long-drawn-out transition from
one epoch of history to another.

In the endowment of the 'middling sort', *honesty* might be said to
claim prime place, as honour did for those of blue blood. From this level
the poet's eye could travel downward to the plain simple qualities of
people of the most ordinary sort, the necessary foundation of any higher
culture. Great art has always, perhaps, had roots in the artist's longing to
reunite himself with the People from whom a divided society cuts him
off, to recapture a primal whole where a poet could address all his
fellow-men, as his forebears once did. Class division brings with it
fissures within the artist's consciousness; it may be surmised that when
Shakespeare tried to reconcile the ideals or standards of Englishmen, he
was at the same time trying, instinctively, to surmount inner discords of
his own.

It is a suggestive though disputable dictum of the novelist Somerset
Maugham (316–17) that all a writer's characters are aspects or particles
of himself. If this is even partially true, study of them offers the best clue
to his own personality. But his consciousness and that of his age are not
sealed off from each other; he must be supposed capable of entering into
the sensations of others, in a measure proportionate to the breadth of his
own sensibility. Thus Coleridge could say that a poet's understanding of
varied emotions grows less by his seeing them in people around him
than by 'the power of imagination proceeding upon the *all in each* of
human nature. By meditation, rather than by observation' (*Shakespeare*
410). And he himself can find outlet and relief for whatever disturbs or
excites him by being able to merge it with a human consciousness wider
than his own. If he can thereby rise above his imprisoned self, both an
artistic and a therapeutic purpose will be served.

It was the natural bent of a society reared on rugged individualism to
view each Shakespearian character as a four-square, free-standing statue.
Shakespeare cannot have thought, or felt life, in such terms; and it is
because his men and women are rooted in the conditions of his time,

most of all in its complex web of relationships, that they are so full of sap or vitality. They are alive, as Pushkin said, vibrant with diverse passions – not simply personifications, like Molière's people, of a single quality (Morozov 85). Shakespeare lived in a comparatively open, expansive society; Molière in one of stricter classification. To the Elizabethan listener emotions unfolded on the stage could have kinship with feelings of his own; the rhetoric of a power-hungry Tamburlaine or Richard III could seem like 'huge cloudy symbols' of his own more modest ambitions of rising in the world and outstripping his rivals. Walter Scott recognized Giles Overreach, the remorseless bloodsucker in Massinger's play, as 'the Richard III of middling life' (Lockhart ch. 25). Shakespeare's royal personages are not a narrow caste, apart from other men; good or bad, they are themselves men; and as M.E. Prior said, he makes use of them to display human feelings and actions at their most intense (102). For the same reasons they continue to have messages for us too: for men and women everywhere.

We must, on the other hand, be cautious of looking for precise 'meanings' in the plays. We must keep in mind 'one of the principles of mature Shakespeare, that of indeterminacy', openness to discrepant interpretations (Daniell 109). Many have been struck by the apparent detachment with which he lets each participant in turn pour out his mind. Very often – though not on essential moral issues – he throws out opposite suggestions as to what we should think, and leaves us to choose. This openmindedness to ideas marks him as a man of the 'interregnum' between old and new, when medieval rigidities were crumbling but modern thinking had not yet taken orderly shape. It was a time when cobweb-covered windows were opening, and far-off vistas were coming into sight.

It may be helpful to conjecture that what engrossed his mind in the act of composition was not the individuals for whom he was finding words, but rather a complex of which each formed a component. How could an author totally immersed in – or self-identifying with – Hotspur, and then Glendower, alternate between one and the other, minute by minute? His consciousness must seem to have been spread over some larger whole, embracing both of them, so that he was concerned not with each of them separately but with their unique interaction – somewhat as Bach, improvising a fugue, would have his subject and countersubject working together in his mind.

Shakespeare was not a preacher with a cut-and-dried gospel, as many of his contemporaries were, but a man who must often have been, like Othello, 'perplexed in the extreme' – about human life, and about his own fellow-countrymen in particular. He, like many who have lived in days when everything has been altering, must have felt acutely the lack of correspondence between things he grew up believing in – and might still hanker for – and newer realities or rationalities he could not shut his eyes to. He can often be quoted against himself, because on many crucial issues he felt, we must suppose – and painfully – opposing affinities. He has been credited with an immense sanity, and sometimes does seem to possess it; but we may need to think of this endowment as wrestling with deeply depressive moods. His must have been an extremely complex nature. Without its fundamental contradictions and extremes he could hardly have been both supreme tragedian and supreme comedian. There must have been saving qualities of balance, a sense of the ludicrous as well as the sublime in human existence, to keep him from being pulled to pieces.

Great poets, English poets especially, have been apt to make their appearance at moments of revolutionary upheaval. Shakespeare did not, as Milton did, live through a period of open conflict, though there was much of this both in the British Isles and on the Continent. But his lifetime coincided with the crossing of a steep watershed, and ended with revolution almost in sight: a return – in changed, but not altogether different, form – of the civil broils he had written so much about. Fractured consciousness in him went with deepening schism in his England. He could not be expected to read the riddles of coming events. No one else, even the philosopher-statesman Bacon, had any inkling of what lay beyond the gathering storm clouds. No one, even today, has a very clear comprehension of why it happened.

3

Shakespeare's Life

Kenneth Muir drew a valid distinction when he confessed that he had come to doubt the feasibility of 'relating Shakespeare's works to his private life', as he and O'Loughlin had earlier essayed to do, though he still held that the outlines of 'his development as an artist and of the development of his mind' were discoverable from the plays ('Shakespeare the Man' 9). What little we know from other sources of Shakespeare's life cannot, of course, be neglected. The outward contours of any artist's career must be important in helping to determine which facets of the life around him will be likely to set up vibrations in his artistic self.

About the middle of the sixteenth century Shakespeare's father John quitted his native village of Snitterfield for nearby Stratford, 'a well-to-do market town of some two thousand inhabitants' (Lee, *Life* 4), where he plied a mixture of trades, that of glover among them, and for nearly three decades prospered. Stratford was granted a charter in 1553, which means that William was familiar from boyhood with a community governing itself, if not very democratically; and his father rose to be an alderman, and in 1568 bailiff, the highest civic post. John's wife Mary was the youngest daughter of a wealthy farmer, Robert Arden, the leading branch of whose clan stood high in the county. William was thus, in a small way, an example of the intermixing of gentry and burghers that went on all over England. Arden was a Catholic, and in 1583 a more prominent Arden was executed for treason (Levi 19). There is reason to think that John Shakespeare, too, was a Catholic in private. With William, a half-nonconformist family background may have resulted in the tolerant spirit, the indifference to formularies, that seems manifest in his plays. They show, however, far more familiarity with the Bible than the works of any other playwright (Fripp 101; Boas, *Elizabeth* 67 ff.).

William was born in 1564, the eldest of five children – four of them sons – who survived infancy; he was no stranger to family life, which figures in so many diverse lights in his plays. Stratford had a free grammar school, where he may be supposed to have become a pupil; he would have acquired some grounding in Latin, and in later years may well have picked up a reading knowledge of French and Italian. Whether he ever became a wide reader has been queried (Hart 9); if not, his vast and ever-expanding vocabulary is all the harder to account for. From about 1575 his father's affairs were going downhill; he was never bankrupt, but for years he was harassed by debts and lawsuits, and lost his place on the town council. This was happening during William's adolescence, a sensitive time for him to be exposed to such a family comedown; it may well have left a permanent scar. Stratford too was going through hard times, and had to petition for tax relief in 1590, urging that with its trade in decay the poor 'now live in great penury and misery' (J.W. Gray 102). Early in his life Shakespeare was familiar with the spectre of poverty; it may have taught him both fellow-feeling with the poor, and a determination not to be condemned to a life of deprivation himself.

If the family's decline had a disorientating effect on him, one result may have been – if we can trust an old story – his poaching escapades and prosecution by the landowner Sir Thomas Lucy. Such an episode might kindle an early and lasting spark of radicalism, resentment at the arrogance of the rich. A less benign consequence of youthful recklessness – or so we can guess – was his marriage at eighteen to a young woman of twenty-six, the daughter of a respectable farmer, which was hastened by her pregnancy. It was a 'most unusual union', requiring, since he was a minor, his father's consent (Bradbrook, *Shakespeare* 18). A daughter was born in 1583, a twin son and daughter in 1585. Sundry touches scattered through some early plays warrant the suspicion that he was haunted by the image of a shrewish woman. 'To be slow in words is a woman's only virtue', says the servant Launce (*TGV* III.i.328). Hotspur thinks Glendower as tedious 'as a tired horse, a railing wife' (*1H.IV* III.i.159–60). 'Women are shrews, both short and tall', sings Master Silence (*2H.IV* V.iii.35). Clearer evidence of regret for a hasty marriage may be the almost obsessive disapproval of pre-marital sex to be found in plays as far apart as *Romeo and Juliet* and *The Tempest*.

At any rate, his wife was unlikely to be congenial company for long for a young man whose mind was developing as extraordinarily quickly as Shakespeare's must have been. From 1585 to 1592 he disappears from view. At some date – which may have been 1589 – he made his way to London, as other young Stratford men were doing. He may have been stage-struck already; touring actors visited his town, where he can be expected to have seen them. We never know him as a very youthful writer; if he made his start about 1590, he was already twenty-six. Plentiful money was to be made in the theatre business, but as Walter

Cohen says, not mainly by writers; he compiles a long list of poor, needy, ill-starred playwrights (171). Shakespeare was one of very few Eliza-bethan dramatists who were also regular actors, though as a performer he was not in the first flight, whereas by 1600 he was the most popular writer of all. No other playwright is known to have become a theatre shareholder, as he was, with an entitlement to 10 per cent of profits, from the opening of the new Globe Theatre in 1599. No one could well be more completely a man of the theatre, even if he was much else as well. His company, the 'Chamberlain's Men' – who on James I's acces-sion became the 'King's Men' – appear to have been a happy family.

He was lucky in entering the theatre about the date when various of its leading writers were disappearing from it; Greene died in 1592, Marlowe in 1593, Kyd in 1594 (Wilson, *Shakespeare* 48; Dobrée 245 ff.). Still, Shakespeare's rise cannot always have been easy going. Malcontents, men disgruntled over exclusion from the position they think due to them, are common in his plays, and in the earlier ones may sometimes be voicing frustrations of his own. Richard Crookback, in a curiously pathetic simile, pictures himself as a traveller

<blockquote>
lost in a thorny wood,
That rends the thorns and is rent with the thorns. (*3H.VI* III.ii.124 ff.)
</blockquote>

Properly licensed players, with a patron of high rank, were accepted by an Act of 1571 as a reputable profession, and might win both acclaim and wealth; but the upper-class view of them remained supercilious, the religious view hostile. It may not be surprising that a quality Shakespeare soon learned to esteem was patience, fortitude in undergoing ordeals. Very early, in *Two Gentlemen*, Silvia's tribulations teach her to bear trouble 'patiently', and Valentine prays for 'patience' (V.iii,iv).

A recurrent cluster of images reveals Shakespeare's detestation of hypocritical flattery (Spurgeon 195); all the stronger, perhaps, because he may have been compelled to have recourse to it himself at times, not only in his sonnets. His provincial origins must help to explain a preference for plain, unpretending manners. He is fond of moralizing on the deceptiveness of 'outward shows', the gap there may be between pretence and sterling worth. Touchstone's peacock airs make little impression on Corin the honest shepherd (*AYLI* III.ii.22 ff.). High-falutin' modes of speech, 'taffeta phrases', are among the bad habits that Berowne resolves to discard (*LLL* V.ii.406).

'Sincerity', in fact, was becoming Shakespeare's moral yardstick. He seems to have had a fixed dislike of vows, because they might prove hollow and, if genuine, were superfluous. 'Do not swear at all', Juliet says to Romeo (II.ii). Crookback can sound exactly like the man who knows how to smile and be a villain, as Hamlet says. Shakespeare must have been making some close friends, or at least feeling a keen need of them. Respect for friendship loyal through thick and thin shines through even so preposterous a metaphor as a lady's hairs 'Sticking together in calamity' (*KJ* III.iv.64 ff.) or so unimpressive a leave-taking as that of Warwick and the two brothers before battle. A 'prentice writer can feel strongly about things he cannot yet clothe in fitting expression. Farewells, separations, exiles were of poignant concern to Shakespeare because they meant disruption of human ties, the essence of human life.

By 1593–94 he was in a position to dedicate two long poems to a wealthy young patron, the Earl of Southampton, a ward of the powerful minister Lord Burghley. He was reaching the fringes of the aristocracy; his contact with it was evidently, from the Sonnets, not to be an untroubled one. What he saw or heard of high life may have helped to colour his picture of a nobility decaying, morally as well as politically, in the Histories. He was not only writing history, but living on its edges. One evening in 1601 his company was performing at Whitehall before the queen on the day when she signed the death-warrant of Essex, who was to be executed within a few hours (Lee, *Life* 376). Southampton was implicated in Essex's mad rising, and narrowly escaped the scaffold himself.

Shakespeare did not bring his family to London – at first if only because he could not afford to. He may not have wanted his daughters to grow up in a city where their father was a well-known stage actor. He may have feared that his wife would be out of place in the company he had to keep, either social or literary. He seems to have lived for the most part in lodgings, with liberty to remove when he liked. 'Shakespeare lived near where he worked'; from Bishopsgate he had crossed the river, by 1599, to be close to the Globe (Schoenbaum 7). One would guess him to have been a sober, methodical worker, but a very different and more 'Bohemian' portrait emerges from a passage in Ben Jonson's commonplace-book, apparently referring to Shakespeare though not by name: it comes only a page later than the celebrated criticism of Shakespeare's style as too copious and florid. According to this account it was hard to get him working, but once started he wrote feverishly, day and night, until exhausted, and then relapsed into 'sports and loosenesse' (589; cf. Wilson, *Shakespeare* 72).

If he was not an authentic puritanizing citizen, dedicated to steady application and thrift, he was living economically enough to be able to save and invest money. His son Hamnet's death in 1596, at the age of eleven, cut short any hopes he may have cherished of being the founder of a family; still, he went on being careful with money. He had two daughters to marry off, but he may have been chiefly saving up for a rainy day. In 1597 he acquired a big Stratford house, New Place, though he occupied it only after his retirement. In 1599 – with his aid, no doubt – his father obtained, after earlier failure, the coat of arms he hankered for; William too probably set store by it as the badge of a gentleman: in English society a hazy but weighty distinction. From this time he seems to have come to Stratford annually, and he was buying land and making other investments there. He inherited his father's litigiousness, and 'stood rigorously by his rights' (Lee, *Life* 341).

He seems to have divided himself into two: one self devoted to mining the gold of imagination, the other to putting together a modest competence. His labours, however irregular, must often have been exhausting. Not seldom he dwells on the wholesome sleep earned by manual toil, by contrast with the restless nights of a weary mind. He seems to have left the stage about 1608 and removed to Stratford, still with a few plays left to write. He may not have found his native place as consoling a retreat as he hoped. Puritanism was gaining ground there, and dislike of the theatre was one of its hallmarks. In 1612 play-acting was banned by the council. Shortly before his death in 1616 his younger daughter Judith, aged thirty-one, made a somewhat irregular marriage, which turned out not too well, with a man four years younger (Levi 338 ff.). It may sometimes have occurred to Shakespeare that he had neglected her in childhood.

When he died, only about half of his plays had been published – some imperfectly. The complete First Folio collection – still very much a novelty at that date – appeared in 1623, two of his old fellow-actors taking the lead. Their dedication contained a regret that he could not have 'set forth and overseen his owne writings' – a phrase suggesting, perhaps, that the project had been mooted before his death, and with his approval. To doubt this is indeed difficult. He had written eloquently in youth on the immortality conferred by verse. It was part of the spirit of his age, or of those many for whom undying fame could be a substitute for what religion no longer convincingly offered. When Bassanio talks of dying to save Antonio, his friend bids him 'live still, and write mine epitaph' (*MV* IV.i.118). Hamlet says the same to Horatio. It was a thought inspired by Shakespeare's strong social sense, in addition to any personal interest. A man and his reputation belong to the common stock; the memory they leave with others matters after they are gone. But the poet may have grown too tired to care about any of this, or to face the labour of revising.

He had written much about the past, and had more leisure now to speculate about the future. A good many thoughts scattered through the plays suggest that he had often done so before, in one mood or another. A quarter-century after his death England was engaged in civil war of a different kind from any he had written of, or any that had ever happened. In July 1643 the queen, Henrietta Maria, on the march with a small army, reached Stratford, and was lodged for three days at New Place, the house of Mrs Hall, the poet's elder daughter Susanna (Lee, *Life* 509).

4

Shakespeare and the Theatre

Most astonishing in the cultural life of Shakespeare's England was its sudden, torrential outpouring of drama. This above all was something cosmopolitan as well as English. Drama was flourishing about the same time over western Europe and as far away as Hungary. English actors toured abroad, English playwrights borrowed from foreign productions (Cohen ch. 2; Chambers vol. 3). English and Spanish theatres had many resemblances (see Rennert). Secular drama seems to have been a phenomenon of the long interval between medieval and modern, part of a convulsive attempt – or compulsion – to escape into a new age. The Greeks had thought of life passing like a scene on the stage; now the image became a commonplace. In *As You Like It* the philosophical duke talks of life's 'universal scene', which launches Jaques on his 'All the world's a stage ...' (II.vii.136 ff.). Sir Henry Vane's speech at his execution in 1662 began: 'The work which I am at this time called unto in this place, as upon a public theatre, is to die' (Willcock 382). There could have been no more potent stimulus than the theatre to aid a people's struggle into consciousness, discovery of itself and its world of good and ill, faculties and weaknesses, hitherto smothered. Centuries later Yeats wanted the Irish Theatre to be 'a place where the mind goes to be liberated as it was liberated by the theatres of Greece and England at certain great moments in their history' (Ronsley 27) – set free, that is, from old grooves and habits, to try its wings in fantasy before it could do so in action.

Like many other great artists, Shakespeare was the heir and consummation of a long tradition, as well as an inaugurator. Medieval England abounded in 'sub-dramatic entertainment'. During the Wars of the Roses there were troupes of actors kept by Yorkist nobles, and by Richard III (Bradbrook, *Player* 17–18, 25). We must wonder how much use was made of these performers for propaganda. In the sixteenth century both partisans and enemies of Reformation knew how useful plays could be (Bradbrook 31). Pageants of the 'Nine Worthies', like the one Shakespeare brought into *Love's Labour's Lost*, were still in his day familiar diversions of country towns. Extempore play-scenes resembling the one between Falstaff and Hal in *Henry IV Part 1* (II.iv) were common. Other Shakespeare plays owe a debt to the old moralizing 'Interludes' which, like *The Taming of the Shrew*, conventionally ended with a lay sermon (Rossiter 151–3).

The England Shakespeare was born into had a many-featured popular culture, where arts like singing, dancing and play-acting found no lack of exponents. By the time he was growing up, entertainment was being provided more than before by professionals, and he belonged to 'almost the first generation in Europe of a predominantly commercial theatre' (Salingar, *Comedy* 221). There was loss as well as gain in the change; amateur performers were liable to be squeezed out. Puritan zeal for sweeping away anything redolent of the old rustic festivals, as bad for morals, was one cause. Another, the most serious, was the gradual crippling of the village community by the segregation of the peasantry into a prosperous upper layer and a rural proletariat (cf. M. Kelly 62–6, 74, 88–9).

On the other hand, the new theatre was releasing drama from its narrow medieval confines, opening up wider perspectives (Weimann, 'Soul' 31–2). London was its focal point, but it was making itself a truly national institution, helping to build a modern national culture. No theatre company stayed in the capital all the year round; any town with a couple of thousand people could expect at least one visit between May and October (Lee, *Life* 81). The provinces came to have some regular theatres, as well as second-rate 'strolling' companies, from whose performances novices like Bottom the weaver in *A Midsummer Night's Dream* must have picked up notions of how things were done. In London some of higher station are likely to have been ready to learn. Acting had much in common with some of their professions: lawyers, preachers – royalty itself – could take useful elocution lessons from the stage. Hooker compared the House of Commons and its seating arrangement to a theatre. Shakespeare was the first professional playwright to indulge in frequent allusions to the actor's art, or stage technicalities (Hart 97).

It has been argued recently that his audience was not a cross-section of society, as many have thought it, but was dominated by 'the privileged playgoer', representing the better-off classes. These, A.J. Cook believes, must have constituted at least one-tenth of the London population, twice as much as anywhere else, and enough to fill up most places in the theatres (8, 93). To suppose that ordinary people had enough sense and taste to comprehend Shakespeare is in her view an illusion of the 1920s and 1930s, disseminated especially by Harbage (4–5). This sounds like a return to the elitist eighteenth-century views taken over, Rossiter remarks, by the Romantic critics (150). His own picture is of a mixed audience, quick-witted and responsive, with no distinct line between the ground-lings' receptive faculties and those of their betters. It may be hard to think of workmen as able to appreciate Shakespeare; no doubt they were not fully able – nor are we; but there seems little reason to suppose that the better-off classes, as we see them portrayed in fiction or sermons or on the stage, were much better qualified. Bradley found it easy to believe that audiences in the public theatres must have had 'the same general character' as those in the 'private', higher-priced ones (364). As to numbers, towards the end of the seventeenth century a single theatre sufficed for the London public, then very genteel; while formerly, as Kenneth Muir points out, there had been half a dozen ('Interpretations'); the contrast surely points to a broad, largely 'popular' audience in Shakespeare's time.

It is undeniable that in the public theatres – as distinct from the private sort, which were smaller and completely roofed over – the audience was in one sense sharply divided. The poorer stood, or sat on the ground, under the wintry sky, while the wealthier were seated under cover; and the two sorts cannot have had the same feelings about contentious subjects such as the drama often threw up. In another sense the drama was an equalizer, a place where the classes rubbed elbows. Anyone was free to smoke, eat apples, hiss or clap. Except in church, occasions for public gatherings of any serious kind were few. A theatre audience might be called an impromptu parliament, and the temporary proximity of classes so discordant could be a stimulus to the minds of all. The theatre would have a special function in helping to induct into London life the swarm of newcomers always arriving, at first uprooted and bewildered. Altogether, as L.C. Knights said, 'the theatre's success lay in the bringing together and the lively interplay of different interests within a fairly homogeneous society' (11). Harbage observed that what its opponents disliked was this audience itself, rather than the plays they watched: 'The theatre was a democratic institution in an intensely undemocratic age' (11).

A trenchant reply to Professor Cook's argument, admitting at the same time some strong points in it, will be found in an appendix to Martin Butler's book. Her estimate of one in six of the London population belonging to the 'privileged', or 'gentlemen', is 'astonishing', he points out; and it is evident if only from the continual denunciations of the theatre that a very considerable number of its frequenters were plebeians.

All performers were male. Boys apprenticed to the adult companies began work when very young, usually in women's roles; though these might be taken by more mature actors – we hear of one aged twenty-four (Gurr, *Shakespearean Stage* 69). In China men two or three times that age have been renowned impersonators of young women. If Shakespeare had no actresses, among his spectators he could count a good sprinkling of women. The epilogue to *As You Like It*, spoken by Rosalind, addresses first the women present, then the men. The former were of all ranks; those more careful for respectability had escorts with them (Gurr, *Playgoing* 8, 57). No special galleries were provided for them, as they were in some Spanish theatres. A playwright-turned-preacher, Stephen Gosson, deplored the scandal of men shoving and elbowing to get a place next to any woman, and the sequel – 'such ticking, such toying, such smiling, such winking' (25). But the women's presence may on the whole have improved the tone of the house, as it has that of the Scottish tavern since they were admitted. Disorder seems to have been infrequent, behaviour reasonably proper (Harbage, *Audience* chs. 3–4).

It was on the stage that Shakespeare had his chief and habitual contact with the 'populace'. He could declaim scathingly about 'The still-discordant wavering multitude' (Prologue to *2H.IV*) without fear of giving offence. We all feel that such criticisms are aimed at other people, not at *us*; and as the most admired of all the dramatists, he was a privileged voice. An average play, it has been estimated, might have been seen in the course of eighteen months by as many as 30,000 people (Beckerman 2). Success required patient study of crowd tastes and moods. An actor who was also an author would be left in no doubt about what was thought of his work. Shakespeare could not foresee that when he and his colleagues recited his lines to the crowded benches of the Globe, they were addressing the entire future world, the human race of centuries to come, but he must at least have been able to believe that a fair part of his audience appreciated him. A willing suspension of disbelief is a need of the writer as well as the listener.

The 1580s were the true inaugural decade. When they began, a drama was not much more than horseplay and blood-and-thunder; a melo-drama as crude as *Titus Andronicus* might still have years of resounding popularity before it, and end up enshrined in the First Folio. From the later 1580s, however, progress was marvellously rapid. Marlowe led the way, Shakespeare was his great successor; and the audience, too, was learning. Whatever its deficiencies, it possessed the supreme merit of being sufficiently close to earlier ages of the world to be able to listen to dramatic verse. About 1580 Sidney was lamenting that poetry, 'the first light-giver to ignorance' among the noblest nations, had sunk in England to being no more than 'a laughing-stock of children' (102–3). When he wrote, a miraculous fountain of poetry was about to gush out from, of all places, the dry bare boards of the despised stage.

It was not to flow for long. Dryden's estimate of his audience, a more elitist one in his day, was low, and helped to make him want his plays to be read rather than performed: poetical beauties could not bloom on the bustling stage (159). 'Poetry and the stage do not agree together', Hazlitt wrote in 1816 (Wells 9), stating what by then had long been an irreversible fact. Rummaging through a bundle of old plays one evening, Walter Scott concluded that 'The audience must have had a much stronger sense of poetry then than now' (*Journal* 1 August 1826). One consequence was the readiness of Shakespeare's characters – Hamlet most of all – to enlarge and generalize, to soar from the particular to the universal. Poetry transformed both its themes and its hearers, lifting them above their commonplace selves.

Actors needed patrons in high positions to give them legal status; they needed, too, the government's protection against their enemies, Puritans and others who formed the ruling interests of the City. Performances at court brought a welcome addition to their takings, but for most of their income they had to rely on the public. If they fell into the hands of a manager like Henslowe (see Greg), they would learn something of what the new capitalism could mean. Shakespeare and his associates escaped this by being able to hold on to an older, co-operative form of organization; though in relation to actors and other assistants who were not 'sharers' they stood in the relationship of a business enterprise to its workers. Actors as a profession were thought of as poverty-stricken, shilling-a-day men (Sheavyn 93–4). Here, as often, we see Shakespeare's place – in the practical affairs as well as ideas of his world – as curiously ambivalent.

A gentleman complained of his young son being got hold of by some actors, to be made use of in the 'vile and base manner of a mercenary player' (Bentley 47–8). City prejudice found succinct expression in a letter from the Lord Mayor to the Lord Chancellor in 1580, referring to actors, acrobats, etc., as 'a very superfluous sort of men' (Chambers vol. 3, 279). Civic topics were not neglected by authors; in 34 out of the 80 plays surviving from 1580–1603, merchants or craftsmen have parts to play (Stevenson 50). But there were complaints that they were too often ridiculed, and this kept some of the 'better sort', though not all, away from the theatres (Wright 604–7, 628). It is not unlikely, of course, that 'prentices and craftsmen enjoyed seeing their employers made fun of. There was a riot of 'prentices in June 1591 after a performance, though its cause was a grievance of their own; five of them were summarily executed after food riots in the summer of 1595. In each case the theatres were closed for a while. In 1597 the Privy Council was induced to order them to be pulled down. This was a sop to the City, clearly; no action followed.

It has often happened (nowhere more than in England, perhaps) that high and low have been able to meet on common ground for recreation – on the turf, at the ring or cockpit, in the music-hall – while the higher-minded middle classes have stayed away. Elizabeth and her courtiers enjoyed the same shows as her subjects; scarcely any of the plays performed before them were written specially for the purpose (Bradbrook, *Player* 76). But apart from this parity of taste, a basic policy disagreement was involved, which went on widening. Like most other monarchies, and every government today, the Tudors acted in the spirit of Machiavelli's advice to keep the public amused with entertainments and spectacles (cf. Underdown). The City, or bourgeoisie, or Puritans, shared in full the government's mistrust of the many-headed beast, or labouring masses; but their preference was for the alternative tactics of discipline, moral reform, inculcation of sober, industrious habits. Their aim was to convert ordinary men and women to acceptance of prescribed behaviour – virtues favourable, on their practical side, to material progress and employers' profits. It is worthwhile to ask how much of this conflict of policies, rival medicines for the body politic, can be recognized in the outbreak of civil war in 1642, when one of Parliament's first measures was to close the theatres. In the meantime one effect was to confuse and divide the political sympathies of playwrights and well-wishers of the drama.

By friend or foe the theatre could be seen as a force to be reckoned with. It could whip up patriotism, as Nashe said in 1592 in its defence (128–32). A play might be commissioned for propaganda purposes, like *A 'Larum for London*, a grisly story of the sack of Antwerp by Spanish forces in 1576, to convince the taxpayer of the need for preparedness. Drama such as Shakespeare's Histories lent itself admirably to dissemination of opinions and sentiments agreeable to the régime. To keep writers from straying, there was a censorship, exercised from 1579 until near his death in 1610 by Sir Edmund Tilney, as Master of the Revels (Boas, *Elizabeth* ch. 2). Shakespeare must be referring to it in Sonnet 66, where he speaks of 'art made tongue-tied by authority'. This is only known to have happened to him once, over his *Richard II*, where the scene of the king's deposition was cut out. Control might not be easy to enforce. Players could serve as mouthpiece for any mood of the moment; they were accused not only of satirizing City worthies but also of disrespect to Church and State, or to foreign governments, which might protest. Actors might drop hints not in the text: they could deride an individual by aping some mannerism. Hamlet cautions Polonius not to fall foul of them (II.iii), and in *Troilus and Cressida* Achilles and his friend are said to be guying the Greek leaders like scurrilous players (I.iii). Shakespeare himself was supposed to have got his own back on his Stratford enemy Sir Thomas Lucy by turning him into Justice Shallow.

As a rule during the 1590s the government felt sufficiently secure to tolerate more frank speaking on the stage than later (Heinemann, 'Drama' 188). History broke in rudely in 1601, on the eve of the Essex rising, when the conspirators induced Shakespeare's company to perform *Richard II*, by way of preparing public opinion for another transfer of power. Elizabeth was sensitive on the subject of Richard's dethronement, and if, as she heard, a large number of performances were given in the streets, it cannot have been by the regular actors, or things would have gone hard with them after the coup. But the episode is a tribute to the influence that the theatre was believed to wield.

Churchmen and pious writers were usually hostile. All the same, medieval drama had a religious framework, and none the less abounded in social criticism and the complaints of the man in the street (Kinghorn ch. 6). Sidney held that comedy, though bad writers had made it 'odious', could usefully combat 'the common errors of our life' (123). This was very much what the preachers were doing, in their own manner, and dramatic language could overflow into divinity (Collinson 233–5; Willey 136, 169–70). John Field was an anti-theatre divine, and one of his sons was a bishop; but another, Nathan, turned actor and dramatist, and wrote in defence of the stage. William Shakespeare and William Perkins, most influential of all Puritan gospellers, can often be heard saying the same thing, especially when it was a question of upholding traditional moral standards or good sense against aberrations. Both were critics of duelling, for instance (cf. Perkins 120, 136, 435). And in the Elizabethan as in the Romantic era, religious revival and romantic love were blossoming side by side, nourished by the same soil and silently encouraging each other. Divine and human love were alike 'infinite' and 'eternal'.

'Shakespeare was a poet before he was a dramatist' (Rylands 89). A writer in whose evolution the dramatic came first would be unlikely to scale the heights of Parnassus. On the other hand a poet dabbling in amateur drama, composing out of sight or sound of the theatre, like Byron, Tennyson, Browning, Bridges, or T.S. Eliot, would be even less likely to excel. As professional playwright and actor, Shakespeare had to be as familiar with stage and audience as with his own house and neighbours. They made it possible for him to combine poetic and dramatic in perfection. Absence of scenery favoured shifts of location from scene to scene and with them – in Shakespeare's plays as in others – a looseness of construction that was sometimes excessive. We may fancy him going to work with the same eagerness as his Mrs Page, when a fresh stratagem occurred to her and her ally – 'Come, to the forge with it; then shape it. I would not have things cool' (*MWW* IV.ii.17–18). His creative flow showed in his habit of writing plays much too long to be performed without cuts (Hart 151); and since he seldom invented stories, but took them ready-made, he had less need to pause and ponder. The fact that they were often familiar to his hearers in advance is a pointer to the presence of a strong 'popular' element in his audience, though also to the ability of the higher sort to share the taste for folk-tale.

Shakespeare had to write for a particular set of actors, Baldwin reminds us (*Organization* 300). Rossini likewise composed each opera to suit whatever set of singers he found. There is evidence, as Baldwin adds, of actors giving their writers advice and suggestions: this must sometimes have been a nuisance, but in the case of Shakespeare and his associates, so long and closely linked together, can have contributed much 'collective invention' (303). We do not know how often Shakespeare's mind turned back to plays he had written a year or ten years before, but theatres worked on a repertory system, with a stock of plays more or less frequently revived. This would oblige him to look through his texts again, and no doubt consult his colleagues on details. Discrepancies in *Twelfth Night* have made readers suspect an incomplete revision (Bethell 138 ff.). Saintsbury felt that *The Merchant of Venice* and other plays contained sections differing so much in maturity that they must have been written at different dates ('Life' 183–4). Evidences of revision can be detected in twenty-five plays altogether, distinct proof in sixteen (Bentley 261). Shakespeare's boast, reported by Jonson (587–8), that he never 'blotted' – cancelled or altered – a line, can refer only to his original drafts.

An instinct of fidelity to life may underlie his apparently casual methods. A well-organized plot must always be unnatural in its singling out of one sequence of happenings from the daily welter. A story told with some of its inconsequences and illogicalities may reflect more faithfully a real world where men more often than not act hastily, forgetfully, failing to see obvious repercussions. As a man of the theatre Shakespeare had his eye fixed on the building up of dramatic situations, giving plenty of scope for the clash of rival wills or hopes. As a student of human nature he was interested, as Scott said, in permanent features, by contrast with Ben Jonson the collector of ephemeral social mannerisms (*Monastery* Introd.). Shakespeare could enjoy – and knew his audience enjoyed – an allowance of topicality, but he freed himself from over-immersion in it by his choice of settings, far away in time or space. They gave him the liberty to concentrate on his chief characters and their relationships, so distinctly drawn that they make up a little world by themselves, as real to us for the time being as our own.

PART II

The Histories

1

Shakespeare and English History

Sir Thomas Elyot's treatise on government in 1531 strongly upheld the doctrine that history can be an invaluable teacher; but his illustrations were nearly all taken from Antiquity, classical or biblical. Chroniclers, and the playwrights who drew on them, were teaching Englishmen lessons out of their own past. Shakespeare above all was enabling them to look back on it. Paying tribute to his achievement, Coleridge observed that much of the knowledge of bygone men and events still afloat in the public mind was derived from his plays (*Shakespeare* 112). They might be called collectively an epic poem; after them the Epic could have only one more appearance in English, perhaps in any European language, and Milton had to remove it from an earthly to a celestial plane. Shakespeare's barons contended for an English throne; Milton's archangel was incited to rebellion by 'no less than the throne of the universe' (Hazlitt, *Poets* 94).

But every now and then in *Paradise Lost*, amid the crash of heavenly artillery, we catch glimpses of terrestrial affairs; and between past and present in the Histories can be felt a similar vibration. Noblemen of 1400 and 1600 are different in many ways, but still alike in others; ostlers, servants, common soldiers, of whom the chronicles had little to tell, have altered much less. It is by breathing impulses and passions of his own day into men and women of old, as well as feelings proper to their place in history, that Shakespeare brings them to life.

Shakespeare wrote nine English Histories and part of a tenth, *Henry VIII*, and three Roman; if to these are added *Troilus and Cressida* and *Macbeth*, we have not much less than half of his total output. In one late work he refers to history as 'devised and played to take spectators' (*Winter's Tale* III.ii); no doubt the business of 'taking spectators', and their money, had to come first with him, as it did with his companions. But study of happenings of the past was an important part of his continuing efforts to comprehend his own world; a fascinating arena in which he could contemplate men and women in action, and the complex relations between them and the families, classes, nations they belonged to. Here he could show himself 'an almost unrivalled observer' (Morris 103; cf. Hill, *Origins* 174). A profound instinct led him to history and helped to make him one of the first great artists of modern Europe, and its greatest writer. Universal art must have a firm local footing.

Both Renaissance and Reformation, in different ways, promoted growth of national feeling, that dangerous but invigorating flame; and everywhere the sense of belonging to a people with a name, and a part to play in the world, fired interest in the collective past. An England often at war in the late sixteenth century could draw assurance of its rights and its claims on divine favour from the memory of a victory like Agincourt. In nearly two centuries since then English triumphs abroad had been few. For fanning patriotic ardour there could be no more effective medium than the theatre. A government desirous of identifying itself with defence of national interests could only welcome the aid that actors could give it; though it had to take care that their trumpet was always blowing the right notes. On their side the theatres had many enemies of their own, grave magistrates and bigoted preachers; they could have no better apologia than that they were helping to forge patriotic unity.

Shakespeare covered the best possible ground: the years of the fifteenth century which saw the later stages of the Hundred Years War alternating with the Wars of the Roses, and ended with the accession of the first Tudor. Material came from a variety of sources, chief among them Holinshed, whose *Chronicles* were first published in 1577 and enlarged in 1587, each time suffering some unkindly cuts from the censor. They marked 'a turning-point in the history of Tudor drama' (Wilson, *King John* xv). In general Shakespeare stuck as closely as he could to the facts as recorded; we may see here a respect for reality, a seriousness about the importance of history. During the 1590s historical drama, fed by the Spanish attack and national excitement, breathed fresh vitality into the theatre and raised its standing and prestige. On the stage an image of 'national character' was taking shape. English soldiers 'hare-brain'd' in their 'courage and audacity' (*1H.VI* I.ii.36–7) were to have many descendants in the fiction of later times.

Hitler is recorded in his *Table Talk* as finding fault with Schiller for seeking a hero in a paltry Swiss instead of a German, and with Shake-speare's English history sources for providing only imbeciles or madmen. Shakespeare learned from Marlowe, and especially in the first and last of the Histories (*1H.VI* and *H.V*) may seem at times to be emulating *Tamburlaine*, published in 1590, with its 'high-astounding terms'. A certain miasma of the insane, of violence out of control, pervades all the earlier Histories, as the spiral of crime goes on mounting. Amid it all the old political order shows itself irretrievably bad, incapable of regeneration. Its animating spirit is an unreasoning, insatiable thirst for power: over foreigners by conquest and over Englishmen by success in winning the throne and riding in triumph through London like Tamburlaine through Persepolis.

Historical drama is always concerned with change, but often leaves its causes mysterious (Lindenberger 99). Shakespeare has no comprehensive explanations to offer, but he strews plentiful hints or guesses. England's failure to hold on to its French domains precipitates civil war. The first sequence of plays rises to its climax in *Richard III*, where Shakespeare takes an amazing stride forward. It is a drama falling·not far short of tragedy, and can be called at the same time the finest melodrama ever written, with an energy ensuring it a permanent place on the stage. Richard, the supreme power-seeker, goes far beyond his forerunners; with him the contest takes on a dimension only hinted at previously. Political intrigue and demagogy have first place over warlike prowess. Thematically *King John*, though of uncertain date, can be placed between the first series and the one starting with *Richard II*. Shakespeare's sole foray into an older medieval era, it exhibits another double calamity. Failure in France leads to French invasion and a near approach to civil war, with a king unfit – like Henry VI, but for very different reasons – to cope with the situation. Here again, success abroad seems necessary to peace at home.

The second series opens on a level again aspiring to the tragic, by very different means than those of *Richard III*. R.L. Smallwood points out that Richard II's queen is virtually an invention of Shakespeare's, and that he was beginning to bring fictional characters into an increasingly complex interweaving with his facts (151, 155). Each play in turn was now a novelty; his imagination was displaying astonishing fertility. His old men in *Richard II*, last of Edward III's overmany sons, are stragglers from the past, and seem to stand for a whole era ready to fold up its tents and depart. The leap from here to the England of *Henry IV*, from stylized altitudes to the rough-and-tumble of common life, is prodigious. History ceases to be simply political and is fused with comedy or social satire, though until Hotspur's death still with a lingering of the tragic.

In *Henry VI* there was humour of a clownish sort, in episodes tacked on to the main story. Richard Crookback revelled in macabre wit; King John's nephew the Bastard in robust jocularity. In *Richard II* anything humorous disappears, as if deliberately repressed. Then, in *Henry IV*, laughter rolls over us in a flood. Each play has been coming to group itself round one outstanding figure, the first of them Warwick the king-maker; now it is Falstaff's turn. He is an outsider, an onlooker, but rubs elbows with people from all walks of life. Much of the play's sparkle arises out of the jostling together of classes and ranks, and the discovery that at bottom all men and women belong to the same species, and sober history and comedy to the same world. Falstaff emancipates Shakespeare and us from any inflated estimate of the great and their doings. Plebeians are not rebelling now, as they did in *Henry VI Part 2*, but we see far more of them – in their ordinary lives, or in the army; we learn something of their hardships, and hear some of their grievances aired.

In *Henry VI Part 1* and *King John*, scenes set in England and France alternated; now the shift is more abrupt: between Eastcheap, home of the comic spirit, and Westminster, where it would be unthinkable for anyone to crack a joke. With this mixing of ranks and medley of moral planes goes a looser, more episodical construction. Shakespeare has come to be concerned less with the outer husks of history, more with its inner reality; he is less its custodian, especially in the Elizabethan official style, and more its interpreter. In spite of all the wit, in *Henry IV* we are emerging not into fresh sunlight but into a grey, overcast morning. Witticisms are sometimes things for people to enjoy together: more often, even in the tavern, they are weapons for them to use against one another. An old feudal world and its ideas, everything from the crown downward, are coming under critical scrutiny. Age and decay have a pervasive presence, which seems to find a bodily manifestation in old buildings gnawed by time: the 'ancient castle' with 'rude ribs' and 'ruin'd ears' (*R.II* III.iv), or Warkworth, that 'worm-eaten hold of ragged stone' (*2H.IV* Prologue), whose condition heralds the approaching downfall of the Percies. What we see of the condition of England is no more cheering. It is another symptom of a vitiated atmosphere that women, except of a disreputable sort, are practically eliminated.

At the outset of Henry V's brief reign, all this seems to have been banished. Exeter talks with ringing confidence about a truly national, united government; Canterbury follows with his glowing picture of class harmony in the beehive. But it includes 'soldiers' who range afield to make booty of the flowers and bring home their 'pillage' to the tent of their 'emperor'. Both men are arguing for peace at home, war abroad; and thinking of the two, evidently, as inseparable. Monarchy has suffered an ignominious collapse with Richard II's fall; Henry IV's reign has been at best humdrum, and marred by the behaviour of his heir. For it to recover credit the king must be the champion, the embodiment, of his people; for this, there must be a foreign enemy in sight.

In Hotspur the heroic virtues remain self-centred, therefore an-achronistic and harmful. What Shakespeare requires is that honour and emulation should transcend this anarchic level and become profitable to the commonweal; but he has no means of bringing this about, in order to improve the people's lot. All he can do is to turn his back on the dilemma, and march his hero off to worsen the French people's lot. The

Histories seem to end where they began; but the problems that Shakespeare, like his Henry V, was trying to escape were still there to haunt him. This is typical of his progress. Each play is pushed forward by its contradictions and their demand for solutions: it has, properly speaking, no end, because it has brought to light more new questions than can be answered within its own limits.

2

The Plays

Henry VI Part 1 (1590)

There have been many doubts about the authenticity of several scenes in the three parts of *Henry VI*; in recent years – perhaps from exhaustion after prolonged debate – there has been more willingness to take the whole work as substantially belonging to Shakespeare, a youthful learner of his craft. Its acceptance has indeed been called a major swing of critical opinion (Bradbrook, *Shakespeare* 55; cf. Ribner 97). One consideration urged has been 'the occurrence of typically Shakespearean clusters' of imagery (Armstrong 185). Construction is loose, in the absence of any coherent train of events; Shakespeare makes up for this at times with formalistic devices, or relies on coincidences to cobble things together, as when all three of the chief participants in a scene at the French court simultaneously receive letters from England at the crucial moment (*Part 3*: III.iii). Hair's-breadth escapes, dizzy ups and downs of fortune, thrills of all kinds, often horrific, provide a rapidly shifting kaleidoscope. One pungent ingredient is the revenge theme so dear to Elizabethans. Dear also was the trick of a foeman's head cut off and displayed on the stage.

Part 1 is divided between growing resistance in France to the English occupation, despite the superhuman exertions of Talbot, and politics at the English court, with feudal magnates quarrelling for first place. In general the English or 'political' scenes are better written than the French or 'military', except when Joan of Arc is in the limelight. Talbot, that 'dreadful lord' (I.i.110) – to one commentator at least (Leggatt 9) a true hero – bestrides the battlefields, knocking over Frenchmen in heaps; he glories in being acknowledged their 'terror and their bloody scourge' (IV.ii). He is above all a man of blue blood, with a long string of titles for Joan to deride (IV.vii); captured, he rejects the indignity of being exchanged for a prisoner of lesser rank, and we never see him fraternizing with the rank and file, as Henry V learns to do – though he is as ready as Henry V, or Cromwell, to give the glory to God (III.ii.117, iv; IV.ii).

No dramatist could fail to make good (or bad) use of so extraordinary a personality as Joan of Arc. In this play the better scenes about her are a remarkable tribute both to her and to French resistance. She is portrayed as so active and energetic a leader that there is no need of witchcraft to explain her successes, except as a salve to English pride (e.g. III.ii.38–40; cf. Warner 107 ff.). Her dignified appeal to Burgundy to come over to the French side, and his response (III.iii), do far more justice to the better side of patriotism than almost anything in the trilogy.

Loss of France is bringing civil war to England, and the blame rests clearly on the 'factious emulations' deplored by the young king (IV.i.111 ff.). Talbot is left to perish because York and Somerset are too jealous of each other to organize a relief force. The soldiers are muttering about the jangling lords' behaviour (I.i.57 ff.); we can hear in this the voice of the common man, and the prelude, misconceived as it may be, to popular criticism of the ruling class. Act II Scene iv, where the red and white roses become the badges of rival claims to the throne, is one of the more impressive. It may be supposed that the audience was ready to be interested by the genealogical details unfolded here, and again (in II.v) by the aged Mortimer, nearing his death in the Tower. England in the 1590s was facing the prospect of a change of dynasty before long, and James VI of Scotland's hereditary right as great-grandson of Henry VII's daughter Margaret loomed over the political scene. In this context Shakespeare's dramas were doing something to educate the public mind – as James can hardly have failed to note with approval – to the benefits of adherence to strict hereditary succession. But so far as the Wars of the Roses are concerned, we are shown only a senseless scrimmage. Neither side raises any issues of public concern, except the war in France.

Henry VI Part 2 (c. 1590)

At the close of the first scene of Part 2 all the protagonists reveal their aims; they are beasts of a jungle where only the most ruthless can survive. In Act III Scene ii Henry prepares to hold the trial of his Uncle Gloucester, whom we know to be lying murdered behind the curtain. Before long the Bishop of Winchester – 'the haughty cardinal' for whom, as in Part I, nobody has a good word – dies raving and sees the ghost of Gloucester, whose death he has connived at, whispering at his pillow (III.ii.370 ff., iii). Of the ill-fated king, Shakespeare's portrait is at times wavering; it is only personalities as crude as Talbot or the bishop that he can as yet see, or draw, in firm outline. Henry soon sinks into dependence on his termagant wife; he appears to be aware of her preference for Suffolk, but shows no jealous resentment. He is a good man who, like one or two others in Shakespeare, fails completely as a ruler; perhaps because only a harsh, even cruel ruler can be an effective one. He pines to be rid of the throne he was born to, while his challenger York is ravenously eager to seize it.

Among the feudalists, Gloucester is the most estimable. More than in Part I, he emerges clearly as a faithful statesman who, as Protector during Henry's minority, kept order well. But he has grown old and tired, and is being pulled down by his enemies; there is real pathos here, and some likeness to the dying John of Gaunt in *Richard II*. His afflictions are worsened by the plotting, and disgrace, of his ambitious wife. This embryo Lady Macbeth warns him that he too will come to grief; she is right. Next in respectability are Salisbury and Warwick, father and son, who seem to accept York's right to the crown, when he argues his case to them, on its merits (II.ii). Salisbury feels duty-bound to resist Henry's appeal to him to stay quiet in his old age, not 'seek for sorrow' with his spectacles, and he fights on the Yorkist side like a 'winter lion' (V.i.165, iii). York himself 'reaches at the moon', like Hotspur, but for power rather than 'honour' (III.i.158). His lengthy soliloquy at the end of Act III Scene i, glorying in his own naked ambition, has much striking imagery and real eloquence. Evidently Shakespeare felt a sort of fascination in such characters and their Nietzschean will to power. York has no compunction about the ten thousand Englishmen whose deaths may be needed to bring him to the throne, any more than Talbot cared about the lives of Frenchmen.

Far the most interesting scenes in Part 2 are those concerned with Jack Cade and his Kentish rebellion; due tribute to their vitality is paid by Leggatt (16–20). To treat them as merely comical, 'anarchy by clowning', may fit into a view of Shakespearean comedy as a sort of humorous purgation, a 'saturnalian release' (Barber 4, 13); but it leaves half of the meaning out. Serious and comic, or grotesque, jostle together in this irruption of rustic mentality and discontent into the feudal or urban framework of the Histories. Shakespeare at Stratford had been close enough to the countryside to learn a good deal about it. It is interesting in itself that he chose to bring in – or drag in – this episode, a miniature drama scarcely connected with the main plot. Such an outburst of class conflict, like the feudal factions in another way, shows something rotten in the state of England. Elsewhere in these plays we have realistic detail about hardships and grievances of the poor; only here is there active revolt against them. Shakespeare had in mind also, no doubt, that the invasion of the capital by the rebels would have a special piquancy for his audience. To see these yokels burlesqued, as they partly are, would be rich entertainment for Londoners high and low, united by the usual conceit of a metropolis. One might indeed expect some of them to be stirred to sympathy with the rebels by hearing them addressed as 'the scum and filth of Kent' (IV.ii.119). Shakespeare may have counted on such language to allay any official disapproval of social revolt on the stage; the poor, like the French, must be denigrated.

Cade's talk is a jumble of sense and nonsense. His turn for rough-and-ready jocularity makes it difficult to know how much he intends to be taken literally. Not all his followers swallow his tall talk about his high birth. Dick the butcher and Smith the weaver, who laugh at it, are of the village artisan or shopkeeper sort; very probably such men were easier than ploughmen for Shakespeare to find words for. Cade himself is first called an old soldier, later sometimes a 'clothier' or cloth-merchant. He has something of the same reckless energy and desire to lead and command as the ambitious lords; but in his bombast about the happiness to be brought by his reign there is an undercurrent of Golden Age utopianism. He is given a deliberate resemblance to John of Leyden, leader of the Anabaptist rising at Münster in 1535 and ever since a bugbear to all the propertied classes of Europe. As John was accused of doing, Cade intends to make all wives 'as free as heart can wish or tongue can tell', but reserves to himself the right of the first night with every woman (IV.vii.114ff.).

The semi-proverbial saying that 'it was never merry world in England since gentlemen came up' (IV.ii.8–9) would have been echoed by thousands of Shakespeare's poorer contemporaries; and Cade's pledge that 'there shall be no more money' (IV.ii.66), and 'all things shall be in common' (IV.vii.16), have a ring of the primitive communism of some Anabaptists, whose propaganda Shakespeare had clearly heard about (Hill, *Upside Down* 114). A clerk or scrivener is caught and, because he can write his name, hanged; and the captured Lord Say, a judge, makes no impression on the insurgents with his plea that he has been a patron of education and knowledge, 'the wing with which we fly to heaven' (IV.vii.21 ff.). Protestant Bible-reading stimulated literacy in the sixteenth century, but Cade's men show no inclination to fly away from their troubles to heaven. The meaning of learning for their class was quite different from its meaning for city folk, to whom it could spell opportunity. Lawyers were the poor man's enemies. John of Gaunt's words about the country being tied up 'In inky blots, and rotten parchment bonds' (*R.II* II.i.64) had far more relevance to the plight of the peasantry than to him and his fellow-nobles. These Kentishmen (though the only distinct grievance we hear of is overtaxation) are alienated from everything in the national life except its worst feature, its bellicose nationalism: a prophetic glimpse of Europe in times nearer our own. They are as ready as their betters to blame those in power – Say is one – for the loss of French provinces.

Authority's first impulse is to resort to threats, and then the mailed fist. But the commons are not to be put down so tamely. Cade leads them into battle, in pell-mell style but boldly, with the cry of 'liberty', to be won by the pulling down of lords and gentry (IV.ii.181–2). They rout their assailants, and enter London. In the scenes that follow, the 'rascal people' join the rebels (IV.iv.), while the mayor and burgesses are with the government: they too are defeated. Resort must be had to diplomacy, and Clifford and a fellow-nobleman are sent to offer a royal pardon, though not much else. What cuts the ground now from under Cade's feet is the jingoistic demagogy he himself has incautiously indulged in. All the colloquy is made to turn on which side is more patriotic, or anti-French, while the people's grievances are pushed out of sight. Cade's men abandon him and appear humbly before the king, with halters round their necks. Henry has just been lamenting his own fate, and wishing he were a private man instead of a ruler. We seem to be hearing a confession of how little monarchy can really do for its humbler subjects. Their leader, now a fugitive seeking food, is caught and killed, defiantly exclaiming that 'the unconquered soul of Cade is fled' (IV.x). His killer, a squire, delivers a violent tirade over the 'damned wretch', in which we hear again accents of ferocious class hatred.

Henry VI Part 3 (c. 1591)

In Part 3, mostly ebb and flow of civil war, Shakespeare must have found his work tedious at times; there is a plethora of uninspired verse, though also some firmer character-sketching. At the outset Henry makes an effort to outface his opponents, and even manages to sound quite fierce. War shall 'unpeople this my realm' before he will give way (I.i.126): a phrase echoed by Cleopatra, and proper for a sovereign because the realm is his patrimony. He is soon pushed into the background by Margaret and her henchmen, and is content to be a resigned bystander. Thanks to this he can learn something, as Lear does later, of the miseries of ordinary folk; watching a battle, he feels as no one else ever does the pathos of the weak suffering for the quarrels of the strong (II.v.73 ff., 94 ff.). But at most he can take comfort from the thought of having at least done his people no harm: he has never overtaxed them, nor denied them justice (IV.ix). In the end, when Richard Crookback comes to murder him in the Tower, Henry defies him fearlessly. In fact he has never shown any fear for himself; he is not a coward, and therefore not contemptible.

Warwick the king-maker has swelled into a grand, commanding figure, as nearly admirable as can be expected against such a background. He is a frank enemy, a loyal friend, who changes sides only once, from motives not discreditable, and receives erstwhile foes with a generous freedom from mistrust. York, the resilient politician, brave soldier and affectionate father of Part 2, meets his terrible end stoically, shaken only by the murder of his youngest son (I.ii). Nearly all these pitiless men are brave; and it seems always an instinctive feeling in Shakespeare that while men possess this bedrock quality, without which they are less than human, there is room for hope of mankind growing into something better. But more than before, assassination has now become a regular part of politics. Blood calls for blood, and Shakespeare has to pile on the agony in order to keep up the interest. With no injury of her own to call for retaliation, Margaret joins in stabbing the captured York (I.iv). Protest is left to boys, like Rutland pleading for his life with the inexorable Clifford, and later Edward IV's young sons in the Tower, followed in *King John* by Prince Arthur. In their prayers and laments can be heard Shakespeare's own protest against man's inhumanity to man.

York's eldest son, destined to be Edward IV, makes his profession of faith early: 'I would break a thousand oaths to reign one year' (I.ii). A sensualist and egotist, he wants the crown as a schoolboy wants a plum pie, and sets about enjoying it irresponsibly. Taken to task by his brothers and advisers over his foolish marriage, he retorts that he is king, 'and must have my will' (IV.i.16; cf. 75 ff.). By comparison with Henry's concept of kingly duties, monarchy is in decay. With the sort of irony these plays abound in, Edward, near his death, is basking in a glow of success and family goodwill, while his brother Richard stands by, plotting mischief (V.vii).

Richard III (1591-92)

Richard had been germinating in Shakespeare's mind for a good while before he came to the front, full-blown. Early on we have seen him effervescing with animal spirits and vitality, but not yet totally self-centred. He has risked his life in battle for his father, and been a Yorkist with a strong family attachment. It is in his long self-communing at the end of Act III Scene ii of *Henry VI Part 3*, when Edward is already on the throne, that he suddenly sheds his old skin. Shakespeare sets himself to chart the inner workings of such a character, his subtlest hitherto, and convincingly links the mania for power with the deformity that cuts Richard off from his fellows, especially from women and love. He is driven on by a demonic impulse in whose grasp he is as helpless as any of his victims. After stabbing Henry he glories in his wickedness, and thinks of himself in a strikingly Byronic style as a Cain, a solitary among men. He is already scheming to destroy his other brother, Clarence – 'and then the rest' (V.vi).

Richard's 'I am myself alone', in the same scene, ranges him with a number of solitary Shakespearian characters. When their aloneness turns into willing self-isolation it is vicious, even if Shakespeare himself can say, in the dark, world-defying mood of Sonnet 121, 'No, I am that I am'. Richard opens his own play with another of the spirited soliloquies in which he takes pleasure in spreading his cards out on the table for us to see. Physically handicapped, he plumes himself on his intellectual superiority, the skill with which he can bend human beings to his will. For monarchy in itself he has no conventional respect; his derisive attitude to the world he moves in is sometimes not very far removed from Falstaff's nihilism. He revels in his work for its own sake, and we rejoice with him, though of course we are glad to know that he will come to a bad end when he has had his fling; this is our sop to the conscience that warns us of illicit cupidities of our own. Charles Lamb, in his essay on Shakespeare's Tragedies, confessed his liking for Richard more candidly than most, his admiration for what he thought most actors missed – 'the lofty genius, the man of vast capacity, the profound, the witty, accomplished Richard' (IV, 203). Trollope paid a similar tribute to Thackeray's Barry Lyndon, a consummate scoundrel for whom 'it is almost impossible not to entertain something of a friendly feeling' (70–71).

The play has unusually many theatrical metaphors (Murry 125), and Richard is an accomplished actor. He has been seen as a descendant of the 'Vice' in the morality plays, but he is a very up-to-date one who has pored over his Machiavelli. Shakespeare had to do his worst for him, because his villainy was the warrant for the Tudors to usurp the throne; Thomas More, the poet's chief source, gave him his cue. But he was growing up too fast to be content with a mere stage villain. He did not make a Richard a 'tyrant' in the sense in which Macbeth turns into one. Those he dooms are few and carefully selected; there is little hint of a reign of terror bleeding the country. Like 'honest Iago' he likes to pose as a rough plain-spoken fellow (e.g. I.iii.45 ff.); really he is a master of words, and loves to juggle with them and make them work for him. He is in his own line an artist, and for us it is a privilege to be taken into his confidence.

Buckingham makes a splendid collaborator, bold and crafty and resourceful. It is fine to watch him playing to the gallery of public opinion, striving to convince Richard of his duty to accept the crown, for the country's sake, while Richard protests his reluctance in tones of vibrant sincerity (III.vii). Mixed with our appreciation of their per-formance is probably a thrill of discovery – that this is what the kind of men who come to the top are really like, and this is how they fool us. But any partnership between two such men is sure to break down before long. For Shakespeare, true friendship can link only good men, joining for good purposes.

Already in *Henry VI* Richard has displayed a vein of sinister humour; it goes well with the dramatic irony that intensifies now, and rubs into our minds the self-destructiveness of this feudal world whose presiding genius Crookback is. Clarence's murderers reveal to him the hollowness of Richard's friendly professions (III.iv.243 ff.); we may feel that Shakespeare misses a chance by not making Clarence sound as thunderstruck as we expect. Hastings foolishly ignores a warning to escape, and in the council chamber remarks on how cheerful Richard is looking, and how his mood always shows in his face – a moment before Richard fiercely accuses him of conspiracy, and orders his execution (III.ii, iv).

Something is needed for the sake of contrast with the hyperactive Richard, and this is supplied by a chorus of wailing women, royal widows and mothers whose lives have been blighted by masculine ambitions – sometimes by their own as well – and who are now reduced to helpless suffering. Their doyenne is Margaret who, with little care for probability, haunts the palace like a living ghost, or living record of the whole span of civil wars. Their long-drawn-out lamentations and denunciations are rhetorical exercises, which must have suited the audience's taste; today their highly artificial style makes them tedious and insipid. One scene in particular, Act IV Scene iv, runs – or crawls – to an immense length of over 500 lines. It fails to extort sympathy, because none of these unfortunates has any sympathy to spare for anyone but herself. With this chorus of 'formal Senecan declamation' (Ribner 104), Shakespeare is attempting to weave a fate-laden atmosphere like that of ancient tragedy, but he has not found the right means.

While the women curse, Richard believes in prompt action, much unlike Richard II or Hamlet: 'fearful commenting/Is leaden servitor to dull delay' (IV.iii). Yet the strain of continual calls on his resources is proving too much even for him. Macbeth and his wife suffer from 'terrible dreams'; unlike them, Richard has no conscience to molest his waking hours, but in sleep his iron nerves are shaken. Anne is wakened in the nights by his 'timorous dreams' (IV.i); she might well have some herself, before becoming yet another of his victims. Towards the end, his firm hold on men and events is failing. He hurries messengers off without messages and loses his temper, like Macbeth, with one he thinks is bringing bad news (IV.iv). He is more and more cut off from others by his crimes; he 'hath no friends but what are friends for fear', an enemy assures Richmond (V.ii).

His breach with Buckingham has cost him his one real ally. He tries unavailingly to keep Stanley loyal by threatening to send his son, kept as hostage, 'Into the blind cave of eternal night' – which he himself is soon to enter (V.iii.54). On the evening before Bosworth he needs wine to make up for loss of his old 'alacrity of spirit', and in his sleep the ghosts of all his victims come to denounce him. He is left to meditate, for the first and last time, on his sins, and his solitude: 'There is no creature loves me'. He quits his tent to go round the camp, in very undignified fashion (and very unlike Henry V before Agincourt), to eavesdrop and hear what his lieutenants are talking about. In the morning – to our relief in a way, because the strength of such a man is part of the strength of the human race – he is himself again, and can dismiss conscience as a bogey 'Devised at first to keep the strong in awe'. This is hardly the best way to cheer his nobles, whom he seems to be addressing as fellow-brigands, but it is his final declaration of independence, a substitute for the dying speech Shakespeare does not allow him. He harangues his soldiers, and takes the field with all his old zest – 'A thousand hearts are great within my bosom' (V.iii). Shakespeare's villains, as well as his heroes, die game.

Anne was queen for long enough to remember how she had once laid a curse on whatever woman Richard should marry, and to feel the curse falling on herself (IV. iv). All the maledictions, or prophecies of woe, and the nightmares that started with Clarence's 'fearful dreams' and memories of his crimes (I.iv.1 ff.), seem to throng together in the ghost scene in a collective vision of a feudal world at its last gasp. For Shakespeare – as for modern historians – a whole epoch is ending at Bosworth, a new era opening. As a sort of public-relations officer to Queen Elizabeth, Shakespeare is clothing the final events in semi-religious guise. Her very worldly-wise grandfather Richmond – or Henry VII, the first Tudor – becomes a saintly champion to whom the ghostly visitants bring hopeful dreams and blessings. He proves himself a true dragon-slayer by killing Richard in single combat. His closing speech is a denunciation of all future renewers of England's 'mad' divisions, now ending and giving place to peace and 'smiling plenty'. Tudor England was indeed to be blessed for most of its time with internal peace; its plenty was reserved for a minority. Shakespeare's hearers knew this; he must have intended them to ponder on his last touch of irony.

King John (1590-91)

In this conjuring up of a remote time, history and drama are loosely, awkwardly matched. John was a usurper, but the crown was not yet fully hereditary, and though he was a youngest son he had been nominated as successor by his brother Richard I instead of the boy Arthur, son of another brother. In the first two Acts John is in France, not as invader but as guardian of territories joined to England in 1066 by the Norman Conquest. France is backing Arthur against him. By 1204 John had been driven out. All this is jumbled up in the play with happenings of a decade later, when his dispute with his barons led to civil war (and to Magna Carta, which the play ignores), and their calling in the French as allies. From lack of time – or of interest in details of things so far away – Shakespeare did not go to the chronicles, but relied on a play published in 1591, perhaps written in 1588–9, *The Troublesome Raigne of John King of England*. His own version may have been produced in 1590–91 and revised in 1594.

It is a poorly constructed thing, revised – if at all – very carelessly. Its second half has little connection with the first; the gap is patched over with the business of papal interference, the staple of what Englishmen since the Reformation associated with John. In the later Acts the three women have disappeared; the denouement is a chapter of accidents and anticlimax. Most obvious of a number of confusions is the way Hubert agrees to kill Arthur and then threatens him instead with blinding. Some characters are indistinct, inconsistent. Yet there are new ideas, new feelings, much splendid writing. Above all there is a spirit of curiosity and inquiry, close sometimes to the critical mood of the later Histories; even more than there, the England of this loose chronicle play is full of discordant elements. Shakespeare's abiding interests – war, kingship, class, women as an influence on men – are handled with striking freedom, and with their good and bad sides both fully in view: with an acute eye, that is, for their contradictions, an invaluable gift of both imaginative writer and historian.

John could not be treated as a thorough-paced villain, like Richard III, because of his reputation with Reformers as an anti-papal champion. He might stray, but he would not be immune to either moral compunction or fear of public opinion. He shows no misgivings about his being on the throne, as his mother and confederate Elinor secretly does. In the first half he is bold and confident to the point of rashness, winning the respect even of the French; in the second he is paralysed by a sense of guilt, becomes incapable of action, leaves everything to his bastard nephew Philip. The turning point comes with the fine scene (III.iii) where he stoops to flattery in order to suborn Hubert, and shufflingly edges towards the ugly disclosure of what he wants: the murder of his young captive Arthur. The dialogue works up to an explosive line made up of five brief speeches, of hinting and compliance. The scene of Arthur pleading with Hubert is the most highly wrought of Shakespeare's variations on the theme of royal fledgelings faced with the rigours of an 'iron age', as Arthur calls it. The poet is voicing his protest against horrors of his own iron age – and, prophetically, of ours. After this John's only independent act is his craven submission to the papal legate Pandulph, without a word to the Bastard, who deems it a shameful national betrayal. John moulders away unheroically, beset on his deathbed 'With many legions of strange fantasies' (V.vii.18). Yet his last thought is of England. Patriotism is the overriding imperative.

The Bastard is one of Shakespeare's creations who impress above all by their abounding vigour and vitality; this keeps us from noticing the contrarieties he is made up of. These derive partly from Shakespeare's model, *The Troublesome Raigne*; he makes use of them to work out some of his historical thinking. The Bastard is a hybrid figure, with one foot inside and one outside an old crumbling feudal world, open-eyed both to its faults and to those of a new age preparing to supplant it. He is delighted, at the outset, to be recognized as a natural son of Richard the Lion-Heart, and welcomed by John and Elinor into the royal circle. His birth and his pride in it stamp him as a free' spirit, unfettered by convention, determined to make his own way; though from a reckless adventurer he will quickly mature into his uncle's right-hand man.

Something here can be traced to the Romance motif of young sprigs of royalty brought up ignorant of their origin, but with an innate royalty of nature. His talk often has a rustic bluntness; the phrase 'fair play', which he uses twice, seems redolent of the village green. He is one of the very few men of rank in these plays to be endowed with a sense of humour, and there is a mocking detachment in his view of the great world into which he has been so suddenly inducted. When he intervenes to prevent Salisbury from attacking Hubert, as Arthur's supposed murderer, his words – 'Your sword is bright, sir, put it up again' – sound like Othello, but his threat to 'maul you and your toasting-iron' belongs much more to the vernacular (IV.iii.79, 99). He brings new blood into a fossilized aristocracy, and an atmosphere of change, renovation. But he has no positive ideas, no armour for the old order against Falstaff's mockery.

France and Austria ostensibly go to war with John for purely chivalrous reasons, on behalf of Constance and her son Arthur. It is 'a just and charitable war' (II.i.35–6). But King Philip, defied by the citizens of Angiers, threatens to 'Wade to the market-place in Frenchmen's blood'. Even Constance, bent on war as she is, has some qualms, and deprecates unnecessary bloodshed (II.i.44 ff.). War is the Bastard's vocation; still, he has an uneasy feeling of how murderous it is, and when he manoeuvres France and Austria into bombarding each other's forces, it is hard not to think that warfare is being made to look grotesque. When the allies have abandoned Constance and come to terms with John, he winds up Act II with a long soliloquy about how 'Commodity' – self-interest, profit – rules everything nowadays. Philip has abandoned his role as 'God's own soldier' in an 'honourable war' for a 'most base and vile-concluded peace'. This was an antithesis that Shakespeare could never escape or overcome; all the same, as an account of the dishonesties of diplomacy the speech is brilliant. Its opening words – 'Mad world! mad kings!' – make a good summary of the state of Europe in Shakespeare's own day. 'I am not worth the coil that's made for me', Arthur is sensible enough to tell his mother. None of these royalties is worth fighting about, Shakespeare may be telling us *sotto voce*.

Later the Bastard becomes the spokesman of patriotism, the ideology destined to be as much that of the bourgeois dispensation as chivalry was of the feudal. It is he who organizes the country's defence when the barons, outraged by the thought of Arthur murdered, join hands with the French. (Shakespeare is regrettably silent about their real reasons for falling foul of their king.) Their dignified leader Salisbury, in a speech originating with Shakespeare, pledges their allegiance to the Dauphin, but bewails the cruel necessity of fighting against their native land. He and his friends are vastly relieved when the treacherous intentions of the French come to light and set them free to forget Arthur and turn back to 'our ocean, to our great king John' (V.iv.47). In reality John has shrunk to a sterile marsh: the true 'ocean' is the motherland.

At the sight of Arthur's dead body, and suspecting Hubert of being responsible, the Bastard himself sounds at first quite religious in his indignation at a crime 'Beyond the infinite and boundless reach/Of mercy' (IV.iii.117–18); but before long the thought of England in danger banishes all else from his mind. John longs to have a united nation at his back, but knows that he has no right to expect it (IV.ii.170–72). It is left to his nephew to blow the trumpet and talk of England's 'victorious hand' terrifying the foe, and of even English ladies donning armour, ready to fight like Amazons (III.ii.127 ff.).

Less chance is given to the French to display a similar love of country. We have no reason to credit King Philip with an ideal of French unification. The Bastard has all John Bull's disdain for the French. 'A cockered silken wanton' is his description of one of them (V.i.70), and it is only because Count Melun has an English grandfather, and hence some spark of decent feeling, that he dies confessing his countrymen's – quite pointless – treachery. The Dauphin shows resolution in face of the loss of his fleet (V.v.20–22); at other times he is easily cast down, and he may be called a stereotype of the mercurial French temperament.

King John is very much a drama of royalty, with its three sovereigns and half a dozen princes or princesses. This collective portrait of 'the anointed deputies of heaven' (III.i.136) and their families is not a flattering one. All three rulers are prepared to kowtow to Rome. Austria shows up worst, because he has bragged too loudly of his knight-errantry. A king's oath is no longer worth much, Constance declares: by deserting her Philip has shown himself a mere 'counterfeit resembling sovereignty'. Yet her denunciation of 'these perjured kings' (III.i.99–100, 107) must strike us as monstrous egotism, by contrast with the compromise peace and marriage alliance that has just been agreed on. It is the proposal of the citizen of Angiers, guided by middle-class common sense instead of royal or knightly punctilio.

John's initial defiance of legate and pope is magnificent, and goes well beyond any requirement of the story. A 'sacred king' cannot be called into question by prelates, he asserts, and he goes on to a sweeping rejection of all the papacy's 'usurped authority' (III.i.147 ff.). It is emerging that monarchs are 'sacred' because they embody their peoples' rights of sovereignty and independence. Pandulph's retort includes incitement to murder as well as rebellion, with an evident topical reference to plots against Elizabeth. His answer to Philip's expostulation against renewal of war with England is full of logic-chopping and quibbling, a Jesuitical argument that ends justify means. Later the Dauphin refuses much more firmly to obey when the legate wants him to leave England alone now that John has submitted to Rome.

Where priests hector and kings falter, the men of the bourgeois future, represented by the citizens of Angiers, stand firm. They sensibly care nothing about the legalist claims of John or Philip: their politics are pragmatic, and they feel as the burghers of Verona do about the brawlings of Montagues and Capulets. The warring monarchs are made to look silly when, after their scrimmage, each claims victory, and the citizens tell them they have watched it all and know that neither side has won; there is a telling image of them looking on from their walls like spectators in a theatre (II.i.300 ff., 373 ff.). Angiers dictates rather than proposes a peace treaty, and adds a challenge as bold as any ever thrown out by an arrogant king or noble. Its men are, indeed, given the *beau rôle*, and they speak the same high-flown verse as the feudalists. The Bastard, iconoclast as he may be, is quick to notice and resent their plebeian presumption (II.i.456 ff.). At Angiers, more daringly than a playwright could have ventured to draw it in a scene of English history, a revolutionary middle class is lifting its head. In later times it was to do so only too seldom.

Richard II (1595)

We see two very different Richards in this play. Either Shakespeare had not decided at the outset what sort of Richard he was to be, or he wanted to show an outward, acquired self crumbling away at the touch of adversity, and exposing a native ego concealed beneath it. In the early scenes Richard is a self-willed, overbearing individual. We know from his own words (I.iv) that he has been reckless with money – 'from too great a Court, and liberal largesse' – to favourites; as a remedy he means to hand over the collection of revenue to tax-farmers; the burden will thereby become heavier. The Duke of York warns his brother John of Gaunt of the futility of giving advice to a nephew whose head is addled with flattery and frivolities. Several touches, left undeveloped, point to criminal as well as foolish behaviour. Richard may like to talk of his sacred self, but his aunt, the widowed Duchess of Gloucester, talks of the 'sacred blood' of all the royal family, and demands punishment for his complicity in her husband's death (I.ii). These hints should not be forgotten when we hear the later Richard pitying himself as a hapless victim – a good deal like Charles I after his fall.

Gaunt's son Bolingbroke and a rival noble, Mowbray Duke of Norfolk, accuse each other of treason, and are to undergo trial by battle before the king. What happens is an anticlimax: Richard forbids the combat when it is about to take place, and banishes both men: why, Shakespeare leaves unclear – a not infrequent feature of his methods. Richard's ostensible reason is that their quarrel is inspired by envious pride and ambition and, if not cut short, might lead to civil broils. In the following scene (I.iv) it is made clear that Richard is suspicious of his cousin Bolingbroke, and has been watching his departure, 'his courtship to the common people'. One of the most brilliant passages in Shakespeare on the modern art of demagogy comes here: Bolingbroke is suddenly transformed, by a couple of centuries, from a cavalier entering the lists to wager his life in true chivalric style, into a wily politician. That he is close in the line of succession, and that Richard, now thirty-two, is childless, is left unmentioned. All this suggests an abrupt change in the picture Shakespeare is planning to draw. His creative growth and interests seem to be pushing him forward towards modernity.

As soon as Richard is confronted he loses his nerve, his bold front dissolves, and each brief fit of resolution is quickly followed by a fresh slump into despair. We might guess that he is undermined by remorse for past misdeeds, but almost until the end he is conscious of no more than unpopularity and isolation. He is sorry for himself instead of for the country he has misgoverned; he retreats into self-righteous hugging of his divine right to do as he chooses. Like all Shakespeare's archetypal characters, Richard is both an individual and a personification of historical change; it was in the same way that the Stuart monarchy was to try to face down opposition. He is the only English king in the Histories who is not a usurper or the heir of a usurper, and has therefore the strongest title to legitimacy. Schücking notes his habit of referring to himself in the third person, like Julius Caesar (52), but may misconceive the reason: it may denote rather a distance opening between king and crown, man and monarchy, an absurd incongruity in the royal pretensions of any human being.

Shakespeare holds up the doctrine of divine right in a very unfavourable light by associating it with a weak, histrionic claimant who loses
himself in poetical fancies as a hiding-place from reality. He is an actor,
instead of a man of action, because it can no longer feel natural for a
mere man to wear a crown. He postures to his subjects, and to himself.
He has no party: scarcely anyone is ready to stand by him. Back from
Ireland, he calls on England's loyal spiders, toads, nettles to bar the rebel
advance – parlous auxiliaries indeed. When he discovers how things are
going wrong, he can think only of 'sad stories of the death of kings'; in
prison he pictures himself as a king long dead, his fall a tale for a winter
night (III.ii; V.i). Monarchy itself has grown moribund, as Richard, in Act
III Scene ii, is the first of all Shakespeare's people to see. Nowhere else in
the plays, Leggatt observes, is it 'subjected to such intense scrutiny' (60).

Richard has shown no sign of religious feeling in Act I, but when
abandoned by men he counts on legions of angels – not spiders and toads
now – to come down and fight for him (III.ii). This militant mood sinks
into one of resignation, and when his faithful consort tries to rouse him
it is too late. He is learning something, however; he is one of a line of
rulers in Shakespeare who are compelled by misfortune, like Lear, or by
danger, like Henry V, to realize that a monarch is only a mortal. 'I live
with bread like you, feel want/Taste grief …'. In the end, chastened by
suffering, he is capable of repentance. He and the queen must atone by
'holy lives' for the 'profane hours' they have squandered. In prison he
quotes Scripture, and looks back on his failure to manage affairs of state
properly. He is a fantasist, but still a prince, who dies resisting his
murderers and winning at least their respect.

What Shakespeare wants now is someone in Richard's place who can
grow into respectability, not tarnished by over-obvious ambition. Bolingbroke shuffles, instead of striding, towards the throne. He returns from
exile professing to want only his rightful inheritance, seized by Richard
and his hangers-on; he may, for all we know, be sincere at first in this
protestation, which his supporter Northumberland vouches for; though
Bolingbroke also declares his intention of ridding the country of
Richard's minions, those 'caterpillars of the commonwealth'. But
Richard's collapse cannot but draw him on, or almost compel him to go
on. It is a vice of the whole monarchical system that a man in his position
can feel safe only when he has the throne to sit on; and then his own
friends cannot feel safe.

Henry IV Part 1 (c. 1596-97)

This play's extraordinary richness of ideas and personalities is emphasized by its background: an England still in confusion, where things

either sombre or ridiculous catch the eye most. In the early Histories nearly everyone belonged to much the same mould; now England can give birth to a pair as antithetical as Hotspur and Falstaff, Borderer and town-loiterer. They are centuries apart in outlook, yet in very different ways both are men of the past, descended from common feudal origins. Hence, though such opposites, they are related to each other, however distantly, and can react dramatically to each other. They combine in a marvellous discord, whose resolution will lead far. Hotspur meets his death from Prince Hal's sword, but morally it is Falstaff who laughs him and all he stands for off the stage of history. His corpse, carried off by the fat knight for exhibition, like a carcass to the market, symbolizes the overthrow of Chivalry. Appropriately, whereas *Richard II* was written almost entirely in verse, *Henry IV* is very largely prose, the language of workaday life. The distance between the two could not be better marked.

Survivors from the past are now aging men, on whom it lies heavily. Henry is a usurper, who can never feel entirely secure. The Percies, who helped him to power, feel cheated and resentful, and Northumberland – Hotspur's father – has a painful sense of guilt as well. The England of common men and women, so skilfully wooed by Bolingbroke, cannot now be ignored by those above; and with the two Englands face to face, acrimonies between them are obtrusive. In the political wrangles each side professes to uphold public interests and welfare; each accuses the other of indulging in empty talk. The action moves back and forth between serious and comic; which of these is the more real, or meaningful, it is hardly possible to tell. From one viewpoint political strife looks portentous; from another it is a farce, absurder than any tavern merriment.

Because powerful currents are dragging the story in various directions, superficial facts of history have to be treated offhandedly. Everything connected with Mortimer and his claim to the throne is incoherent; Shakespeare is no longer interested in such cobwebs, if he ever was. Prince Hal undergoes fairy-tale metamorphoses. Closer scrutiny of the dramatist's handling, however, reveals a careful dovetailing of his two series of episodes, in such a way as to show high life and low life as really two versions of the same thing. As Gadshill says, ' "homo" is a common name to all men' (II.i.94).

Thus the first scene is about wars and disputes among the great; the second – surely meant to be heard as an echo – is about highway robbery. In the third scene the conspiracy of the Percies takes shape; in the fourth the plan for the robbery does the same. The humbler miscreants call it their 'plot': Hotspur has just been lauding his own 'plot' as a fine one, and reiterates the term four times in a soliloquy not much later. (This meaning of the word was new, as also was 'plot' as the outline of a play.) Gadshill talks of the prince robbing for 'sport' (II.i.77); and 'sport' – Hotspur's notion of war – was the last word of the previous scene. Act II Scene ii ends with the prince laughing at the nervous fears of his fellow-thieves; the next scene begins with Hotspur growling to himself about the cowardice of a timid friend unwilling to join in his adventure. Early in the following scene we have Falstaff's repeated 'A plague of all cowards', to uphold his own pretence of valour on the highway. In the next, Hotspur makes a joke of Glendower's still more preposterous assertions. In Act III Scene ii Hal is promising his father to turn over a new leaf; Act III Scene iii opens with one of Falstaff's rueful fits of wanting to do the same: his resolve to repent and go to church.

At the outset English forces have defeated the Scots, but have been defeated by Welsh rebels. Fighting is to be expected now only in the country's outskirts, it seems; and the northern rebellion that soon breaks out gets no nearer to London than Shrewsbury. Hotspur is facing 'the lion's armed jaws' (III.ii.102), and he alone is filled with unclouded determination; his elders are doubtful and hesitant, pricked on more by fear of the king turning against them than by any positive motive. Henry, for his part, is uneasy about them, and helps to provoke them into revolt by what looks like unreasonable harshness towards Hotspur after the hero's defeat of the Scots. On the other hand, we can sympathize with Henry for rejecting Hotspur's anachronistic plea that it was all right for his brother-in-law Mortimer, having been wounded and captured by the Welsh chief Glendower, to go over to him and marry his daughter.

Hotspur was in fact older than the king; but whereas Shakespeare's Henry looks aged and worn out, Hotspur can be thought of only as brimming with buoyant youth and its 'idealism', however irrational. He dies lamenting that he is being robbed of his youth. His father and uncle share with the king the spirit of 'base and rotten policy' that he detests (I.iii.108); much of his attractiveness lies in his openness and freedom from calculation. By nature he is a border baron of old times, cherishing almost sovereign rights. One of Shakespeare's sharpest social antitheses brings him together with the foppish courtier whose silly chatter infuriates him on the battlefield where he has just been grappling with the Scots (I.iii.29 ff.). But Hotspur is a composite portrait, native to a time of change, as Shakespeare's more original creations are apt to be. He is a man of the Renaissance as well as of the turbulent frontier – full of its intense consciousness, intoxicated with the dazzling mirage of Fame. His two selves together breed the restless temperament of one living too much on fantasy. It shows in his wife's account of his 'cursed melancholy' during the long painful waiting for action, his dreams of battle (II.iii): a picture of nervous tension rather than the pleasurable excitement of a healthy fighting animal. This, more than overconfidence, is what must be supposed to have made him engage the enemy precipitately at Shrewsbury, where he 'leap'd into destruction' like a madman, 'with great imagination' but with too few men (*2H.IV* I.iii).

His old antagonist and now ally Douglas the Scot praises him as 'the king of honour', and his widow as the inspiration of 'all the chivalry of England' (*2H.IV* II.iii). With him the idea of 'honour' soars to a semi-mystical height, as all values which have outlived the conditions they sprang from are apt to do. But his tactless contradicting of Glendower shows a more modern quality, the sceptical rationalism that was another part of Elizabethan culture. Glendower boasts of the wondrous portents that surrounded his birth and marked him as outside 'the roll of common men'; Hotspur pooh-poohs them as merely the effects of an earthquake that made Nature shake 'like a coward' (III.i.15 ff.).

He has the same scornful disbelief in Welsh demons. This is in part a lordly indifference to hell or heaven; he never turns to God or asks for divine aid, as his opponent Hal learns to do so fluently. In politics this wilful self-sufficiency leaves him, as his wife says, 'altogether governed by humours' (III.i.233). At his first entrance he is reproaching his father and uncle for having helped Bolingbroke to the throne, and thus incurred a 'detested blot', 'a world of curses' (I.iii). They admit this, and it becomes their main justification for revolt that Bolingbroke, after pretending on his return from exile to be claiming only what was his, had seized the crown. Hotspur, addressing his friends before the battle, assures them that their consciences can be at rest, because their cause is 'fair' and 'just'. Despite this legitimist pose, he intends to make Mortimer, whose right to the throne he seems to recognize, only king of southern England, while he himself reigns over the North and Glendower keeps Wales. Thus the rebels are guilty of treason not simply against Henry IV, but against England. Shakespeare did not invent this atavistic plan of partition (Wilson edn 159), a flat negation of the rising spirit of nationalism; it stamps the conspirators as stragglers from a bygone age, as well as from remote frontiers. But with one of his many puzzling silences, Shakespeare makes no comment.

Hotspur may be 'the perfect mirror of honour', as Norman Council dubs him (42), but only in a very out-of-date sense. In his company we are nearing the end of an era. He may be one of Shakespeare's best poets, as another critic says (Van Doren 121), but he resembles Henry V in drawing his rhetoric from the past, while affecting on weekdays a love of plain blunt language. He carries the aristocratic virtues and foibles to their furthest point, where they hover between grandeur and folly. His ambition is a quest for 'glory' more than for power; there are no brutal crimes to be laid to his account. He has something of the look of a

youthful English Don Quixote, with a head turned by too much reading
of old romances: Cervantes's novel was to come out half a dozen years
after Shakespeare's play, and to win speedy popularity in England. But
for Hotspur 'honour' can be little more than vainglory; it is extravagant,
easily caricatured because destitute of any social or moral purpose. True
'honour' is rescued only by the *coup de théâtre* of a dissipated Hal
transformed by a wave of the wand into an ideal hero.

Shakespeare was adding social to political history, long before professional historians thought of any such thing. The two could not be
fused; to bring their two spheres together, and those of high and low life,
he had to resort to the awkward – if theatrically effective – artifice of a
legendary Prince of Wales dividing his time between court or army,
and disreputable haunts and escapades. We may be meant to surmise
that he – or Shakespeare – considered the court as disreputable a place as
any. The story's requirements oblige Hal to treat his poor careworn
father as heartlessly as later he treats his companion in idleness, Falstaff.
Already near the close of *Richard II* Bolingbroke was lamenting the
behaviour of his 'unthrifty son' (V.iii). Early in *Henry IV Part 1* Hal is
given a soliloquy, which critics (e.g. Schücking 220) have laboured
needlessly to interpret, offering us an explanation of his conduct. It is
highly unconvincing, and brings in very inappositely the Puritan maxim
of holidays being better when they are rare (I.ii.187 ff.). His father's
sermonizing in Act III Scene ii and later shows that Hal's life is all play
and no work; also, in the king's opinion, he has been fooling too much in
public, as Richard II did, and making people sick of the sight of him and
his japes. Hal does not try to rebut this, though he denies some of the
graver charges against him as slander. There are hints, all the same, that
the robbery at Gadshill was not the only escapade of its kind (I.ii).

In the tavern, it is true, Hal is never drunk or silly, never gambling or
in pursuit of women. He is habitually cool, self-possessed, looking down
with more or less disdain on those he is consorting with. We seldom, if
ever, see him really at his ease, in unbuttoned enjoyment of life. At times
he has the air of a shrewd observer looking through the shams and
posturings of the great world – as when he burlesques his father, or
laughs at Hotspur as a mindless fighting machine. His temporary
reformation, for the campaign, is reinforced by a laughable description
of him and his madcap playmates vaulting into their saddles in full
armour – which might weigh from 70 to 130 lb. Most of this piece of
claptrap was borrowed from Nashe and Spenser (Wilson edn 172–4), by
a Shakespeare with his tongue in his cheek.

Still, under the test of war we are shown a Hal with worthy
antagonists. He can feel true respect for Hotspur, which the latter in the
end can return. Both are soldiers who can talk finely about their calling.

Hal shows his only touch of real feeling for Falstaff when he thinks he has been killed in the fight. He sets the captured Douglas free, without a ransom, in recognition of the bravery he has displayed; it is a lesson in 'how to cherish such high deeds', even those of enemies (V.v.29–31). This, Shakespeare is telling us, is how war between gallant opponents ought to be fought.

Henry IV Part 2 (c. 1597-98)

Part 2 is an epilogue, whose chief purpose is to gratify the public with another chapter of Falstaff. It is even more lacking in unity than Part 1; Shakespeare is using up ideas and situations he had no room for there. None the less, the humorous scenes are brilliant, the serious ones full of political insight. After years of reflection on English history Shakespeare has learned, like his Cassius, to look 'quite through the deeds of men', and the play is a compendium of the qualities of a late feudal epoch – through whose final stages he himself was living. Tudor manuals of statecraft are anaemic by comparison.

Heroic and Comic, the two continents between which the action moves, are drifting further apart. Hal is now a less habitual visitor to an Eastcheap that is going downhill. Its revels take on a more sordid look when someone dies after a row with Pistol and Doll, and she is brought out to be whipped by the beadle. But Falstaff is more sparkling than ever in his running exchange of fire with the Chief Justice, that pillar of right thinking. Fresh entertainment is provided, far away in Gloucestershire, by Justice Shallow, a very minor representative of the governing classes; an old dodderer at whom Falstaff can only poke fun, not share flights of fancy with as he could with Hal. Connected with this is the business of Falstaff misusing his commission to impress men for the army, and pocketing bribes from those who can afford to buy themselves off. This is very diverting from his point of view, very pathetic from that of the men taken: we know from Part 1 what their fate is likely to be. In many ways this is one of Shakespeare's most pessimistic plays. Its mood is reflected in the fact that, still more markedly than Part 1, it is a play about old men and women, and their weaknesses and fears. Shallow's maundering reminiscences are mixed with delusions; Falstaff's comment – 'Lord, Lord, how subject we old men are to this vice of lying!' (III.ii.275–6) – may be meant for seniors of higher rank as well.

At the top, the king is always ailing and lamenting under burdens from the past and anxieties for the future, as he totters towards the grave. He is not, like King John, tormented by conscience; he is satisfied that it was 'necessity', rather than ambition, that guided him to the throne; though he still has misgivings over what the country thinks about it

(III.i). He has loyal ministers and reliable younger sons, and is ready to leave most of what has to be done to them. But he has no intimates, and it pains him to recall that Northumberland, now his foe, was not long ago his sponsor. Over him hangs, as over the Shakespeare of the Sonnets, the pervasive Renaissance feeling of the instability of all human things, whose old religious foundations have crumbled.

Warpings within the old order have their counterpart in disruption of the family; the tension between Henry and his heir persists almost to the end. Waking to find the prince gone from his bedchamber, and the crown with him, he meditates on how impatient greed sets sons against aging fathers. It must be said for him that his anxieties are more for England than for himself; his dread is that when the Prince of Wales comes to the throne, the worst can be expected. Hal's exculpation is a laboured piece of rhetoric, seasoned with pious sentiments.

Here is one of the relationships, and the strains they are subjected to, that Shakespeare is more concerned with in this play than with men's actions. These strains, and the heaviness of age, afflict the opposing camp even more than the royal palace. Far more than the feuding nobles of *Henry VI*, the rebel lords are flesh-and-blood creatures, not walking suits of armour. Family revenge is again a prime motive. At the tidings of his son's death Northumberland falls into a paroxysm of fury and despair, and raves about anarchy and destruction (I.i). As Morton tells him, this is not of much help to his party; and before long his wife and Hotspur's widow persuade the timorous old man to run away, leaving the others to bear the brunt – a flight which only postpones his death and renders it less honourable.

We are told of little more than private grudges as causes of the rebellion. Shakespeare neglects what Holinshed had to say of the public grievances alleged against the government. He may have wanted to put the rebels in a bad light: his own government can hardly have wanted rebels to be put in a good light. It has been argued, with force, that there are signs of mutilation by censorship in Act IV Scene i. The archbishop's brief and obviously defective speech, lines 94–6, may be one such. In his longer speech to the royal envoys (53 ff.) the second half is a statement of grievances, but the first – which makes nonsense of it – is an unexpected sermon about England's civil broils having for their real cause a kind of 'burning fever'. 'We are all diseased' – *we* can mean only the self-indulgent ruling class – by 'our surfeiting and wanton hours'. Shakespeare is ensnared in a medical metaphor of luxurious living to be cured only by bleeding: he cannot (or has not been allowed) to turn it into plain terms of needed reform. But there is a glimpse here of the real situation: an aristocracy pushed by its appetites into a struggle for the sweets of office. Such an idea, far above the ordinary ding-dong of the Histories, can most safely be entrusted by Shakespeare to a churchman whose eminent virtue is recognized even by his opponents. There is something like a kindred thought in Henry's words about the rich having food but no stomach for it, the poor sharp stomachs but no food (IV.iv).

In Part 1 rebellion was crushed far away from London; in Part 2 it is nipped in the bud. Henry's chief lieutenants now are his son John of Lancaster, and Westmoreland. Prince Hal has to be kept in the background, reserved for higher things. It is these others who are made responsible for the treacherous seizure and execution of the rebel leaders, after terms have been agreed on. A bloody encounter is averted, and Shakespeare seems to invite us to see this as a good thing, whatever the means; but clearly there is not much 'honour' left among these Honourables of the ruling class. Civil war may be over, but this has taken the 'rotten policy' of the king, the treachery of Lancaster, the cowardice of Northumberland. Beyond political discord, there is spiritual decay for England to be rescued from; suppression of the old insubordination has almost suppressed the old virtues with it.

Hal is in effect waiting for his father to die; Shakespeare's pretext for bringing him back to Eastcheap, his fear of being thought hypocritical if he shows grief at court over the king's illness (II.ii), is clumsy, though it may shed some light on court mentality. His father seems to understand his character when he calls him a mixture of good qualities with passion and caprice (IV.iv). One display of temper that Shakespeare turns to good account is his striking the Chief Justice in an altercation about Bardolph, of all unworthy causes, and being arrested. This is only reported to us, and briefly (I.ii.46–7), but it puts the prince in a very degrading position.

On his accession Hal has to reassure his brothers that England is not Turkey, where a new sultan's brethren are summarily put to death (V.ii). The man with most cause to be nervous is the Chief Justice; and the new king's promptness in not only pardoning but commending and reappointing him sets the key for a new reign. Monarchy as arbitrary autocracy has had its day, and in its place the impersonal State is emerging, with law as its grand regulator. In sixteenth-century England and Europe, justice could be reckoned the principal responsibility of government, at any rate in peacetime. This worthy judge with his civic courage represents a settled, orderly world of self-respect and honesty – or men's aspirations towards such a public life. We never hear of him by name, only by his office, another reminder that the law takes no account of persons.

Folklore required the young ruler to pretend resentment and then be nobly reconciled; Shakespeare takes the opportunity to preach a salutory lesson on law and order and the duty of men of every degree to respect them (V.ii). The judge's long speech defending his action is one of Shakespeare's most splendid political utterances. He reminds Hal that the offence took place while he was in his courtroom, 'busy for the commonwealth', as the king's deputy and upholder of 'The majesty and power of law and justice'. He has prepared himself to face loss of life as well as office. Harry, in his still lengthier response, says everything he ought to; it is noticeable that he twice uses the word 'state' in its modern sense of political nation, just emerging from the earlier usage seen in the judge's speech.

Order has triumphed over anarchy, in the moral sphere as previously in the political. But order and justice have never agreed more than approximately in the modern State. Shakespeare does not mean us to forget how many injustices can flourish under the cloak of legality, or how 'Order' may in practice be only an orderly robbing of the many by the few, the shearing of a docile flock. Falstaff's daydream of having the laws of England at his commandment when Hal is king (V.iii) only magnifies things familiar lower down. In Gloucestershire Justice Shallow is easily persuaded by his man Davy to favour one party in a dispute against the other. The man to be favoured as a knave, they agree, but 'God forbid, sir, but a knave should have some countenance at his friend's request' (V.i).

One writer on the Histories decided to pass over Falstaff as irrelevant, 'historically an intruder' (L.B. Campbell 213). This was to take a very narrow view both of 'history' and of Shakespeare's genius as an interpreter of it. Of the nineteen scenes of *Henry IV Part 1*, ten might be classed as historical, six comic, three mixed. Falstaff is on the stage in eight of them, and altogether for rather more than a third of the play's duration. He also has a prominent place in Part 2. In the company of the self-important men of action, he lends a flavour of silliness to their doings and pretensions. He makes fun of everything, good or bad, in an obsolescent society of which he himself is a maverick member. All theatregoers loved him; spectators of the poorer sort must have liked him all the better for the way he exhibited the follies and malpractices of their superiors. Shakespeare was not a professed satirist, but with Falstaff's aid he could be the master satirist of the age without exposing himself to attack, because Falstaff's random commentary on human behaviour is always light and tolerant, and his creator could disclaim his opinions. If Queen Elizabeth really appreciated Falstaff, she must be credited with enough clear-sightedness to see through the glittering falsity that surrounded her.

Falstaff refuses to take serious things seriously, Bradley wrote (262–3); Shakespeare could let him do so because many conventional notions of what was 'serious' had worn thin. Falstaff is the great jester, but not a court jester. He has a prince for companion rather than patron; both of them are usually under a cloud. He gets some help from Hal in – occasionally – paying his bills (*1H.IV* I.ii.49 ff.), but we never hear him ask for money. He values his independence; his casual mode of existence, with all the discomforts of which he complains, has been his own choice. He has not been expelled from society but has, in the modern phrase, opted out of it. He has a good share of intellectual vanity, and plumes himself on his wit, the best ever to come out of 'the brain of this foolish-compounded clay, man' (*2H.IV* I.ii.1–2): a good summary of his estimate of the human species. He is delighted with Shallow as a butt for witticisms almost more than as a source of easy cash (1:V.i). With Doll on his knee, and Hal and Poins listening unseen, he talks of them both with lofty superiority (2: II.iv.194 ff.). A solitary being, though far from unclubbable, he is fond of talking to himself – less often, like Richard III or Iago, about his nefarious schemes than, like Hamlet, about his philosophy. The secret of his magnetism is the fund of humour he adds to his wit; he disarms us by his willingness to see himself as others see him, to laugh at himself; this sets us free to enjoy his roguery, and let our critical morality sleep.

Poins smiles at Sir John's habit of letting everyone know that he is a knight, just as others let everyone know that they are related, however remotely, to the royal family. (2: II.ii). 'Dropout' though he is, and mocker of the society he has turned his back on, he holds firmly to his title. He rebukes the servant who proposes that he should waive his rank and fight him man to man (2: I.ii). Social status can, of course, be of some assistance to him in trying to remedy the 'perpetual consumption' of his purse. 'As I am a gentleman' he says to the angry Hostess, assuring her that he means to pay her bill. Snare, coming to arrest him for debt, is hesitant: 'It may chance cost some of us our lives, for he will stab' (2: II.i). He does indeed resist. Snare and Fang, the sheriff's men, are underlings, and his self-respect will not let him truckle to them. Shallow remembers him in youth as quite a blade (2:III.ii.26–8). In his verbal set-to's with the Chief Justice he is perfectly cool in his assumption of equality, and once winds up with an impudent suggestion that the dignitary should lend him a thousand pounds (2: I.ii).

As a gentleman he keeps a few tatterdemalions for retinue, a parody of the throngs of servitors kept by the great. When exercised on them his wit is not always good-humoured; he derides Bardolph's red nose without mercy (1: III.iii). But they too are dropouts, living not unlike him, some degrees lower, and remember him after his death with a grumbling affection (*H.V* II.iii). His talk of his luckless conscripts is as cold-blooded as any of Crookback's jibes at his victims (1: IV.ii; V.iii). What is prudence in a knight is disgusting in a plebeian; he is contemptuous of recruits who buy themselves off – exactly what he would do if he were in their shoes.

Every society has its loose fringes, especially in an age of change like Shakespeare's, or our own. Falstaff is their supreme representative, with a perennial appeal as a sceptic, a nonconformist, such as we all are at times, if only covertly. He and Hal burlesquing the court, with Falstaff for once orating in verse, his bald head for crown, a stool for throne (1: II.iv.370 ff.), reduce the pomp and paraphernalia of monarchy to nonsense. It is the same with all the strutting and stiffness of conventional life. Falstaff used to live, he tells us, as 'virtuously' as a gentleman need, with not much swearing, gambling not more than once a day, and so on. It is not on any points like these that his notions of conduct diverge from upper-class standards. They are heterodox most of all over the neochivalric code of honour which in Elizabeth's time was being enshrined in the duel.

Shakespeare made a mock of 'honour' more than once, as not a few other writers did; he owed something to Montaigne's essay on Glory, and the picaresque novels of sixteenth-century Spain were fond of ridiculing heroic posturings (Valbuena Prat 164–5). He takes his first quizzical look at the subject in the scene in *Henry VI Part 3* (IV.iii) where sentries on night duty are comparing peaceful comfort with 'dangerous honour', just before Warwick rushes in with his shout of 'honour now or never!' Falstaff on campaign, with his unsentimental view of warfare, must be expressing thoughts afloat in the minds of many ordinary soldiers. Every great character of fiction draws together, in some such way, the thinking or feeling of many. His monologue on honour at Shrewsbury marks a crucial point in the unfolding of Shakespeare's ideas. It is quickly followed by the death of that champion of honour, Hotspur.

'But yet no coward, Hal', Falstaff protested (1: II.ii). No one believed him until after Maurice Morgann's essay appeared in 1777, and even since then not all readers do. A coward is a man who dare not do something he feels he ought to do. If Falstaff is to go on being Sir John, he must be ready to show proper spirit, or something like it, when he thinks it necessary, though without running himself into any superfluous hazards. Before the Gadshill affair Poins speaks of two of the band as 'true-bred cowards', and of Falstaff as a man who will not fight 'longer than he sees reason' (I.ii.175 ff.): an exact distinction. Whatever may be said of his humble companions, a really craven Falstaff would scarcely be engaged in such a 'vocation' as highway robbery. It carried more risks than one. 'If I hang, old Sir John hangs with me', one of the others declares: in other words, he will 'peach' (II.i.66–7).

Falstaff joins in the attack on the travellers although he is warned that there are eight or ten of them, and he has only three men with him. Waylaid in turn by the disguised prince and Poins, and deserted, he strikes a blow or two before taking to his heels. A fat old man need not be expected to stand and fight a pair of young swordsmen. When it came to making up a tale about what had happened, his purpose was of course, as Morgann pointed out, to amuse, not to deceive (140–41). Hacking his sword-edge as testimony of a stiff resistance, and multiplying men in buckram by leaps and bounds, were comic fictions on a par with Pooh-Bah's 'corroborative detail' about an imaginary execution. Poins had predicted that he would have 'incomprehensible lies' to tell of a struggle with 'thirty at least' (I.ii.178 ff.), and Falstaff had a golden chance to live up to his inventive reputation. Hal labours the obvious when he refuses to believe a story that would not deceive a child.

At Shrewsbury too, Falstaff's demeanour is that not of a poltroon but of a cool level-headed man who will do what he must and no more. He has 'led' his men under fire, and left them dead or crippled, presumably withdrawing in good time. (Are we to guess that he hopes to go on drawing their pay and keeping it, as Elizabethan officers frequently did? If so, the more killed the better.) He looks around him at the heavy-handed heroes, as unperturbed as though taking his ease in his inn. At Douglas's approach he lies down, pretending to be dead, as sensible men have done when approached by a bear. Still, he will be happy if people think that by some fluke he has managed to kill Hotspur, and earn a reward.

Falstaff makes game of Hotspur's Honour just as Hotspur does of Glendower's magic (so does Falstaff: II.i.v.331 ff.) – on this point at least, the ill-matched pair agree. Puritan writers and preachers were attacking atavistic notions of honour, but they were doing so from the firm standing-ground of a new class with new values, whereas from Falstaff we hear the self-criticism of an old class whose values are rusting away. He is fond of Puritan jargon, tags and fragments of Scripture, but only as figures of speech; he would be quite ready to sell his soul to the Devil for a cup of Madeira and a capon's leg, as Poins accuses him of having done (1: I.ii.111–13). He affects indignation at the sad discovery that 'Virtue is of so little reward in these costermonger times' – so little that purse-proud tradesmen are impertinent enough to insist on gentlemanly customers giving them 'security' (2: I.ii). Here is the cry of a whole class of decayed gentry, swept away to make room for the moneybags.

Sir John has to be thankful for an invitation to dinner at a tavern from Master Smooth the silk-dealer, hoping no doubt for a suit of clothes on credit as well as a free meal (2: II.i). He is stranded between two eras, with no place in either, yet always unblushingly ready for a laugh. 'They hate us youth', he exclaims as he and his band attack the pious well-fed pilgrims: 'young men must live!' (1: II.ii). Young men *were* discontented; and in his freakish way Falstaff is a true rebel against a grey, cramping environment. He is an old scamp, to be forgiven because he is an amusingly unsuccessful one: all his schemes go awry, as they ought to for a man to whom life is a farce.

Still, life on his Bohemian plan must also be a long train of petty makeshifts and annoyances, ending in catastrophe. His self-pityings are a ludicrous counterpart to King Henry's. In his very first meeting with us he is a prey to low spirits, and is deploring his bad reputation (1: I.ii). 'Sighing and grief' are his excuse for corpulence. He likes to harp on his age, but he does not relish anyone else hinting that he is old and decrepit. He was angered once by the prince comparing him to 'an old, withered applejohn' (2: II.iv). Bardolph irritates him, when he is feeling sorry for himself, by saying 'you are so fretful you cannot live long' (1: III.iii).

Bradley – and, more surprisingly, Hazlitt – thought him unfailingly good-humoured, or pretending low spirits only for fun (Bradley 261; Hazlitt, *Characters* 146, 148): as great an error, surely, as to reckon him a coward. We never dream of seeing him drunk, but he is a toper, one of the very few in Shakespeare, and a philosophical one, as true a disciple of Bacchus as Hotspur is of Mars. Without sherry-sack life would scarcely be bearable; it is his refuge from the squalor of his surroundings. It purges the brain of 'all the foolish and dull and crudy vapours which environ it' – another hint of moods of depression. More positively, he pays tribute to it as the inspirer of his wit, as of warlike valour in others (2: IV.iii).

Falstaff's spells of self-reproach, and talk of reforming and recovering his name, are not purely jocular (cf. Salingar 41). He is fond of blaming others – 'Company, villainous company' (1: III.iii.9) – for leading him astray: at one moment Hal, at another Poins. But a return to a state of grace, or genteel living, has no real attraction for him. Employment as a hangman, he tells Hal, would suit him quite as well as 'waiting in the court' (1: I.ii.65 ff.). But in the end his philosophy of life breaks down – under the weight, we must think, of increasing years and needs, and of temptation: news of the king's death, and the sudden rash hope of court favour. Now at last he is ready to sell himself for a mess of pottage, disguised as luxury, influence, patronage. This is his real fall; his rejection by the new king only caps his self-betrayal. Our idea of him is sadly tarnished by his indecent haste to get back to London and make his fortune, with an unworthy revenge on the Chief Justice to sweeten it. By repudiating him Hal saves him from sinking into a hated court favourite.

Commissioned by the now ostentatiously virtuous Hal to see to Falstaff's reformation, the Chief Justice orders him to jail as a first step in improvement; much as in the beehive fable in *Henry V*, the Justice hands over the lazy drone to the executioner. What we hear of Falstaff's last days is painful. Like the past he belongs to, he has to be left sternly behind. 'His heart is fracted' (*H.V* II.i) – not by sentimental regrets, for which he has little room, but by disappointment, and the shame of ruthless public disgrace; above all, we must hope, by the thought of how he has lowered himself to the level of a vulgar fortune-hunter. His deathbed is a troubled one, and there are only his old disreputables to regret him. 'Would I were with him', says Bardolph, though all he ever got in Falstaff's service was drink and a red nose (*H.V* II.iii).

Henry V (1599)

Hazlitt, the great dissenter, refused to see Henry V as an ideal patriot, and objected to his bloodthirsty speechifying (*Characters* 156–8). Infatuation with Empire restored the victor of Agincourt to his pedestal. Sidney Lee rejoiced at his display of 'the higher potentialities of human character', particularly as they are found in England (*Life* 252). World Wars of the twentieth century did him further good – in his native land, at least. Shakespeare's play could be extolled as 'a new epic and heroic drama, blending Christian virtue with martial prowess' (Knight, *Sovereign Flower* 37). Since then there has been a relapse. One pair of critics find symptoms of boredom on the author's part, covered by forced metaphors (Muir and O'Loughlin 112–13). Another complaint is of an 'astounding inflation' of language (Van Doren 172). Leggatt goes so far as to call the play a 'satire' (121). It does indeed often seem as if Shakespeare – fresh from writing a work as iconoclastic as *Henry IV* – is ranting to conceal his own disbelief in his recantation, even parodying his heroic style by turning it into bombast. Graver still is the charge that he is the herald of a historical ideology 'destructive and ultimately self-destructive' (Stribrny 101).

The anniversary of Agincourt was still being celebrated in the sixteenth and seventeenth centuries. It was a triumph of aggression; unfortunately, before the Armada year England had scarcely any defensive struggle to look back on. From *Henry IV* Shakespeare had perforce to go on, as pledged in its Epilogue, to *Henry V*, for a grand finale to his Histories. Equally inevitable was his failure to make a coherently credible drama of it. His play contains thrilling poetry and pointed thoughts, but a time-honoured tale of conquest could not be a fitting place for them. The Chorus's appeals to the audience to assist the author with its imagination may be a sign that this author is often wrestling with an uncongenial task.

Edward Hall's chronicle had given Tudor Englishmen a Henry V who was 'the mirror of Christendom and the glory of his country' (Wilson edn xviii). With this eulogy Shakespeare could not openly disagree; he could only lend it some shade as well as light, by touches here and there. As with Prince Hal, the result is an unconvincing medley. Early on he takes pains to colour his picture of Henry as a reformed or newly revealed character. We are told, as impressively as if Shakespeare really believed it, how well he can discourse on theology or political or military affairs, in spite of the fact that his time has all been frittered away on 'riots, banquets, sports' (I.i.37 ff.). His lengthy denunciation of the 'English monsters', or traitors, suborned by French gold is a lecture on patriotic loyalty; he bespeaks our sympathy by telling us pathetically of his very intimate friendship with one of them, Scroop, a Judas who had known the very bottom of his soul (II.ii.79 ff.). This is news, for we have previously heard Henry say that he had no better friend than Poins (*2H.IV* II.ii), and he never seems like a man capable of close friendship. His heart is not 'fracted', at any rate; Scroop and the betrayal are not given another thought. Even an admirer who believes in his 'genuine love of public service for its own sake' finds something missing, an absence of human reality behind the mask of the successful ruler (Ellis-Fermor 43–5). It should be noted, however, that the villains are not condemned to death out of hand, but remitted 'to the answer of the laws': law is a higher authority than the king, even if we know well enough what their fate will be.

It may be conjectured that some in official quarters were displeased by the levity of *Henry IV* in the matter of army recruitment, for instance; and that its author was given a hint to be on his best behaviour next time. In any case, this play is stridently nationalistic. Throughout it the French are denigrated; care is taken to blunt any better feeling we may have for them. Their attempt to procure Henry's assassination warns us what to expect of them, like their vile plot in *King John*. Yet despite all the patriotic noise and heat, the public seems, to its credit, not to have been enthusiastic. There appear to have been few performances in Shakespeare's lifetime, or for long after. Disappointment at the loss of Falstaff must have been a main cause; a further instalment of his doings had been promised in the Epilogue to *Henry IV*. Shakespeare must have understood when he set to work that Falstaff in France would cast a blight over the whole campaign. He offers a sort of apology when Fluellen, discoursing on Macedon in the midst of the Battle of Agincourt, and on Alexander as Henry V's peer, refers inadvertently to Alexander's hasty temper and killing of his best friend, and goes on to compare it to Henry's turning away 'the fat knight' who was 'full of jests, and gipes, and knaveries, and mocks, I have forgot his name' (IV.vii.31 ff.). No one else had forgotten it.

Once more, as when Talbot was in his stride, an English army is marching and slaughtering on foreign soil. There is, however, a vast change of atmosphere, and an audible undercurrent of criticism of both war and royalty. Each of these twin institutions is far more complex now than it used to be. Henry wrestles with God; Shakespeare can be seen wrestling with himself. Often he is writing far too well to be doing mere journeyman work; but his words may sound double-edged. To suppose him a simple-minded cheerleader, wanting everything he says to be taken literally, would imply as abrupt a transformation of Falstaff's creator as of his Hal. On the surface the play is a straightforward exercise in drum-beating, but scattered through it are asides to us by the author that give it a very different complexion. War-weariness was growing in England in the few years before Ireland was 'pacified' and James I put an end to the fighting with Spain. Shakespeare was thinking of ordinary folk who suffered under the burdens of war, as well as of the warlords. The superheated rhetoric of Henry's speech to his men at Harfleur borders on caricature.

After Agincourt, not much is left. Shakespeare apologizes for leaving things out; he may have been wearying. He might have ended on a note of blood-reeking triumph, but preferred a fifth Act tranquillizingly bland, only half the length of Act IV, and nearly all in prose. Its business is to arrange a French surrender, but Shakespeare gives this the air of an amicable settlement of claims, with Henry eager for peace. Nothing tactless is said to ruffle tempers. What overshadows all the rest is Burgundy's speech, as mediator, about the torment that France has undergone. In Act I we heard Henry threatening France with all the horrors of war; now we know that these horrors have in fact been inflicted on that hapless country. A jocular courting scene makes a poor sequel, a worse comedown than almost any other important Shake-spearian play's conclusion. Henry, bluff and self-satisfied, has no remorse for the devastation he has caused; Katherine is a mere stage doll. To have to descend to this was a confession of failure; and the Epilogue reminds the spectators of how quickly, with Henry's infant son on the throne, France was to be lost.

It was on 'high moral grounds', according to the faithful L.B. Campbell, that the decision to invade France was taken (263–4). Yet Shakespeare offers no acceptable explanation; what he does give us is a sight of the kind of secret history that played a large part in getting the wars of his own era going, as it still does now. In the background is the lesson Henry had learned from his father: that the way to avoid trouble at home was to pick quarrels abroad (*2H.IV* IV.v.209 ff.). For too long England had been a prey to feudal factions; an attack on France would unite all these, wash away their guilt in French blood, and refresh and legitimate the monarchy.

Foreign war was counted on by contemporary wisdom to purge the realm of discontents of the poor as well as of the powerful. New social forces were emerging, but nothing yet of a social programme, apart from the prescriptions held out by Puritanism. Henry's incursion into France will enable some social rubbish – like Bardolph – to be got rid of; more respectably, it may draw high and low (and likewise the component regions of the British Isles) together in a common endeavour: all are to have a place in Henry's band of brothers. The archbishop's idyllic beehive, with order and obedience for keynote, is – like Menenius's fable in *Coriolanus* – a panegyric on social harmony, all classes blending into one: a vision always dear to conservatives.

Fullest justification of a war of aggression could come only from religion. The Henry V of history did make a parade of piety, and advertised it by persecuting heretics. Shakespeare's Henry, with his incessant applications to God (for a further credit, so to speak), his insistence that heaven is squarely on the English side, sounds incongruously like a militant Protestant. It was Protestant animosity against Catholic Spain and Ireland that supplied most of whatever popular approval England's wars, at the time when this play was written, enjoyed. Henry's opponents are not allowed even to beg for divine favour, and Frenchmen are too frivolous even to think of doing so.

Shakespeare might have given Henry a better-sounding claim by arguing that France was under bad or weak rule, and he would govern it better. Instead, he thinks of the country as crudely as an animal-tamer: 'France being ours, we'll bend it to our awe,/Or break it all to pieces' (I.ii.226–7). Only here and there in Shakespeare's Europe were people learning to object to their countries or provinces being handed down or bandied about among kings just as estates were by landowners. His audience may well have taken an interest in his genealogies of its own rulers, but it is not likely to have felt nearly so much in the archbishop's antiquarian rigmarole about Henry's rights to France. Shakespeare took it straight from Holinshed, and left it 'very imperfectly dramatised' (Raleigh 69), as if deliberately making it sound nonsensical. Henry's envoy tries to convince the French that his claims are not mere rubbish 'Picked from the worm-holes', or 'dust of old oblivion' (II.iv.85 ff.), but that is what they obviously are; and the bloodthirsty threats that follow – with the responsibility, as usual, laid entirely on the victims – belong to an age that Shakespeare must have wanted England to leave behind.

Shakespeare seems to relish the opportunity afforded him by the chronicles to begin his play by showing a pair of supple prelates scheming to avert a sweeping confiscation of church wealth proposed by Parliament by egging Henry on to war and promising financial support. After this, Henry's earnest exhortation to Canterbury to pronounce on his claims with religious impartiality, and the anxious wish he professes not to offend heaven by starting 'unjustly' a war whose bloody consequences he vividly foresees, can only sound like Shakespearian irony. The response is unctuously reassuring; and on one point, the plunder to be won from war, the Metropolitan is franker than anyone else, even if he wraps it up in his parable of the bees. What real gains will accrue to the nation, except a surety against civil war, he and Shakespeare refrain from any attempt to show. That there will be a positive loss – of the church wealth that Parliament could have applied to useful purposes – is not emphasized; but we may suppose that a post-Reformation audience would be alert enough to see such points.

By offering no public justification for war, Shakespeare leaves Henry to appear as a ruthless egotist demanding his pound of flesh. This does much to nullify the appeal of the synthetic hero he is trying to produce, a compendium of admirable qualities from previous plays. There is no room for a Hotspur in England; only in a foreign war can his dashing courage be put to good use. Prince Hal overthrew Hotspur; Henry V dons the skin of the dead lion, and talks about his thirst for Honour in exactly the same strain. Englishmen were being invited to see themselves as a collective Hotspur, as they were to become in empire mythology. In Henry royalty is taking on a partially modernized aspect. He is a feudal monarch fighting for hereditary rights, and playing the knight errant. But once in the field he becomes the leader of a State with a swelling nationalist spirit to be played on; and he has a strong infusion of the middle-class virtues, united with the older ones of sword and lance. The England of his successors is to be a nation of well-armed shopkeepers, a land of imperial grocers.

Unlike Richard III before Bosworth, Henry before Agincourt goes out to mingle incognito with his soldiers, and then prays himself into the proper mood of self-righteousness. His small army is cut off, hemmed in by superior forces; he is alone. He does not kneel to ask forgiveness for the selfish ambition that has brought his men to this pass; it is no sin of his own that weighs on his mind, but his father's sin of usurpation. He has nothing to reproach himself with. After all, he wants no more than his God does – the kingdom, the power, and the glory. British empire-builders of later days could have no better patron saint than Henry V.

A king going about in disguise among his people had long been a popular ballad motif (Holt 103). Here it leads to an argument, one of the passages that make this a 'problem play', and a partial rebuttal at least of Bernard Shaw's charge against Shakespeare of having (unlike Ibsen and himself) no *ideas* (*Shakespeare*). Doubts in the soldiers' minds combine with Henry's own uncertainty about his title to the throne, and bring on his brief loss of confidence. The debate, however, is an unsatisfactory one. Tillyard found it chilly (*Historical Plays* 309); it is so because Henry can only be evasive – which, moreover, is less easy in prose than in verse.

Bates and Williams have a sour conviction that if the English are beaten the king will be ransomed and go home, while common soldiers are left to rot. They go on to thoughts of the battlefield, with its maimed and dying men, who may have left unprotected wives and children; the king, they argue, if right is not on his side, will be responsible for all this. Shakespeare does not let them talk about responsibility for the evils the invasion is inflicting on France; he may wish his hearers to think of it. With the skill in theology we have heard him to possess, Henry turns the whole question into an abstract one of divine purposes. It takes a form where the new individualism shows once again, more morbidly than usual. God has his eye on every single soldier, and battle is his opportunity to punish those who are guilty of crimes – committed not during this blameless campaign, but before it. Each man is answerable for the fate of his own soul, Henry insists, and must not think to put the blame on his leader: it behoves every soul to be in a state of readiness for death, so that death can come as a blessing.

Henry's prolix reply may sound to us 'poor, muddled and irrelevant' (Palmer 238), but it is really a skilful piece of casuistry. His subjects may think they can blame him for everything that befalls them; he transfers the blame to God: 'War is His beadle, war is His vengeance.' Bates and Williams are easily convinced (was Shakespeare's audience?), though other anxieties still rankle in their minds. The question of widows and children left unprovided for has dropped out of sight; so has that of responsibility for crimes committed on orders from above. Shakespeare had brought this up earlier – in Act I Scene iv of *Richard III*, where Clarence's murderers met his expostulations by saying that they were only carrying out the king's command, while he urged that murder was forbidden by 'the great King of kings'. In our century this has grown into a worldwide issue.

After these nocturnal scenes, the battle itself is uninteresting. There is not much of it that Shakespeare can put on his stage, and he seems not even to want to. In the play as a whole fighting enters into only two Acts, and then with a refreshing infusion of lighter business. Henry's blood-curdling threats to the citizens of Harfleur had the warrant of a rule, coming to be accepted in Shakespeare's time, that a beleaguered town which refused to capitulate when it had no chance of being relieved could be given up to 'military execution', or sacked, as Badajoz was by Wellington as late as 1812. But Shakespeare must surely have expected some of his hearers to wonder whether Henry's antiquated 'rights' in France were worth such atrocities as 'naked infants spitted upon pikes' (III.iii.38).

There must have been some smiles at the announcement, after the fierce fighting at the bridge, that French losses have been heavy, while the English have not lost a single man; but clearly part of the aim is to depict the campaign as costing England very little in blood. Agincourt is a mere walkover. Ten thousand Frenchmen are killed, nearly all of them of blue bood – commoners have not suffered much – and only twenty-nine Englishmen (IV.viii). 'O God, thy arm was here', Henry may well piously exclaim. Shakespeare makes a muddled effort to discredit the enemy again, but he really brings out Henry's streak of ferocity, with his order to kill all prisoners. Fluellen angrily accuses the French of a massacre of English baggage-boys, but Henry has given his order a scene earlier, simply because the French seem to be rallying, and later threatens to give the order without any allusion to their crime (IV.vi, vii). And in the end the English are left with 1,500 gentry prisoners, besides others. To lend the battlefield a sentimental touch we have a description of York and Suffolk expiring in each other's arms, like brothers. Shake-speare calls this 'pretty and sweet' (IV.vi). He must have forgotten that his Duke of York is the craven Aumerle of *Richard II*, Act V.

There is no Falstaff now to laugh at his protégé's declamations, but his seedy followers are still with us – a walking commentary on the glorification of war and a picturesque contrast with the sturdy, sober men-at-arms whom Henry meets. At the start they are taking leave of their London tavern, and Pistol of his newly wed Hostess. He warns her to be on her guard, and cautious about giving credit – 'For oaths are straws, men's faiths are wafer-cakes' (II.iii.49): a comic echo of Henry's denunciation of the traitors in the previous scene. There is another Beggar's-Opera sort of parody in Bardolph having to reconcile Pistol and Nym after a gambling dispute, so that they can go off to the wars 'all three sworn brothers' (II.i), much as Henry is going to war to unite his quarrelsome nobles. The trio are off to France 'like horse-leeches.... To suck, to suck, the very blood to suck!' (II.iii; cf. IV.iv.65). Pistol is as realistic as any prelate about the fact that the purpose of war is plunder.

The boy they take with them is one of the sharp-eyed youngsters whom Shakespeare makes use of as reporters. He is soon wishing himself back in London: 'I would give all my fame for a pot of ale, and safety' (III.ii); he must have listened profitably to Falstaff. At Harfleur Henry's 'Once more unto the breach' is promptly taken up by Bardolph: 'On, on, on, on, on! to the breach, to the breach!' – but he and his comrades at once find good reasons for *not* going on, until Fluellen appears and beats them forward (III.ii). Shakespeare has tried in this play – maybe half-heartedly – to kindle something like the exaltation of 1914 and Rupert Brooke's sonnet about Honour coming back into the world. But Hotspur, its standard-bearer, perished at Shrewsbury, and Falstaff gave his corpse a parting stab as though to symbolize the moral death his satire had already inflicted on the heroic dream-world.

The last we see of the unheroic group, after Bardolph is hanged for pilfering, is Pistol getting a well-deserved thrashing from Fluellen, for insulting him and Wales. 'All hell shall stir for this!' – his furious threat, on being released, sounds as if it is borrowed from some of Henry's earth-shaking menaces; but he soon collapses. 'Old I do wax, and from my weary limbs/Honour is cudgelled': once more the heroic is deflated by association. His wife has died of the 'malady of France'; Doll Tear-sheet has sunk to 'a lazar kite', a low prostitute; and he is going to sneak home and live by begging and stealing (V.i). Another pathetic remnant of an older time has come to the end of its tether.

Englishmen of Henry's time and later were taught that 'he had ruled spectacularly well'. He was a winner, and 'conspicuous worldly success is demanded of kings' (Saccio 88). He has a kindred spirit in the Richmond who, on his way to the throne, assures himself that he is God's appointed 'captain' (R.III V.iii). He has a successor in Cromwell, the crusading imperialist, and all his brood of empire-builders for whom Henry V was to be something like a camp bible. Through it we have a good view of the feudal perversions which were bequeathing to later times a mentality of conquest cemented by Christian conviction, or a pretence of it. As a resounding climax for the whole series of plays, Henry V has a historical veracity. It was written when England was on the brink of three centuries of imperial expansion, beginning with Ireland, settlements in North America, buccaneering expeditions round the globe. But no worldwide expansion could ever lay to rest the contradictions planted by Shakespeare in his drama.

3

Historical Themes

Monarchy

'Hath he deserved to lose his birthright thus?' Queen Margaret exclaims, when her husband signs away their son's title to the succession (*3H.VI* I.i.229; cf.II.ii.35). The crown is the supreme emblem of the divine right of property; it is the 'birthright' of whoever has the best claim to it by descent. Each landowner's title to his estate or fief rested on the same basis: the two species of right evolved together. But when the crown is disputed in the Histories, men take sides from varied motives, as they always have done when societies are divided by fundamental issues.

Henry VI himself is weakened by an uneasy conscience on account of his grandfather having been a usurper. His scruples are Shakespeare's own invention, not derived from the chroniclers (Council 13). This has helped to inspire a conception of the Histories as a kind of *Oresteia*, a record of a royal house under a curse from its founder's guilt. It is a notion rightly rejected by W.R. Elton (30). Shakespeare's view of history is pragmatic, not mystical. Kingship may be 'divine', but only in so far as it is useful; though he is quite ready to make use of any striking ideas for the sake of dramatic effect. Made prisoner by some gamekeepers, Henry VI is confronted by the alien way of thinking of these commoners. When he taxes them with their oath of allegiance, their answer is that they must take orders from whatever king may be in power; and they seem to care very little which king this may be (*3H.VI* III.i). Englishmen of the sixteenth and seventeenth centuries were obliged to acquiesce in a shuttlecock alternation of regimes and creeds; these plays brought on to the stage a similar spectacle, which must have had a similar psychological effect. On balance Elizabeth could feel satisfied. She was the granddaughter of another usurper; her right to the throne rested very much on her own prowess, as Henry V's was vindicated by his conquest of France. In any government's eyes the best lessons of history are those that tell in its own favour.

Philip in *King John* can discourse impressively on a king's duty to right wrong, as deputy of the 'supernatural judge' (II.i.112–14), but the prime function of kingship is to keep order. In *Henry VI Part 2* York rhapsodizes about the sceptre not only as the supreme possession but as the means 'to act controlling laws', 'to govern and rule multitudes', which he declares Henry incapable of (V.i.91ff.). In the very first scene of the Histories Henry V's memory is evoked by his brother Humphrey of Gloucester, as that of a model ruler. It is a fearsome enough picture: menacing eyes, 'brandished sword', 'arms spread wider than a dragon's wings'. There is a clear implication that unless a king knows how to play the dragon, anarchy will quickly ensue: in other words, the State has little cohesion of its own, but can be held together only by unremitting coercion. Clifford the younger, in his dying speech on the battlefield, mourns Henry VI's fatal weakness in not destroying the Yorkist faction out of hand (*3H.VI* II.vi). Richard II's gardener knows that plants growing too tall must be lopped off, like overmighty subjects (III.iv). Richard has obeyed this rule of thumb by banishing two such men; but that was not enough.

An heir coming to the throne while still a minor could not be a vigorous ruler; here was a failing of hereditary monarchy, nowhere more prominent than in Scottish history. It might, therefore, be deemed sensible to pass over a minor and install the competent man nearest to the succession. This is Richard III's contention, and John's; and as John's enemy Constance complains, the sovereigns she is appealing to ignore legitimacy when peace with John suits their interests. His seat on the throne is unquestioned until he comes under suspicion of having had Arthur murdered. This distinction between ousting an heir and making away with him may be illogical, but it may well have weighed with public opinion, never much guided by strict logic. Even the hardened Buckingham jibs when it comes to Richard wanting his nephews killed, and his defection is the beginning of Richard's downfall.

Similar mixed feelings might be aroused by removal from the throne of adult rulers, and their subsequent fates. Shakespeare said quite enough about the sinfulness of usurpation to placate an Elizabeth to whom Richard II's deposition was a sore subject; her appetite for flattery had early won her the nickname 'Richard the Second'. Shakespeare could also write impressively of the sanctity of a king's person; this was a theme that could have potent mythic or poetic force, in union with the religious or magical virtues of anointment. His murderer's hand will 'burn in never-quenching fire', Richard warns him, and Exton shudders at the thought (*R.II* V.v). Richard's death seems to weigh more heavily than his deposition; and at Agincourt, when Henry V is troubled by the memory of his father's 'fault' in 'compassing the crown', it is the shedding of royal blood that is uppermost in his mind (*H.V* IV.i.). Yet the practical difficulty remained. A dethroned monarch left alive would always be a focus of conspiracy – hence Elizabeth's execution, after many hesitations, of her prisoner Mary Stewart. It was an advantage in this case that Mary was a foreigner, already rejected by her own country. Still, Elizabeth had to disclaim responsibility; as Holland says (128), Shakespeare may be politely subscribing to this pretence when his King John laments 'the curse of kings': that their officers are always ready to exceed their instructions (*KJ* IV.ii.208). Cromwell was to learn that Charles I's deposition and execution could seem two very unequal things to his people.

As a political study *Richard II* is less a drama of one king's overthrow than a rejection of an archaic pattern of kingship, or the idea coming to be known as the 'divine right of kings', which was to cost the Stuarts so dear. Richard is an unstable, self-absorbed individual, under the sway of favourites and flatterers. His challenger Bolingbroke, by contrast, is a man of will and action, such as the times require, as well as a first cousin of Richard, with blood almost as royal as his. It may be noted as another part of Shakespeare's elastic conception of what is due to rulers – and from them – that foreigners have no claim on his advocacy, though they may have received, or be entitled to, the same mysterious ointment from the same Church.

If the preoccupation of the earlier Histories is with the need for strong government, capable of maintaining law and order, it is not long before an opposite danger shows itself: of government becoming too strong and arbitrary. This may come about whether the man on the throne is strong or weak. Richard II's frivolity allows his minions to persuade him into, or themselves indulge in, all kinds of misuse of authority. John is an energetic ruler who provokes chaos by abusing his power, until factions are snarling like dogs, the Bastard grumbles, over 'the bare-picked bones of majesty' (*KJ* IV.iii.148). Pandulph has predicted that John, as a usurper, will have to maintain himself by ruling despotically, and argued that tyranny can never make itself safe by killing (III.iv). When John has done no more as yet than resolve on a single crime, in imagination Shakespeare sees him, his people see him, he seems to see himself, as already drenched in blood. His foot 'leaves the print of blood where'er it walks', cries Salisbury (IV.iii.25). John himself is driven to recognize that bloodshed can be 'no sure foundation' (IV.ii.104). What, then, can? Monarchy seems to demand mutually exclusive qualities. A king must be strong and resolute – 'glister like the god of war', as the Bastard tells his uncle (V.i). But the greater his strength, the likelier he is to resort to arbitrary methods. Only a good man is fit to hold sway, but no ruler could be a better man than Henry VI.

Strong rule may bring order, at least for a while, but Shakespeare is far from admiring power for its own sake; and greed for it can lead to crime, and thereby liberate fresh disorder. After changing sides in the Wars of

the Roses, Warwick at once denounces Edward IV as a 'tyrant', and
Edward's queen, Elizabeth, applies the same epithet to Warwick himself
(*3H.VI* III.iii.206; IV.iv.29). It meant properly a usurper, but was loosely
used in a sense more like ours. Edward's brother Clarence, in the Tower,
protests that he has had no trial, no jury: it is 'most unlawful' for him to
be condemned without being 'convict by course of law' (*R.III* I.iv).
Edward on his deathbed will soon suffer painful regrets for his hasty
suspicions of Clarence. The whole play may be called a warning against
the irremediable acts of violence that unfettered power seems doomed to
give way to.

Richard Crookback, once on the throne, is in every sense an authentic
tyrant, though able to style himself (with a sardonic chuckle, doubtless)
'the lord's anointed' (IV.iv.151). Tudor lawyers struggling with their
often-changing law of treason faced the dilemma of how to distinguish
the due rights of *de jure* and *de facto* wearers of the crown. Shakespeare
seems to be left stranded between two contradictory ideas: it is not on
the whole wrong for an unsuitable ruler to be deprived of the crown, but
it is wrong for any other man, however suitable, to take it. Common
sense has to brush such difficulties aside, and treat the problem as a
simple one of expediency. In a crisis of battle during the civil wars
Edward of York kneels to God, the 'setter up and plucker down of kings';
a little later, Margaret vituperates Warwick as 'Proud setter up and
plucker down of kings' (*3H.VI* III.iii). Their almost identical words can
mean only that if a crown topples from a royal head, its wearer must
have proved unworthy of it. In the end Richmond is the country's
heaven-sent deliverer. His lack of a royal pedigree is kept out of sight.
Clearly the mandate of heaven has been given to him, and he demon-
strates it by slaying Richard in something like a ritual trial by battle. At
Shrewsbury Henry IV likewise confirms his right to a stolen crown by
facing the redoubtable Douglas in single combat; he has to be rescued,
but it is his son and heir who saves him. Personal courage is a quality no
king worth the name can be without.

In the heady days of civil war, to heedless aspirants the crown is an
irresistible magnet. Richard of Gloucester, urging his father to break the
pact with Henry VI, expatiates on how sweet it must be 'to wear a
crown,/Within whose circuit is Elysium' (*3H.VI* I.ii); but once won, it
makes its fatal Midas touch felt. It may prove a heavy burden to those
under its sway, but it is certain to be one for its wearer. All princes pay
for their empty honours by undergoing a 'world of restless cares', the
governor of the Tower reflects over his sleeping prisoner Clarence (*R.III*
I.iv.78 ff.). Henry VI groans under the painful insecurity of 'kings that
fear their subjects' treachery' (*3H.VI* II.v.45): one of many passages where
monarchy seems to suffer from an incurable disease.

At the close of *Henry VI* Edward IV, safe on the throne and happy with his newborn son, is looking forward to 'stately triumphs, mirthful comic shows' (*3H.VI* V.vii.43). But when the sequel begins, in his gloomy last days, he is sunk in idle fears of 'prophecies and dreams' (*R.III* I.i.54), and his consort laments her elevation to so giddy a height (I.iii.83–4). Richard III in turn is to learn that once power is gained, the fruit turns to ashes. For each of the many royal personages in *King John*, before long some blight or other 'hath spoiled the sweet world's taste' (III.iv.110). Even the Bastard, at first so jovially full of animal spirits, staggers under the cares of state which soon devolve on him.

By degrees as the epic story advances, the focus is shifting from the right to be king to the duties of being king, or an understanding that the ruler exists for the benefit of society, not the other way about. Shakespeare's Elizabeth told her last Parliament what a heavy burden the crown was, and his Henry IV would have agreed from the bottom of his heart. Already in Part 1 his opening words – 'So shaken as we are, so wan with care' – show him approaching exhaustion, as perhaps monarchy itself is. In Part 1 he is gloomy; in Part 2 almost tragic. He dominates the stage less and less, though his shadow hangs over it; in Part 2 he does not appear until Act III. There his first words are a lament over the anxieties that keep him sleepless. If a young man could see in advance, he says, what fate and the strange whirligigs of time had in store for him, he would 'sit him down and die'. Before long Henry himself is lying down to die, worn out by 'The incessant care and labour of his mind' (IV.iv. 116 ff.). His undutiful son, at his bedside, repeats his thoughts about the cares of state banishing sleep (IV.v.20 ff.).

Henry V is 'the mirror of all Christian kings' (Act II.Prol.), but we never see him governing England. He is off at once on a wild-goose chase after glory abroad, his so much admired reformation no more than a skip from his former pranks to war, the sport of kings. Yet he manages to take himself very seriously. In his mouth the theme of the sovereign as a public servant dedicated to unselfish toil is carried still further. Bent under the load of one crown, he is straining every nerve to gain another, which will be vastly more onerous. A labourer can little guess 'What watch the king keeps to maintain the peace' (IV.i.239); but Henry, in fact, is running away from his duties and dragging his people into war. He is devastating France in order to compel the French to admit his sacred right to submit to the painful duty of ruling them for their own good.

It may well be true that for Shakespeare the crown had a symbolic meaning, and could be associated with anything precious (Knight, *Crown* 107, 116, 119). Yet the conservative who was indignant in 1605 about kingship, government, religion being held up to derision on the stage, might well have included these Histories in his censure (Dollimore 8). On the whole, they give us anything but an edifying picture of monarchy. A feudal regime in a malign condition is generating little but divisions and hatreds. The long stretches of insult and recrimination among the royal ladies in *Richard III* are an undignified washing of dirty linen in public. In *King John* too the royal wranglings are on a level certain to corrode any superstitious reverence for crown or throne. Shakespeare is demystifying, demythologizing, purging it of the aura that still clung to it in Europe. Throughout, monarchy is held up as a hazardous form of government, unstable because it kindles excessive love of power in the ruler, guilty ambition in others. It warps family affections. It requires successful war to bolster it. It cannot conceal a widening gap between magnificent appearance and sordid reality. Nothing it is ever likely to do will remedy the social ills so unblushingly displayed in *Henry IV*.

Henry V's mind never turns to such things, but he has a chronic uneasiness. Throughout the three plays he figures in we are hearing 'speeches of self-justification' from him (Palmer 185). Among all the seven English and three French crowned heads in the Histories (Margaret's name might be added), very few can be considered passable rulers, none as an 'ideal' ruler. Hereditary succession could be no guarantee that authority would fall into the worthiest hands. Henry IV's mistrust of his scapegrace son drives him to think that Hotspur has a better natural right (*3H.IV* III.ii.97 ff.). Court life surrounds the ruler with 'smiling pickthanks and base news-mongers', by whom 'the ear of greatness' must often be deceived (ibid. 24–5). Falstaff's amusement at a self-important ass like Shallow being a squire and a Justice (*2H.IV* III.ii.275 ff.) is a reminder of what royal authority was likely to be in the hands of its delegates.

There is still something to awaken awe in the omnipotence that lies in 'the breath of kings' (*R.II* II.i), but such power is coming to seem excessive; and the king who listens to these words is soon compelled to remember that within the circle of the crown, death is waiting for its mortal wearer. It has become a curse; stories throng into his mind of kings deposed, slain in battle, poisoned by their wives, haunted by ghosts. What Richard learns painfully, Henry V knows as a plain matter of fact, having acquired in Eastcheap a taste for small beer (*2H.IV* II.ii). 'The king is but a man', as he says to his soldiers. 'The violet smells to him as it does to me' (IV.i.100 ff.) – as Shylock would say, 'Hath not a Jew eyes?' And the grand eminence that kings attain at the expense of 'infinite heart's ease' is not something for others to envy (IV.i.232). Henry's speech on 'ceremony' (*H.V.* IV.i.226 ff.) – one of Shakespeare's supremely great political utterances – is a declaration that kingship can no longer rest on royal titles and trappings. By the end of the sixteenth century it was growing self-conscious, conscious of critical eyes on it. Shakespeare was, it seems, doubtful of any future king being equal to the demands on it. What was called for now was not new candidates but a new political system for them to be part of. Henry takes care not to appear desirous of the rank of Renaissance superman, like Machiavelli's Prince or Marlowe's Tamburlaine. He modestly gives all the credit for the carnage he is committing to God, and to his band of brothers; at most he will confess to being more covetous of 'honour' than any man alive (IV.iii. 28–9).

When Richard II's willingness to abdicate is announced, the Bishop of Carlisle is the sole protesting voice. For him a king's right to his throne is God-given and indefeasible; he is 'the figure of God's majesty'. He prophesies civil war as the dire consequence (*R.II* IV.i). He is almost the only prelate in the Histories whom we can respect; but we need not suppose Shakespeare to be endorsing his stand. The good bishop is being left behind by history, like his non-juring successors after the deposition of James II in 1688. In the earlier plays interest had been fixed on rulers or would-be rulers; now the focal point is monarchy as institution. It was easy for official Tudor doctrine to extol order and social harmony, but the lesson of history seemed to be that monarchy could not be depended on for those blessings. It might do better if it tried, as the hapless Henry VI knew when he told his queen they must 'learn to govern better' (*2H.VI* IV.ix.49). He was given no chance, and few others ever thought of trying. When Shakespeare enlarges on the hardships and cares of state, he is telling us not that kings all tug so hard at the oar, but that they *ought* to.

But even if they were willing to wear themselves out in the service, as Henry IV might be said to have done, it could not be enough. Only 'Atlantean shoulders', as broad as those of Milton's archangel, would be strong enough to bear the weight of a kingdom. Shakespeare could not tell his audience this too bluntly, and cannot have grasped it fully himself. With the growing volume and complexity of affairs, England was stumbling awkwardly between two eras. Nothing could be accomplished without a ruler playing a strong part, but the more he did so the less freedom there would be for institutions, from Parliament down, to develop, and for administration to evolve on lines according with the interests of the classes that had weight in the country. The revolution, when it came, was to be over the working and programming of government, including its ecclesiastical department.

It was time, in other words, for the frown of majesty to be transferred from king to State. Impersonal authority, working within a regulated framework, must cease to be arbitrary. While he is putting Henry V on the throne, Shakespeare gives us repeated assurances that government in England is to be the antithesis of Turkish despotism. 'We are no tyrant, but a Christian king', Henry tells the French envoy who asks leave to deliver his insulting message in plain terms (*H.V.* I.ii.242): 'Christian', as often, meaning *civilized*. One of his first decisions is to call a Parliament, and seek wise councillors.

But there was, as there has always continued to be, another aspect of the building up of state machinery. No government allows itself to be always bound by law. Cade's captive Lord Say, a seasoned minister of state, when asked whether he has ever struck a blow for his country, gives a grim answer:

> Great men have reaching hands: oft have I struck
> Those that I never saw and struck them dead.
> (*2H.VI* IV.vii.76–7)

In *Henry V* the traitors are unmasked 'By interception which they dream not of' (II.ii.7). Guilty and innocent might be caught in the same snares. The king 'Sought to trap me by intelligence', Hotspur alleges (*1H.IV* IV.iii.18), as many who ended on Tudor scaffolds might have done. Any prominent man might learn, like the younger Mowbray, what 'slight and false-derived cause' could bring him under suspicion (*2H.IV* IV.i.189 ff.). In 1599 Thomas Nashe was denouncing informers who were out to fill their pockets by alarming government with fabricated tales (Wilson, *Life* 193–4).

Shakespeare could scarcely point out – but he knew his audience was well aware – that the government they lived under was a past master of such methods, which were needed all the more because above-board means of policing the country were scanty. There were murky depths of secret-service activity (e.g. Boas, *Marlowe* 25–7, etc.). Burghley was at the centre of an elaborate spy ring. When Shakespeare talks of the State he may seem to be making something portentous of what was really, by later standards, quite exiguous; but he was seeing it through a mist of the unknown or half-known that magnified its dimensions. It has been conjectured that his father came under suspicion of complicity in a Catholic plot in 1583 (Levi 3, 17 ff.).

Elizabeth knew how to strengthen her position with the applause of the multitude; the 'lesson' of *Henry V* – its better one, in contrast with its rampant jingoism – is that government needs more than bursts of cheering, the active support of ordinary men and women. The martyred brothers Crispin and Crispian on whose feast day, as Henry reminded his men, Agincourt was fought were the shoemakers' patron saints. Fluellen upholds the rights of the common soldier by saying that Williams ought to strike the man wearing his gage, of whatever rank he may be: it is, of course, the king. Henry speaks to him in verse; Williams replies in equally dignified prose (IV.vii.35 ff.), and they part good friends. The episode makes an interlude, which Shakespeare plainly relishes, after the uproar of battle. The last friendly face Richard II sees is that of a devoted groom who has got leave to visit him (*R.II* V.v). This is the old feudal fidelity; but such a virtue has a place to fill in the coming age too.

Feudal Nobility and Politics

A king stands over and above his peerage, as the precursor or crude embodiment of the modern polity. In ordinary affairs, on the other hand, kings and magnates in these plays are birds of a feather, and the arrogance of rank and power is the hallmark of the nobility as a class. From early in the Middle Ages it had been developing an image of itself – and not in England alone – as a superior caste, far above ordinary humanity. Its pretensions stand out in the reluctance of Shakespeare's noblemen to submit to law, a humiliating shackle on their independence. In the rose-garden scene (*1H.VI* II.iv) two lawyers are present, but are only perfunctorily asked for their opinion about the rival claims of York and Lancaster. The aristocratic temper shows in Suffolk's indifference to law, to which he has been a 'truant': he is accustomed to make it bend to his will, instead of bending to it. Warwick boasts of being a better judge of hawks, horses and girls than of any 'nice sharp quillets of the law'. Somerset, asked where his argument is, replies tersely: 'Here in my scabbard'.

With this attitude goes an immense disdain for social inferiors, given vent especially in the first set of plays; when these were written Shakespeare's notion of how great men behaved may have been a little overstrained. Good Duke Humphrey flies into a passion when 'dunghill grooms' obey their orders to bar his entrance to the tower (*1H.VI* I.iii). York addresses Peter the armourer's man as 'Base dunghill villain and mechanical' (*2H.VI* I.iii.191). This epithet is a favourite one. Lord Bigot bestows it on Hubert de Burgh, a royal officer not of the lowest grade – 'Out, dunghill! dar'st thou brave a gentleman?' (*KJ* IV.iii.88). Suffolk is contemptuous of 'worthless peasants', and highly indignant at finding himself in the hands of a rabble of seamen, one of them an old servant of his. He cannot believe that such a set of 'paltry, servile, abject drudges', led by an 'Obscure and lousy swain', can mean to take the life of an earl, and he would rather lose his life than plead to such wretches for it (*2H.VI* IV.i.121 ff.). Richard Crookback stops the hearse carrying a prince's corpse and, when the guard remonstrates, calls him an 'unmannered dog' and 'beggar', and threatens to strike him (*R.III* I.ii.39 ff.).

It can be supposed that this abusive language, instead of striking awe into the humbler part of Shakespeare's audience, had an opposite effect on it; we may even guess that this was what he intended. His frequent guying of the French aristocracy might be patriotically John Bullish, but to see foreign grandees ridiculed might be a step for English spectators towards seeing their own peerage in a similar light. They may have wondered, too, why Humphrey of Gloucester's wife Elinor, the guiltiest of her crew of plotters, should be let off with the lightest sentence because 'more nobly born' (*2H.VI* II.iii.9); or why the notables killed at Bosworth, including those on the wrong side, should be given a more honourable burial than the rank and file (*R.III* V.v).

In a late feudal society, 'honour' might be called the true religion of the upper classes. It was closely allied to 'glory', in a complex of ideas of great importance to Shakespeare's England and Europe; they were at the centre of the aristocratic code, and as such a keystone of a feudal society no longer in its prime. They signified all that was due from a man of 'gentle blood' to others, especially to his equals, and all that was due to him from his inferiors. Inspired by these self-advertising values, the world of the Histories is a bleakly masculine one. Noblemen feel a strong sense of family, expressed in loyalty to their fathers; their mothers seldom come into anyone's mind. Young Clifford's threats of vengeance, over his father's dead body, are impressive, except when they lapse into classical tropes (*2H.VI* V.ii). Apart from family ties, there are few signs of any close personal bonds; we are among a race of Hobbesian egotists. Shakespeare is only on the threshold of his task of spinning threads between human souls. He is quicker at learning to assign motives. Clarence deserts his brother Edward IV from resentment at not being rewarded with a rich heiress. Buckingham has very definite expectations in return for helping Richard III to the throne, and rebels when he is disappointed of them.

Past politics fascinated Shakespeare from the beginning – so obviously that it is scarcely possible to think that he was not interested in the politics of his own time. Cut-and-thrust debate of the kind met early in *Henry VI* (1: II.iv) was the precursor of many such scenes to come, in the Histories and beyond. The politician's psychology was one of his fields of study. York's long soliloquy at the end of the first scene of *Henry VI Part 2* is a masterly dramatic monologue, the self-revelation of a bold and adroit schemer with strong passions held in check by calculation. High politics, national and international, are the great game. As Warwick lies dying he is still under its spell, the sensation of open power and subterranean combat: he can boast of how he has learned 'To search the secret treasons of the world' (*3H.VI* V.ii.18). When Salisbury in *King John* sheds tears at the thought of having to take up arms against his own countrymen, the Dauphin tells him he should leave tears to

> those baby eyes
> That never saw the giant world enraged,

never looked higher than the mirth and gossip of private life. Excitement and gain go together; he ends by promising the earl a good share in 'the purse of rich prosperity' (V.ii.54 ff.).

The great game is not for weaklings. Humphrey of Gloucester's virago wife thinks him, as Henry VI's wife and friends think him, too mild and unsuspicious. She is quite right when she warns him that his enemies are on his trail, and he is foolish when he relies on his innocence to safeguard him. His last words are those of a man hemmed round by unpitying foes, with no one to take his part, alone with his fate (*2H.VI* III.i.142 ff.). Competition is increasingly savage. Shakespeare is very unlikely to have known Machiavelli's *Discourses* at first hand, but there is plentiful evidence of his familiarity with their doctrines (Melchiori 91–2). Best fitted by nature to feel at home in the jungle is someone like Richard Crookback, who revels in the thought of outdoing 'the murderous Machiavel' (*3H.VI* III.ii.193). Resolving to murder his wife and marry his niece, he reflects, very much like Macbeth, that he is 'So far in blood that sin will pluck on sin' (*R.III* IV.ii.62): a lesson of all these plays. John, unlike Richard, is capable of repenting – or at least regretting – a wicked design, and realizing that there is 'No certain life achieved by others' death' (*KJ* IV.ii.105). If Elizabeth Tudor ever listened to these words, they may have reminded her of Mary Stuart's head on the block.

Few of Shakespeare's characters, good or bad, need Joan of Arc's reminder that 'Of all base passions, fear is most accursed' (*1H.VI* V.ii.18): a succinct statement of the code of honour. Noblemen are stoical in adversity, defiant in face of death, even while baited by their enemies like Red Indians at the stake, as York is. 'True nobility is exempt from fear', declares Suffolk, in the hands of his captors (*2H.VI* IV.i.105). He, like many others, is at his best or boldest when he is about to die. Richard II's favourites hear their sentence without a tremor, and Green is sure that 'Heaven will take our souls' (*R.II* III.i). Worcester submits to his fate briefly and – one of Shakespeare's great words – 'patiently' (*1H.IV* V.v.12). This physical courage is a virtue that Shakespeare can admire and extol, but it can go with a brutality relieved only by occasional gleams of generosity. Suffolk has been responsible for the strangling of his far more deserving enemy Humphrey. Young Clifford is a Tybalt, a devotee of the blood feud at its worst, as his murder of the boy Rutland shows.

Treason is a 'labyrinth' where 'Minotaurs lurk', Suffolk warns himself (*1H.VI* V.iii.188–9); it does not take him long to overcome any scruples.

Short of treason, there is a great deal of treachery and bad faith in the record. Casuistry allows the Yorkist party, after its agreement with Henry, to decide without waste of time that its oath is not binding on it. Alençon is a 'notorious Machiavel' or treaty-breaker on the French side (*1H.VI* V.iv.74, 163–4). 'Trust nobody, for fear you be betrayed' (*2H.VI* IV.iv.58) is a seasonable warning to all. 'There is no wrong, but everything is right', a Lancastrian accuses the other side of believing (*3H.VI* II.ii.132). In one of the finest passages in *Richard III*, Hastings bewails the folly of relying on the faithless favour of men (III.iv.91–2). 'There is neither truth nor honour in all these noble persons', Hazlitt comments on a scene in *Richard II* (*Characters* 139–40).

There are moments when a feudal lord can be heard striking a note of principle – or 'taking the high moral ground', as politicians say nowadays. Warwick urges Gloucester and Winchester not to injure king and country by their wranglings; but we have lately seen him in private as a heated Yorkist partisan (*1H.VI* III.i; II.iv). Gloucester seems to have earned some respect as Protector, by contrast with Suffolk, who is an oppressor of the poor, an enclosing landlord or stealer of village commons. Generally the individuals who show some better feeling are minor figures. There is patriotism of a sort – mostly a very aggressive sort. It attains a better quality in the later part of *King John*, but the English nobles there are indistinct, unconvincing. Salisbury's 'holy vow' to deny himself every pleasure of life until he has paid dead Arthur 'the worship of revenge' sounds histrionic, like the high-flown chivalry paraded at first by King Philip and Austria (IV.iii.66 ff.).

As a class this nobility seems incorrigibly vicious. Crimes meet with retribution, but can hardly be said to be expiated. 'Measure for measure must be answered' (*3H.VI* II.vi.55) is the keynote throughout: revenge exacts revenge. Some of these bad men feel retribution falling on them in *Richard III*, with the prophetic curses of Margaret and others coming true. There is no Christian forgiveness among any of these men and women, and we have little inclination to forgive them. Shakespeare was no medievalizing romantic, and his procession of snarling, squabbling, school-bully lords looks deliberately unpleasant. The Histories may teach that Englishmen are superior to Frenchmen, but they also teach that England's masters are – or were until recently – far worse men than most other Englishmen, and perfectly indifferent to the hardships or grievances of those below them. *Richard III*, concluding the Wars of the Roses, is the culmination, a kind of suicide of an archaic feudal order, with Richard a wild beast turned loose against the others, splendidly destructive and, in the end, self-destructive. There are still troublesome nobles in store for us, but they are both less villainous and less resolute than those we have seen perish.

Poor folk are only onlookers at history, like spectators in a theatre, Thomas More wrote in his *History of Richard III* (about 1513). His assumption was the general one, and sufficed for chroniclers concerned with not much more than the doings of the great. Shakespeare's principal authority, Holinshed, had little to offer him of the social or economic information needed by the modern historian. His own curiosity led him towards such matters, and we may suppose that he had thought much more about them than he could bring into his plays. He was not alone – indeed, in his social criticism he was more restrained than some of his fellow-writers (see Heinemann, 'Drama'). He was fonder than most of them of exhibiting, in men on the lower or lowest rungs of the feudal ladders, virtues of common humanity that those above them have been losing. Retainers can show more loyalty to their lords than these do to their king, and are ready to take up their masters' quarrels as their own. Winchester's men and Gloucester's brawl in the streets, and profess their willingness to fight and die for them.

This is admirable, but also – as in *Romeo and Juliet* – stupid, a symptom of social distemper. Individuals show up better. One of Humphrey's murderers, humble tools of Suffolk, regrets the deed the moment it is done; scarcely any of the great are ever touched by such remorse. One of Clarence's murderers has to struggle in a style of black humour with conscience – a little like Falstaff with Honour – as something enfeebling that a man who means to rise must hold in check; after the work is done he feels like a Pilate, and renounces his share of the reward (*R.III* I.iv). Hubert's assistant is horrified at the idea of Arthur being blinded. Hubert himself spares Arthur; he wins our further esteem, when threatened and insulted by Salisbury, with his retort that his sword is as sharp as the earl's, and that although he would not beard a nobleman from choice, he would defend his good name 'against an emperor' (*KJ* IV.iii.81 ff.).

In Shakespeare's day the party, destined to take shape from the 1640s onward as the decisive factor in political evolution, was not yet much more than a religious or court camarilla, looking around for backing. In the course of the Histories the inchoate growth can be traced, with its managers accumulating a fund of tactical skill. Worcester admonishes his fellow-conspirators that insurgents must take care not to let prying eyes see or suspect any disunity among them (*1H.IV* IV.i.60 ff.). Just as monarchy has to broaden itself out into state power, with an ear open to public feeling, feudal faction widens into the beginnings of a party by discovering the need for a popular base, and the arts of demagogy.

Even in the first stages there is sporadic recognition of the utility of an appeal to something like 'public opinion' (an entity still highly in-coherent and volatile in our own day). Charges are often bandied about –

though we never get to the bottom of them – of embezzlement of army funds meant for the French wars, overtaxing of 'the needy commons', and so on (e.g. *2H.VI* III.i.108 ff.). Leaders profess at times – as in the opening scene of *Henry VI Part 2* – a disinterested regard for the public good, and accuse one another of 'ambition', greed for 'preferment'. Allusions to the importance of conciliating the commoners multiply as time goes on. Salisbury commends his son Warwick for having won esteem by his 'deeds', 'plainness', and 'housekeeping' (*2H.VI* I.i.189–90) or open-handed hospitality, including food for the poor at the rich man's gate. Even the wicked Cardinal of Winchester thinks it worthwhile to angle for street favour, by calling Humphrey 'a foe to citizens' and saying that his war policy cripples them with taxes. Humphrey retaliates by coming to Parliament with 'written pamphlets' or posters against his enemy (*1H.VI* I.iii; III.i). His popularity can have been gained only by 'flattery', Margaret asserts, and it will enable him to draw the multitude into a 'commotion' whenever he pleases (*2H.VI* III.i.28–30). Down to the eighteenth century any public applause could be looked at askance.

In the end it is not Humphrey's pamphlets but his murder that excites a tumult at Bury St Edmunds, with a clamorous demand for Suffolk's banishment: if the king does not give them satisfaction, the people will take their own measures to shield him from evil advisers. This nerves Henry to get rid of Suffolk, the chief culprit and Queen Margaret's lover (*2H.VI* III.ii). These demonstrators have noblemen to speak for them; but as a rule, suspicion and hostility are habitual between nobles and commoners. The crowd expresses its resentments as it can, which may be brutally enough, as when it laughs and jeers at Elinor, sentenced to barefoot penance in the street (*2H.VI* II.iv). Her husband's presence, although he is the good Duke Humphrey, does not restrain the mob. But Humphrey's noble foes bait him in defeat just as unfeelingly, and just as her English captors bait Joan of Arc.

When Edward IV is seeking a marriage alliance with France, King Lewis inquires whether he is 'gracious in the people's eyes', and is given suitable assurances; but Warwick, having broken with him, accuses him – in quite modern accents – of not knowing 'how to study for the people's welfare' (*3H.VI* III.iii; IV.iii). There is nothing to show whether in reality one faction is any better at government than the other; and since there is no sign of promises of better times ever being fulfilled, the people may be excused if they are as fickle in their preference as their betters complain. They might well be expected to relapse into indifference; instead, Shakespeare's picture is of mass feeling continuing to ferment, but taking unexplained, seemingly irrational courses.

To the power-seekers – themselves often quite changeable enough –

the people appear to be weathercocks, turning in the direction of each new wind. Henry shrinks from a trial of strength with the Yorkists in London because 'the city favours them'. London *was* Yorkist, according to the chroniclers. But later on, Warwick talks of leaving him there in safety among his 'loving citizens'. They do nothing for him when, while he is congratulating himself on the goodwill his just rule must have won him, Edward breaks in and seizes him (*3H.VI* I.i; IV.viii, ix). Captured earlier on, he had bewailed 'the lightness of you common men' (*3H.VI* III.i.89). Clifford, dying, has bitter words for 'The common people' turning towards the new sun. Two Acts later the 'common people' are swarming to desert the Yorkist cause and join Warwick; yet when Edward IV comes back to England, 'many giddy people flock to him' (*3H.VI* II.vi; IV.ii, viii). Such experiences help to explain why a man like Henry VI sighs for the tranquil life of a shepherd, far from all the 'care, mistrust and treason' that surround a king (*3H.VI* II.v).

Much of the talk about the fickle masses sounds like literary stereotype. In *King John* the feeling of the streets is – as usual – only reported to us, and leads to nothing positive; but the report is much more detailed and vivid. Confused the mass mind may have been, but it is not dully apathetic; there is a lively, if elementary, interest in public affairs, a sense of involvement in them. Tillyard may be right in saying that the artisans we hear of as so avid for news are bystanders, not 'members of the body politic' (*Historical Plays* 233); but men so eager to learn about events may be relied on to want a share in making them before long. They are most easily roused by happenings or rumours of the sort we call 'sensational' and, as is still the case today, not by ideas and principles but by personalities, stories of men or women. Just as excitement was kindled by Humphrey's murder, now it is the suspected murder of Arthur. Pandulph predicts the effect: a restless populace, uneasy and unsettled, ready to interpret any happening, natural or unnatural, as a portent (III.iv.149 ff., 164–6).

This must have been a state of mind familiar to Shakespeare, in an England under stress of little-understood change, to which erratic moods or wild guesses were an unsurprising response. At the climax, when John is 'giddy' with a press of bad news, the Bastard brings in a 'prophet', Peter of Pomfret, who 'in rude, harsh-sounding rhymes', has been foretelling calamity and leaving his hearers 'strangely fantasised' (IV.ii.131 ff., 193 ff.). There follows Hubert's famous description of a people seized by strange fears, a kind of vertigo; a blacksmith letting his iron cool on the anvil as he listens open-mouthed to the news told by a tailor who has run out in haste with his slippers on the wrong feet. In *Henry IV Part 2* Rumour, as Prologue, censures the spreading of baseless tales, frivolous alarms. Elizabeth's government can be expected to have approved. Shakespeare's interest in this feature of mass psychology shows more humorously in Dogberry's nonsense about somebody called 'Deformed', whose genesis is his misunderstanding of a word (*MAAN* V.i.300 ff.).

A single passage of *Henry VI Part 2*, not followed up, tells us that the Cade outbreak is being instigated by the Yorkists (III.ii.355 ff.). There is deep discontent in the Kentish countryside, which mischief-makers might think of exploiting. But the rising and its leader are depicted as a mixture of brutality and childish folly. Shakespeare, it has frequently been repeated, could esteem individuals of any rank, but not the crowd or mob; and the dictum is not without warrant. Knowledge of national events might be spreading, but people's collective ties and experience of organizing were narrowly local, When men under some extraordinary impulse flocked together in numbers, like Cade's host or any London mob, they were only a chance collection of strangers, and their be-haviour was incalculable. Considering this, Shakespeare does not display an undue mistrust of the 'people', or panic fear of it. His crowds go astray less from listening to leaders of their own, like Cade, than when they let themselves be taken in by deceivers from the ruling class, like Clifford in *Henry VI Part 2*, or Antony in *Julius Caesar*.

The wealthier citizen class, already important in fifteenth-century England, was a class that Shakespeare and his fellow-actors had no cause to love; and the only members of it who are allowed to win our admira-tion are not Englishmen but the burghers of Angiers in *King John*. Indeed, their role is so commanding as to look like a foretaste of things to come about in England's not too distant future. But when English burgesses make an appearance they are sober men, douce householders fond of a quiet life, opposites in every way to the fiery aristocrats. Their senior representative, the Mayor of London, does intervene in a resolute style to stop the brawl of feudal retainers (*1H.VI* I.iii): he reads a riot act, threatens to 'call for clubs' – a turnout of 'prentices, who could be a formidable force – and gets them to disperse. He is left shaking his wise head over their cantankerous behaviour: 'I myself fight not once in forty year'. A little later he attends Parliament to petition the king against the disturbers of public order. The Mayor of Coventry is tongue-tied while the nobles wrangle (*3H.VI* V.i); his brother of York is easily hoodwinked by Edward IV into opening the city gates – he is a good old fellow, Hastings comments, happy to see all well so long as he does not have to take part (IV.vii).

With Richard Crookback we take a big stride forward in the technique of politics, or political manipulation; he is its first real master, and revels in his virtuosity. Act III of *Richard III* in particular is a thrilling spectacle of plotting and scheming, with judicial murder for accelerator.

Richard's situation obliges him and Buckingham to pay court to the respectable citizenry of London, and its spokesman the mayor, rather than to the populace; and they are not easily swayed, even if they are hesitant about speaking their minds. We hear three of them anxiously discussing things – 'the souls of men are full of dread' (II.iii) – but they have no notion of men like themselves taking a hand; they can only leave God to dispose. The mayor can be bullied into acquiescence, but the citizens maintain an obstinate silence. A lawyer employed to forge a long indictment against Hastings, designed to show that he had a regular trial instead of being executed out of hand, reflects that everyone will see through this 'palpable device', though no one will dare to open his mouth (III.vi).

Richard Crookback finds no national grievances to make capital out of; in *Richard II* private wrongs merge with discontents of a public nature. When York remonstrates against Richard's seizing the belongings of the dukedom of Lancaster, now Bolingbroke's, as soon as the breath is out of his father John of Gaunt's body, he dwells on its bad consequences as an affront to all property rights, certain to raise up countless opponents. Northumberland talks to his friends about how other noble houses are being despoiled, for the benefit of royal favourites who lodge false accusations against them (II.i). At the same time, ordinary folk are being harassed by 'grievous taxes'. The favourites know how they are hated, and are in fear of being torn to pieces by 'the wavering Commons', whose love, Bagot naively complains, 'lies in their purses' (II.ii).

Bolingbroke's core of support is a group of fellow-grandees, but he needs the man in the street on his side, to make sure of being the foremost candidate when the throne falls vacant. He has no need to stir up disaffection, but only to put himself at its head. Again – and still more acutely than in *Richard III* – we are made to feel that we are standing on the boundary between two epochs when we first watch the champions ready to fight in the arena, then hear of one of them setting out into banishment amid the clamour of the streets, and of his 'familiar courtesy' to 'poor craftsmen', draymen, oyster-wenches (I.iv).

Contrasting eras stand out again when Bolingbroke is on the throne, and Hotspur, as incapable as a Coriolanus of stooping to cajole the rabble, pours contempt on him as a 'king of smiles', a 'fawning greyhound', and on his tactics after his return from exile, when he declaimed against abuses of government and pretended to weep 'Over his country's wrongs' (*1H.IV* I.iii.246, 251; IV.iii.81–2). No one has ever drawn a more living picture than Shakespeare of this style of aristocratic demagogy, destined to flourish long in England. We can already descry in the distance Dryden's Achitophel, bowing popularly low, and even catch a far-off glimmer of the Primrose League. Henry IV lectures his undutiful son about 'Opinion that did help me to the crown', and the 'courtesy' and 'humility' he cultivated in order to win it. He points out at the same time that while royalty must stoop to conquer, it must maintain at most times a dignified aloofness (*1H.IV* III.ii.29 ff.).

Richard II's queen is not surprised to hear her gardeners talking of affairs of state, because everyone does so when political change is in the offing (III.iv). Shakespeare does not think of opinion as a matter of settled conviction; under Henry IV it is still a 'wavering multitude' that we are faced with (*2H.IV* Prol.). Both the government and its ill-wishers are nervous and mistrustful of it – a symptom, as Shakespeare must in some degree have recognized, of a gulf between the whole ruling class and the rest of the country. It is Henry's turn now to denounce those who would incite 'fickle changelings and poor discontents', penniless men longing for 'pellmell havoc and confusion' (*1H.IV* V.i.72 ff.). In the long-drawn-out disintegration of the feudal order there was inevitably a dangerous mass of discontent, the unlucky ones left without a perch to cling to; and the same label could be conveniently pinned on to social grievances of any kind.

It might be asked what danger such riffraff could be to law and order; but considering that part of the royal force at Shrewsbury consisted of soldiers like Falstaff's scarecrows, it must be allowed that any outbreak could be – at least temporarily – a menace to be taken seriously. At the prospect of disturbances, 'Rich men look sad, and ruffians dance and leap' (*R.II* II.iv): everyone with something to lose would see the point of such a warning. This meant not the rich only, even if a good many had nothing to lose but their lives. In a free-for-all breakdown of order it may be the poor, least able to protect themselves, who come off worst. Shakespeare must have had this in mind in his eloquent condemnations of disorder (on which see Muir, in Kettle), though on the surface they may seem to echo official anathemas. Society in his time was in a chronic condition not of regular class struggle, but of a more elemental tension and instability.

In these plays it is naturally spokesmen of the ruling class whom we hear drawing the moral. Henry IV's commander reproaches rebel leaders with fomenting a revolt that ought to be left to 'base and abject routs', 'boys and beggary' (*2H.IV* IV.i.32 ff.). Revolt, in other words, was no longer a pastime to be carelessly indulged in by great men: all men of weight should close their ranks against it – as in Tudor times they were learning to do. All the 'absolute monarchies' arose on the basis of aristocratic fear of the poor, as well as middle-class disgust with feudal disorderliness. On the other side the Archbishop of York, while declaring that he and his friends must broadcast their reasons for taking up arms, seems to have no inkling of the real ills that the people are smarting under: what sets them in motion is mere irresponsibility, restless love of change. They hated Richard; now they regret him, and are tired of Henry. 'What trust is in these times?' (*2H.IV* I.iii.85 ff.). The conspirators do talk vaguely of misrule, and a suffering country, but they have to eke out their appeal with dried blood said to have been scraped off Richard's prison wall, under the sanction of the archbishop's name (I.i.204–5).

Outwardly, nobility in the later plays is still a distinct, separate caste. It goes with Hotspur's feudal arrogance to reprove his wife for using mealy-mouthed middle-class turns of phrase (*1H.IV* III.i.247 ff.); the great should be free to use any swear-words they choose. There is less contemptuous treatment of inferiors now, however, than in Henry VI's reign. When kings or would-be kings are learning to be civil to commoners, the blue-blooded must trim their tongues likewise; Worcester reproves his nephew Hotspur for lacking the self-control proper to his rank. But on the battlefield, gentility keeps its pride of place and its disrelish for plebeian company. At Shrewsbury, what Hal finds regrettable is that 'Many a nobleman lies stark and stiff', 'stained nobility lies trodden on' (*1H.IV* V.iii.41, iv.13). The fate of men like Falstaff's recruits does not call for notice. After the rout of the French at Agincourt their herald comes to beg permission for them to 'book' and bury their dead; the fact that many of the highest 'Lie drowned and soaked in mercenary blood' (*H.V* IV.vii.70 ff.) seems an indignity more tragic than the loss of the battle. We can read into these attitudes an oblique censure of the ostentatious self-conceit of Elizabethan England's elite.

Whatever its trappings and pretensions, the inner vitality of aristocracy, like that of monarchy, is visibly decaying. The poor old Duke of York, left in charge by Richard II, fumbles and bumbles, unequal to emergency and divided in sympathy. Schopenhauer took the character of Northumberland, in this play and *Henry IV*, as an example of a weak man repeating one cycle of conduct, entering the scene with a weighty, impressive air, failing to live up to it, and finally coming to grief (231–3). It is really not so much the individual as his political setting that has altered. Northumberland's son Hotspur scarcely belongs to his; he is a throwback to an older life still persisting until James I's day in the wild northern borderland. He has a romantic, chivalrous streak, but also more than a touch of the barbaric.

The Percy rebellion will be formidable, Blunt remarks, 'If promises be kept on every hand' (*1H.IV* III.ii.167–8); but they are not. After Hotspur's death his widow's eulogy of him throws into relief the poor quality of those left behind. She reproaches his father with his craven absence from the field at Shrewsbury, but now that a second attempt is being planned she counsels him not to throw in his lot with the rebels until he is sure they are winning (*2H.IV* II.iii). When the rebels are tricked into laying down their arms, and led away to execution, feudal insurrectionism is ending with a whimper. A minor figure, Coleville, surrenders tamely to Falstaff, much as the French gentleman at Agincourt surrenders to Pistol. Coleville too is sent to the block, leaving his captor to sing the praises of sherry (IV.iii).

Mortimer pictures Wales in English feudal terms when he urges Glendower to gather his 'tenants, friends, and neighbouring gentlemen' (*1H.IV* III.i.88). But these satellites of great men are not so ready now to answer their call, when it comes to taking up arms against the government. Hotspur is disgusted to find one man he has approached putting him off with a letter of civil excuses, while protesting his 'love' for the Percies, and suspects that the writer will inform against him (*1H.IV* II.iii.1 ff.). Feudal ties in the North of England were weakening in Elizabeth's time, though even then they were stronger than in areas nearer the capital (James); the northern rising of 1569 and its failure were evidence of this.

It is against the background of an old society crumbling that its concept of Honour, all through *Henry IV*, is being called into question. Falstaff, the renegade gentleman, derides it. Hotspur idolizes it, but makes it look silly by his extravagance, and with him it lacks any serious meaning; it has sunk into mere vainglory, or a figment of fancy to be snatched from the pale-faced moon. One indication of this descent is that the old chivalric linkage of Honour with Love, Mars with Venus, and both of them with the minstrel's art, has broken down. Hotspur has only a rough-and-ready regard for his wife, thinks oftener of his horse, and makes mock of 'mincing poetry' (III.i).

In the Histories, through which Shakespeare was working his way towards an understanding of his society, manifold meanings of the word 'Honour' jostle together. It might mean a man's inner sense of duty and right action; more usually it meant some token of his outward standing. As the badge of gentility, honour was fraying at the edges; what was left was chiefly its central value, courage, readiness to face death without flinching. Even this ultimate virtue is wilting. In the Parliament scene in *Richard II* the exchange of insults and challenges, one lord after another throwing down his gage, serves no purpose except to show the nobility in hopeless disarray. Worse follows: the first loud challenger, Aumerle, is soon taking part in a plot against the new king: his timid father York gets wind of this, and hurries off to denounce his son as a traitor, while his wife follows to beg her son off, and Aumerle, who has lost his nerve, gets there first to kneel and plead for pardon (V.iii). Anything more humiliating for noble breeding – indeed, for royal blood – can scarcely be imagined.

In *Henry IV* the shadow of cowardice lengthens, among men of high degree as well as thieves at Gadshill. The recreant who declines to join Hotspur is 'a shallow cowardly hind' (*1H.IV* II.iii.17). When Northumberland talks of his 'honour' compelling him to fight, Lady Percy declares that he has thrown it away already by leaving his son in the lurch. His final defeat and death are reported, as they deserve, in a few offhand words (*2H.IV* II.iii; IV.iv). Nothing tells us more about the moral debility of the old ruling caste than the fact that it extends even to loyalties within the family.

It was an adage old enough to be cited by Aristotle that a ruler must be on his guard against 'over-mighty subjects', as Tudor writers called them. In the later Histories we see an inevitable contradiction between these great families and a swelling state power, each side convinced of the other's hostility. Worcester may be sincere when he says that he would have chosen a quiet old age (*1H.IV* V.i.22 ff.); but he feels that he and his clan must strike, or be struck down themselves. Before the battle Henry offers pardon, but he offers no guarantees, and there could be none for their future safety. In Hotspur's love of honest fighting, and his hatred of a 'vile politician' like Henry, an antithesis between two epochs can be seen. It is in favour of established authority that the scales are tilting. Northumberland's allies Morton and Lord Bardolph agree that their party had ventured on 'dangerous seas', where failure was far more probable than success. Morton sets great store by the archbishop's reputation for piety; it will counteract the damaging associations that the word rebellion has acquired, which unnerved Hotspur's followers at Shrewsbury or 'froze them up' like fish in a pond (*2H.IV* I.i). In another consultation someone expatiates on the thorough preparations that must be made for a task like theirs:

> Which is almost to pluck a kingdom down
> And set another up.
>
> (I.iii)

War

Shakespeare's classical allusions show him an admirer, above all other gods or demigods, of Hercules (Boas, *Elizabeth* 79). Heroic bravery and strength ranked very high with him. Wars, soldiers, and their problems had a prominent place in Elizabethan drama, nowhere more than in his plays (Langsam 1–2, ch. 2). The tread of marching – or stumbling – armies resounds through the Histories. War is the native haunt of the feudal classes, the vocation where their endowments find a channel. It is the first theme that stirred Shakespeare to true eloquence, well in advance of love, though the feelings it aroused in him might be contradictory. Yet in its details or mechanics he shows little interest. His imagery of war reveals no particular acquaintance with it (Spurgeon 36). Some plays from other hands tell us much more – Beaumont and Fletcher's *Bonduca*, for instance. Only hand-to-hand fighting really fired Shakespeare, because better than any other kind it brought to light the true metal of the warrior – and, of course, because it was the only kind he could exhibit on the stage. A battle was thus reduced to a simple slogging match, uncumbered by niceties of tactics.

Talbot does 'wonders with his sword and lance', and derides the French for skulking behind the walls of Rouen like 'base muleteers' or 'peasant foot-boys', instead of coming out to fight 'like gentlemen' (*1H.VI* I.i.122; III.ii.68–70). Logistics are treated very offhandedly. York, appointed Regent of Ireland, expects to have an army, recruited from all the shires, awaiting him at Bristol within a fortnight. He brings an Irish army back with him and casually dismisses it somewhere between St Albans and London, telling the men he will pay them the next day (*2H.VI* III.i.313, 328; V.i.44 ff.). Shortly afterwards the truce between him and the Lancastrians breaks down and he embarks on a battle, quite forgetting that he has already disbanded his forces. (Shakespeare is doing some drastic compression of events hereabouts: Holinshed 285 ff.). Reconnaissance work is equally neglected. 'Where slept our scouts?' Warwick may well ask when an enemy host suddenly appears under his nose, or under the walls of Coventry (*3H.VI* V.i.19); and King John is equally taken aback by the abrupt apparition of a French army:

> O, where hath our intelligence been drunk?
> Where hath it slept?
>
> (*KJ* IV.ii.116–17)

Richard III is an exception. He makes careful preparations at Bosworth, surveying the ground and settling the disposition of his troops (*R.III* V.iii.15 ff., 291 ff.). For him war is a complex business, calling for experience and skill – even if dramatic effect requires him, when the battle comes, to fight and die like an ordinary soldier.

As for long-range weaponry, there is scarcely more mention of archery than of musketry. Artillery furnished Shakespeare chiefly with thunderous imagery. There is an awkwardly overstrained metaphor in *Henry VI Part 1* of eyeballs turned into bullets; more eloquently Burgundy, persuaded by Joan to abandon the English alliance, says that her words 'Have batter'd me like roaring cannon-shot' (IV.vii; III.iii). Gunnery makes itself felt at Orleans, besieged by the English. Not surprisingly, Talbot regards gunpowder as vulgar; this was the attitude of all the European aristocracy to the grand leveller of the battlefield. When a French master-gunner hits the tower from which English commanders are observing the town, and one of them is killed, another wounded, Talbot is outraged by 'this woeful tragedy', and breaks into bloodcurdling threats of retaliation against 'these dastard Frenchmen' for their 'treacherous' conduct (*1H.VI* I.iv; II.ii). (In colonial campaigns British officers always considered it treacherous of natives to ambush them.)

For us, and perhaps for Shakespeare, there was something emblematic in that gunner's cannonball, heralding the downfall of the old military feudalism. Gunpowder was dehumanizing warfare, nullifying its heroic qualities. In his – or Hotspur's – account of the Battle of Holmedon (*1H.IV* I.ii.30 ff.), Shakespeare altered bows and arrows to cannon, so as to enable the foppish courtier to talk of his dislike of 'villainous salt-petre'. We are breathing a modern air now. Hotspur has feverish dreams about 'palisades, parapets, culverins' (II.iii.52 ff.). At Shrewsbury Falstaff makes use of a pistol-holster to carry his bottle of sack (V.iii). In his next campaign he gives one of his recruits a caliver, or small musket, and bids him show how he can use it; familiarity with firearms must have been spreading in Shakespeare's countryside. His men are given 'coats', uniforms of a sort – another important innovation (*2H.IV* III.ii).

In *Henry V* Shakespeare moves forward somewhat, though partly in quest of humorous material. Fluellen and his companions are officers with a pride in their expert knowledge, and their talk is of mines and countermines rather than of honour and glory, even if the Welshman always wants to drag in the disciplines of the wars as practised by Pompey. Controversy still raged over the merits of Roman and modern methods; Fluellen is a classicist, Captain Macmorris the Irishman a modernist (Langsam 60–61). Longbow and musket still competed. Gunpowder and mining are prominent in the siege of Harfleur, and the Duke of Gloucester, to whom its planning is entrusted, is 'altogether directed' by Macmorris: ill-advisedly, if Fluellen is right in thinking this engineer 'an ass, and as ignorant as a puppy-dog' (III.ii.61 ff.). Generalship is making no similar progress, because it is still the province of the feudal elite. At Agincourt, when action is about to commence, York requests and is granted command of the vanguard (IV.iii.130–32), nobody having thought about such a detail before. We do not see Henry fighting, but he rushes off to lead the assault at Harfleur, and after Agincourt we hear casually from him that he had a hand-to-hand grapple with Alençon (IV.vii.151–2).

There is a pretty touch of the romance of war in the 'dancing banners' of Philip's army (*KJ* II.i.308), and in his vow to win the day or throw

away his life. The Bastard hails this joyfully: true 'glory' shines out
'When the rich blood of kings is set on fire!' (II.i). He is not Coeur de
Lion's son for nothing. John has brought with him a flock of 'Rash,
inconsiderate, fiery voluntaries', young hopefuls who have sold their
patrimonies to equip themselves. The Dauphin Lewis boasts likewise of
the 'fiery spirits' he has gathered 'to win renown/Even in the jaws of
danger and of death' (II.i; V.ii). But it is in a crisis of battle, while trying to
rally his broken troops, that Clifford the younger, in some ways
Hotspur's precursor, pays the finest tribute to war. It sounds the first
authentic note of Shakespeare's long endeavour to moralize war by
endowing it with a true mystique. The poet's divided mind shows in
Clifford's cry that war is the 'son of hell', but also (as Henry V too
proclaims it) the 'minister' of heaven; and that its acolyte can have no
thought of seeking safety in flight:

> He that is truly dedicate to war
> Hath no self-love.
> (*2H.IV* V.ii.31 ff.)

In more philosophical terms, the individual self cannot fully realize itself
except by rising above itself, ceasing to be merely individual. Battle is a
collective ecstasy, whose intoxication can satisfy man's craving both to
assert himself and to escape from or surrender himself. Mars and Venus
can be seen not far apart; Elizabethans spoke of the act of love as a 'dying'.

Less dignified motives, revenge and profit, have more sway over most
of the cavaliers. John's volunteers are not too 'inconsiderate' to think of
recouping their fortunes in France; in other words, they are going there
to loot the country as well as for the sake of adventure and renown. As to
the common soldier, in what we see of his lot there is not much either of
glory or of profit. Usually English soldiers, whether at home or abroad,
seem to be serving for pay; and there is a curious hint of the commercializing of warfare, like everything else, in Shakespeare's day, when Richard
II takes comfort in the thought of a host of angels 'in heavenly pay',
ready to fight on his side (III.ii.58–9). But in the stylized battle scene of
Henry VI Part 3 (II.v) a son and his father, whom he has unwittingly
killed, have both been serving under compulsion: one in the royal army,
the other in that of his 'master' the Earl of Warwick.

Here and there are signs of common soldiers feeling that they are
exploited. French sentinels pity themselves for having to be out in rain
and cold while their superiors sleep comfortably (*1H.VI* II.i.5–7). No
great zeal is ever displayed by the rank and file; their leaders are often
dissatisfied with their performance. Talbot and the Dauphin each curse
their soldiers for hanging back. Sometimes it occurs to a commander to
make an effort to improve their morale. Warwick relates ruefully how at

St Albans he found his men fighting half-heartedly, striking their blows 'like an idle thresher' – a telling image from rustic life – and tried to hearten them with talk about 'the justice of our cause', and, more realistically, 'with promise of high pay' (*3H.VI* II.i.111 ff.); but to no avail, perhaps because they have been scared by Clifford's threat to kill all his prisoners. Edward IV assures his recruits of 'large pay' if they win, as they move off to an engagement (IV.vii.83); in such contests, of course, only the winner would be able to pay anything.

Other governments often found their own subjects too unwilling, untrained, perhaps mutinous, to make serviceable soldiers. From the later Middle Ages reliance on professional troops drawn from a large cosmopolitan pool was growing, and Shakespeare lived at a time when foreign mercenaries were in action all over Europe. In the Histories they are often at work on English soil, without their presence seeming to call for any comment. In *Henry VI Part 3* the two factions compete for French aid: Warwick invades England with troops supplied by King Lewis; Edward IV returns from exile at the head of 'hasty Germans and blunt Hollanders' supplied by the Duke of Burgundy; Queen Margaret lands with forces 'raised in Gallia' (IV.iii.3, 7–8; V.iii). Only fifteen years before Shakespeare's birth Italian and German mercenaries were being employed to suppress risings of common people in Cornwall and Norfolk.

Such professional troops were expensive, and to make native levies more useful, morale had to be improved. Demagogy could be practised on soldiers as well as citizens. At Bosworth both commanders exhort their men to do their duty. Richmond's long harangue is in a highly religious strain. Heaven and its saints are on their side, while Richard is God's enemy as well as a tyrant; they are fighting to protect their wives and children, though Richmond does not forget to add that the merest soldier will have his share in the 'gain' of the victory. Richard's speech is less religious, more nationalistic. The enemy are invaders, foreign brigands like the 'bastard Bretons' often defeated by Englishmen in their own country; they want to seize on our lands and our 'beauteous wives', and 'ravish our daughters' (*R.III* V.iii.238 ff.). Modern war propaganda has struck many of the same notes, and the similarity between the two orations suggests intentional irony on Shakespeare's part.

He must have had recurrent misgivings about war, in spite of its glorious outside and its higher function as the ultimate test of the human spirit. He could not help seeing that many of its cruelties fell on ordinary human beings who had no concern with it. After Clifford's dithyramb there is an abrupt change of key when he comes on his father's corpse, and breaks into one of those threats of slaughter that are Shakespeare's most horrific utterances. At times even the warlords themselves are visited by thoughts of what their ambitions are costing. Starting in *Henry VI*, there is an imagery of war as an uproar of wild beasts preying on one another (Knight, *Flower* 17). In *King John* death itself becomes a monster. The Bastard has been hailing the 'glory' of combat, but he goes on to a grisly speech about death preparing to 'line his dead chaps with steel' and devour men's flesh (II.i.352 ff.).

Shakespeare's self-imposed task of refining warfare, preserving its astringent virtues without its barbarities, is an arduous one. In *King John*, more directly than in *Henry V*, the morality of war is under debate. Philip pleads with Pandulph, vainly, not to disrupt the 'smiling peace' by renewing 'The fearful difference of incensed kings' whose hands, 'besmeared and overstained' with blood, have only just been washed clean (III.i.224 ff.). In England, after John's abject submission to him, Pandulph tries, equally vainly, to call off the Dauphin, and exorcize 'the savage spirit of wild war' that he was recently bent on inflaming (V.ii. 69 ff.). In this play belligerents make the welkin ring with their rhetoric, but the fighting is fragmentary and inconclusive. We have a deepening impression of Shakespeare growing distrustful of war altogether, not simply of civil war. Shifting pressures push governments on; humble folk have to pay for their rulers' caprices.

He wanted to breathe new life into the old chivalric tradition, to make a reality of what had always been mainly fantasy. A reconciliation between two old enemies like Douglas and Hotspur, each the other's warm admirer, has the true flavour of romantic legend. So have Hotspur's brief words to his companions before the battle – addressed to the 'gentlemen', not the rank and file – ending with his cry: 'Sound all the lofty instruments of war!' (V.ii.83 ff.). But all this belonged to a heroic past whose feet of clay Shakespeare was being compelled to acknowledge more and more. Meanwhile we have been learning something of the seamy side of war, which found a place in some of the many military writings of the Elizabethan period: that of Gervase Markham the 'muster-master', for instance (cf. Langsam 29). Charges of embezzling army funds, bandied about among the magnates in *Henry VI*, are repeated by Bolingbroke against Mowbray.

Peculation lower down was notoriously rife in all sixteenth-century armies, but never so inimitably portrayed as in Falstaff's doings as a recruiting officer. In the Shrewsbury campaign he makes £300 by letting men bribe themselves off from service, and fills the gaps with riffraff – runaway tapsters, penniless younger sons, jailbirds, 'the cankers of a long peace' (V.ii.11 ff.). There was manifestly a floating population of broken men ready to serve any employer. Then, as for centuries to come, the army was the last refuge of a pauper. In London Falstaff pretends to mistake the Chief Justice's servant for a beggar, and reproves him for his

shiftlessness: 'Is there not wars? Is there not employment?' (*2H.IV* I.ii).
That Shakespeare's picture was no caricature is shown by a report of
1602 on a contingent of eight hundred recruits gathered at Bristol; the
commissioners declared that they had never seen 'such strange creatures';
all the able-bodied men had managed to dodge the call-up (Boas,
Elizabeth 163, 170; cf. L.B. Campbell 245–54; Cruickshank).

Falstaff's men look 'pitiful rascals' to Hal, but as their captain coolly
rejoins, 'they'll fill a pit as well as better' (*1H.IV* IV.ii.62 ff.). Men of rank
fight with swords; Falstaff's rabble are 'peppered' – bullets are good
enough for them – and left dead, or helpless cripples, beggars for the rest
of their lives (V.iii.35 ff.). Such treatment of soldiers was a crying evil of
Tudor times. Raleigh was one who denounced it (Hill, *Origins* 169), and
Shakespeare deserves commendation for giving it such scathing
publicity. This would have a special meaning for playgoers, some of
whom might chance to find themselves impressed into an army very like
Henry IV's; it must have been well enough received to make Shakespeare
stage a recruiting scene in Part 2, where there is no fighting but plenty of
military business. How the rebel chiefs have got their forces together is
not made clear, but as soon as they are disbanded the men hurry away
homeward, not waiting for any pay, as gleefully as boys running home
from school (IV.ii). Altogether, Shakespeare's shining vision of war,
always blurred, was in danger of fading out; illusion and reality were
drifting in opposite directions.

Henry V is his last grand attempt in the Histories – a too galvanic one –
to reflate the cult of honour and glory. With cleavage growing in
England in the late 1590s between a war party and those impatient of the
burdens of war, a propagandist note must have been obvious in the play.
Much as in *King John*, the army bound for France has plenty of
enthusiasts, adventurous young gentlemen who 'sell the pasture now, to
buy the horse' (Act II.Prol.). In every breast 'honour's thought reigns
solely', though once more it is quickly followed by the thought of rich
prizes to be won. There is much talk of making prisoners; a man of good
birth might be above looting, but there was no bar to his taking ransoms.

However, Shakespeare is doing his best to give us a reformed soldiery
as well as a towering hero, and national purpose (of a dubious sort) in
place of feudal ambition. During the campaign we see very little of the
English noblemen with the army; Shakespeare has to respect the
proprieties by giving them the limelight occasionally, but they are only
figureheads, even if we are not told that the real victors at Agincourt
were the English and Welsh bowmen. The French army is far more an
elite force, with only a small proportion of privates serving for pay, and
no technical services; its miserably poor performance is no advertisement
for blue blood as an asset in war. Shakespeare refrains from pointing out

that a feudal array has been routed by a more modern and plebeian one, but the lesson stands out clearly enough.

Henry addresses his troops at Harfleur as 'yeomen', and declares that none of them is 'so mean and base' as to be incapable of noble emulation. Elizabethan writers often ran into extravagances when flattering those above them, and the same might happen when they were learning to flatter Demos. Shakespeare gets into a preposterous comparison of a soldier's frowning eye to a cannon protruding from a cliff above a wild ocean; an image on a par with P.G. Wodehouse's of a choleric old duke snorting through his snowy moustache until it foams like a wave breaking on a stern and rockbound coast. Henry is for 'modest stillness, and humility' as the proper behaviour for peacetime, tigerish ferocity for war (III.i.3 ff.). Similarly, Warwick the king-maker wanted his neigh-bours 'Not mutinous in peace, yet bold in war' (*3H.VI* IV.viii). It was a well-worn idea; Chaucer and Malory had long before held up as model the knight who was 'lion in battle but lamb in the hall' (G. Hughes 42). This, needless to say, could be the ideal of every government: any grievances that its subjects might nurse they should work off against foreigners.

Henry's soldiers, he tells them before Agincourt, are his 'band of brothers', and the meanest will have a chance to 'gentle his condition' by his feats, or qualify as a gentleman (*H.V* IV.iii.60–63). It was a rule in some early modern armies that good service entitled a private soldier to challenge even an officer to a duel. Seeking to rekindle the torch of chivalry, Shakespeare saw a need to extend the 'honours of war' beyond the charmed circle to a new breed of soldier, plebeian but soberly self-respecting. Williams and his comrades provide the only serious portrayal of common soldiers in the Histories, probably the earliest in English literature. They are the vanguard of a New Model Army. Who they are, what they have come for – except to earn their bread – or what weapons they are armed with, Shakespeare does not tell us. He must be partly inventing a species of men he feels ought to exist, as much as describing a kind he knows. He wants men with whom the king can have a frank, edifying exchange of views. Before Agincourt the army is painfully short of supplies, but we hear no grumbling about food; these men's minds turn to weightier questions – of conscience, of the rights and wrongs of war, and who is responsible for it. Henry, for his part, is the forerunner of a long line of British generals who did not pretend to much technical knowledge or tactical skill, but prided themselves on their gift of 'leader-ship'.

Dover Wilson hailed the play during the Second World War as 'Shakespeare's message' to his countrymen in peril, as *This Sceptred Isle* was subtitled. If so, it must be called a very confusing one. What cannot be gainsaid is that between *Henry VI Part 1* and *Henry V* there has been a great change of atmosphere. A strong undercurrent of criticism of war makes itself felt. Shakespeare may have believed it scarcely possible to eliminate war; in view of his reverence for valour, we cannot safely assume that he wanted it to disappear. In his mind it often seems transformed from reality to symbol, an expression of feelings not easily put into any other form: an ideal touchstone of mankind's fibre. It is noticeable that he often sends his favourites off to the wars, to win their spurs, at a very early age. The Bastard has only just left home. There is some lack of realism in the prowess of such striplings, but youth must prove itself on the battlefield, as a rite of initiation into manhood.

In *Henry V* Shakespeare resorted to various means of softening the more aggressive aspects of what the play would be assumed by most of his audience to teach, besides the too obvious device of spreading an aura of divine favour over the English cause. An English army is now a citizen army of patriots, even if no plans for better treatment of injured ex-servicemen are being matured. An English soldier is hanged for theft. The French have learned less; their nobility is frivolous, whereas in the English camp even common soldiers can be 'touched to fine issues'. Agincourt fits in well with Shakespeare's scheme, because there the English are cornered, taken at a disadvantage; the battle made a good starting point for the tradition, so dear to later-born Britons, of their thin red line defying fearful odds. And at the end we are invited to suppose the two sides quitting the stage arm in arm, henceforth to live in amity.

Yet with all this, the dominant impression left behind is a sombre one. Henry is far too easily convinced that he is entitled to go to war, his Christian conscience intact. In Act II Scene ii he accuses conspirators of wanting to sell England to a foreign enemy whose coming will mean massacre, rapine, destruction. Some conspirators in Shakespeare's England really were trying to do this, in the name of religion. But Henry is about to descend on France, as a foreign enemy, and the consequences will be – as he knows – just as lurid. The two-facedness of nationalism could hardly be more clearly revealed. His accommodating archbishop can savour the thought of Edward III at Crécy smiling as he watched his son the Black Prince 'Forage in blood of French nobility'; the French king has a more painful thought of Edward smiling to see his son 'Mangle the work of nature' (I.ii.108 ff.; IV.ii.60). 'Famine, Sword, and Fire' are to follow the hero to France, like hounds, we are promised at the start; we may need to recall that Shakespeare's audience revelled in bear-baiting and cockfighting.

Henry himself dwells often and feelingly on the horrors of war, but finds it easy to shuffle the blame on to someone else. It is the French

government, or the governor of Harfleur, whose duty it is to take pity on
their people and avert the terrific consequences which must otherwise
fall on them, by surrendering. If Harfleur has to be stormed, it will be
impossible for him to hold the inflamed soldiery back from every
outrage. But 'What is't to me?' It will not be his fault (III.iii.19 ff.).

War is an 'impious' thing, he admits, 'Arrayed in flames, like to the
prince of fiends' (III.iii.15–16). Peace, on the contrary, says Burgundy in
his eloquent tribute, is the 'Dear nurse of arts, plenties, and joyful births'
(V.ii.35). Peace by honourable accord is the best kind of conquest, we
have heard the virtuous archbishop in *Henry IV Part 2* say. This note, as
well as its opposite, has been heard in the Histories from the beginning.
Pope and emperor join to advocate peace in *Henry VI Part 1*; good Duke
Humphrey agrees, saying that he has always thought these wars between
Christians 'impious and unnatural' (V.i). Certainly the lesson meant to be
heeded most in the Histories is that civil war is a horrible calamity, but
its evils are not easily distinguished from those of foreign war. Hotspur
left a widow to bewail the cruelty of 'the hideous god of war' (*2H.IV*
II.iii.35); so, no doubt, did many of the fallen at Agincourt.

Nationalism

Humphrey of Gloucester, traduced by malignant tongues, assures the
king that he would willingly die if his death could end England's misfortunes (*2H.VI* III.i). This king, exiled to Scotland, steals secretly back,
with no aim of recovering power but simply for the happiness of
treading his native soil once again (*3H.VI* III.i.12–13). Young Arthur's
last words are 'England keep my bones' (IV.iii). Mowbray takes a feeling
leave of his homeland, lamenting that he will no longer be able to speak
his 'native English'; Bolingbroke, likewise banished, vows to be always 'a
true born Englishman', loyal to his country's 'sweet soil' (*R.II* I.iii).
Richard, back from Ireland, 'weeps for joy' and caresses the earth with
his hand (III.ii.4 ff.).

In the Histories, Shakespeare is the most eloquent of all poets of
English patriotism, with an emotional, idealizing sense that wells up now
and then of what England is, or might be. It overflows in lyrical speeches
that may have little dramatic relevance; above all, John of Gaunt's
apotheosis of his motherland as he lies dying. This ideal England, a
rainbow or dream of the future more than a present reality, often calls to
mind the country's protective barrier of the sea, the gift of Nature or
Providence. It is thought of as an island, Gaunt's 'sceptred isle', with
Scotland ignored, and with evocations, lit up by the fate of the Armada,
of stormy waves and impregnable cliffs. 'England is safe, if true within
itself', Hastings declares (*3H.VI* IV.i.42 ff.) – much as the Bastard does in

the closing lines of *King John*. An enemy too, the Duke of Austria, talks of the 'roaring tides' that are England's 'water-walled bulwark' in its 'Utmost corner of the west' (*KJ* II.i.23 ff.) – though in fact in this play the waves devour English and French ships impartially.

All this would seem to recommend policies of splendid isolation; and a speech like Gaunt's breathes a civilized, non-belligerent spirit more agreeable to associate with Shakespeare than any braying trumpets. But love of country has everywhere been fed by hatred of foreigners. His audience was blessed with a polarized mentality, a product of changing times, which enabled it to love Falstaff the great sceptic as well as to admire Henry V the great tub-thumper. With one half of its nature it wanted action, and blood. In 1592 Nashe reported that Part 1 of *Henry VI* had been seen by ten thousand spectators in all, in tears as they watched their idol Talbot, covered with blood. Throughout the Histories runs the theme of the superiority of Englishmen over Frenchmen. When France is being lost it cannot be admitted that this is the result of French bravery and patriotism; it can only have been caused by a stab in the back, misconduct among the English nobles.

Here is the sole issue on which the feuding lords can take a public-spirited stand. Warwick actually sheds tears over it; York bewails 'the honour of this warlike isle' and dreams of recovering France (*2H.VI* I.i). His son Edward, in a very Shakespearian speech, avows that but for Henry VI's disastrous marriage and its results in France, his family would have let its claim to the throne sleep (*3H.VI* II.i.144 ff.). So obsessive is the issue that a Lancastrian envoy soliciting aid from a French king bases his party's right to the English throne, very tactlessly, on the victories of Henry V; for good measure he throws in John of Gaunt's mythical conquest of Spain (*3H.VI* III.iii.81 ff.). The boy prince Edward thinks about Julius Caesar, builder of the Tower of London, where he is soon to perish, and shows his royal spirit by resolving to 'win our ancient right in France again' (*R.III* III.i.84 ff.).

Shakespeare can sing the praises of peace; yet a persistent conviction among his contemporaries, that peace brings national degeneracy, too often finds its way into these plays. He never seems to feel any need to give reasons for what is really a very startling belief. Like others, he was unconsciously looking at such things from a point of view borrowed from an upper class whose traditional function was fighting and which was in fact liable to decay, loss of morale, when deprived of opportunity. Sometimes Shakespeare clothes the idea in medical language: peace breeds plenty; surfeit breeds disease. But any notion of the mass of Englishmen sinking (as the archbishop in *Henry VI Part 2* seems to suppose) into gluttonous self-indulgence and sloth is ridiculous, when a large proportion of them were famishing. 'The fat ribs of peace' sound more convincing when John talks of the Church, and of subsidies to be extracted from it (III.iii.9–11).

Peace, being so unwholesome, must lead to civil disorder. At first this meant feudal faction-fighting; but as time goes on there seems to be some deeper-lying peril, something lodged in the nature of society itself. Again, little logic is discernible. If peace brings material comfort, swinish content, it may be bad for the human spirit, but there seems no reason for it to be bad for law and order; except that there will always be some who are dissatisfied with their share, and whatever distempers appear may be worsened by subversive thinking having more freedom to spread. In his defence of drama in 1612 as a teacher of good civic conduct and respect for authority, Thomas Heywood wrote of seditious sectaries sprouting like weeds 'in the fatness and rankness of a peaceable common-wealth' (16).

What all this meant at bottom was that Englishmen might love their native land, but they loved one another much less, because of the social inequalities and clashing opinions that divided and estranged them. Hence national unity could only be precarious. The Histories are full of uneasy presentiments of civil strife, always thought of as a grim prospect. To Henry VI it is a 'viperous worm', and his great-uncle, honest old Exeter, has much to say of 'base and envious discord' (*1H.VI* III.i). Richmond concludes *Richard III* with a condemnation of civil strife; Richard II denounces the 'sky-aspiring and ambitious thoughts' that awaken the 'grating shock of wrathful iron arms' (I.iii). His uncle York reproaches Bolingbroke with coming back to England to stir up broils, 'Frighting her pale-fac'd villages with war' (II.iii). Such fears find vivid expression in the Bastard's image of 'vast confusion' ready to fall on the country 'like a raven on a sick beast' (*KJ* IV.iii.152–3).

All the same, in Tudor official presentation the peril may have been magnified somewhat, because of its usefulness as a bugbear; and in this Shakespeare may be said to have had a dutiful hand. In his plays hostilities are regularly prefaced by the direst threats and counterthreats. Between the rival chiefs in the Wars of the Roses, these are as regularly carried out; more and more, as time goes on, the same ferocious treatment is promised to everyone on the enemy side – though we are left to wonder whether it is actually inflicted. When Warwick and the Yorkists prepare to march on London, he intends to execute all those in towns on the road who fail to applaud them (*3H.IV* II.i.194–7). Bolingbroke threatens that if his banishment is not repealed and his rights restored, he will 'lay the summer's dust with showers of blood' from the veins of 'slaughtered Englishmen' (III.iii). Richard II is ready for similar reprisals if his sacred prerogative is infringed. Falstaff observes – a more modern touch – that even a rumour of political disturbances will depress the market value of real estate; Hal adds a humorous forecast of girls being raped *en masse* (*1H.IV* II.iv.35 ff.). His father, king now instead of rebel, inveighs against those who are unleashing 'all-abhorred war' (V.i.16). After all this, the only crime we hear of during the rising is a shirt stolen from an inn by one of Falstaff's ragamuffins (he expects other linen to be removed from hedges on the march) (IV.ii.49 ff.). Even the invaders from Scotland are not taxed with misconduct.

However, the stolen shirt may serve as symbol of a real fear of political dissension opening the door to social disruption. Pandulph, egging the French on to attack England, talks graphically of how a discontented people will seize any chance to get in a blow at their government (*KJ* III.iv). Insurgents will always meet with a welcome, Henry IV is gloomily aware, because there are always

> moody beggars starving for a time
> Of pellmell havoc and confusion.
> (*1H.IV* V.i.81–2)

And from here the argument leads back with renewed force to the necessity of war. A state is strongest, Nashe wrote, that 'lives every hour in fear of invasion'. There are always some men 'for whom there is no use but war' and who, if not employed against foreigners, will be fighting their compatriots (127–8). In an era of surplus population, prone to lawless behaviour, such reasoning was plausible enough to be very tenacious.

Shakespeare's patriotic Englishmen are just as ready to threaten their fellow-countrymen with fire and sword as to threaten foreigners. Clearly, then, it was best to find foreigners for them to fight. In *King John*, when English swords are about to be turned against each other, Salisbury sighs for a united crusade against the Turks (V.ii). Henry IV hunts the trail of policy in the same direction. Part 1 opens with a long address from him about his preparations for a crusade, designed to heal the 'furious close of civil butchery'. The sum of his statecraft, as he delivers it on his deathbed to his son, is that it is futile to rely on the loyalty of friends or the favour of 'giddy minds': hence to distract attention from affairs at home he has kept up a talk of leading an army to the Holy Land, and his successor too, if he would be secure, must seek 'foreign quarrels' (*2H.IV* IV.v).

Triumphs abroad are the best guarantee of a throne, and for a usurped throne the single justification strong enough to bar the claims of legitimacy. It was only fitfully beginning to dawn on the Elizabethan mind that the best way to forestall social unrest lay in finding social remedies, measures such as curbs on enclosure of village commons or profiteering in times of food scarcity. That the masses will and must always be painfully poor was an axiom. Maladies of peace could be 'purged' only by war. A country 'o'er-cloyed' with inhabitants does well when it 'vomits forth' its surplus on 'desperate ventures', says Richard III (V.iii.316 ff.).

In one of his medieval novels Walter Scott remarks that the loss of French provinces was felt throughout England as 'a national degradation'; he points out that nobles were losing fiefs they had acquired in France, and that squires and yeomen had also made something out of the conquest (*Anne* ch. 7). There could be no benefits to the vast majority of Englishmen from feudal acquisitions in France, though they had to bear a good share of the costs. A few lucky ones among the rank and file must have got home with some plunder; others with at least a right to boast of their feats among gaping neighbours, as Henry at Agincourt pictures his men doing. On this shallow foundation a mythology could be reared about France (as later about India) as a great national property shared by all Englishmen, and the duty of their sons to hold on to what their fathers had won. Much help in keeping the tradition alive must have come from the multitude of local entertainers – minstrels, actors, performers of all sorts, professional or amateur, feudal or civic.

There is thus an underlying realism in the fiasco of the Cade rebellion, as an object-lesson in how useful nationalism can be for diverting mass resentments. Cade himself has some respect for his sovereign for the sake of his father, 'in whose time boys went to span-counter for French crowns' (*2H.VI* IV.ii.154 ff.). Clifford, as royal deputy, has only to take up the glorious theme of how Henry V 'made all the French to quake' in order to set the crowd cheering; and he plays an easy trump card by asking whether Cade will know how to defend them against a French invasion, or to lead them into France, and make all of them 'earls and dukes'. It is God and the King who will carry them to victory. 'To France, to France, and get what you have lost!' This blatant trickery (as Shakespeare must surely have meant it to be seen) wins the day, and Cade is left deserted, ruefully reflecting on his Kentishmen's folly: 'The name of Henry the Fifth hales them to an hundred mischiefs' (IV.viii).

Each of the first two Tudors tried his hand at invading France, and must have counted on popular approval; Mary Tudor, as schoolboys learn, died with the name of lost Calais engraved on her heart. We may think of the fantasy of a lost France as an outlet for grievances for which ordinary Englishmen could find as yet no rational expression or cure. It is in some such fashion that all garblings of mass discontent into fiction must be interpreted. England's supposed need of France was a distant forerunner of Cecil Rhodes's teaching that Britons could prosper only if their rulers had a far-flung empire to rule as well. By Shakespeare's time France was turning into a symbol for hazily grandiose aspirations to worldwide expansion, just taking shape and evolving with scarcely a break out of the old feudal instinct of conquest. Ireland was the bridge, as Granada was for Castile. Appropriately, the Prologue to Act V of *Henry V* does its best to work up enthusiasm for the coming conquest of Ireland along with the bygone conquest of France.

All such national daydreams could be dramatized – allegorized, almost – in the shape of an old legend like Agincourt, brought up to date by a writer of Shakespeare's skill to herald a new era. A strong 'colonial' tinge colours nearly all the French scenes in the Histories – from the outset, where the French are England's 'oft-subdued slaves', and any resistance on their part is 'treachery' (*1H.VI* I.v.32). Since then the author of *Henry V* has learned much: he is a better historian or political observer now, and a great deal in this play is serious study of a war of aggression. It ends with an urbane mirage of France not as a conquered dependency but as a partner with England in an amicable 'league' (V.ii.356 ff.). Whatever the connection between the two, it was destined to break down before long. Foreign war appears to lead nowhere; yet if abandonment of it must lead to civil war, the condition of Christendom appears altogether morbid and unstable. It is a dismal confession for a patriotic poet to be forced to make.

Religion

Kenneth Clark deemed Shakespeare unquestionably a sceptic, of a kind 'more complete and more uncomfortable' than the Montaigne whom he admired; he was 'the first and may be the last supremely great poet to have been without a religious belief' (163–4). There is a great deal of Christian feeling in Shakespeare, in terms of ethics and a philosophy of life: it is religion refined, held in solution, without doctrinal colouring. His good men and women are good spontaneously, thanks to their own natures, and because they feel sufficiently in tune with life to be above petty spites and jealousies. In an age of religion – or rather, of theology and clerical self-assertion – he created extremely few characters with a recognizably religious temperament. He could think himself into many varieties of mind or mood, but not easily, it seems, into this.

Religion in the Histories, especially the early ones, is chiefly a wing of the feudal edifice, and its representatives are at first simply feudal nobles in other costume. When Humphrey of Gloucester produces in Parliament his indictment of the wicked Bishop of Winchester, the prelate snatches it from him and tears it up: he will have no truck with 'written pamphlets studiously devised' (*1H.VI* III.i). Not content with this, he challenges Humphrey to single combat (*2H.VI* II.i.36 ff.), as if

Shakespeare wants to make him look grotesque as well as villainous. This arrogant, ruffling priest, whom we see paying down money for a cardinal's hat (*1H.VI* V.i), stands for Rome as well as feudality, and the anti-popish note often struck in the Histories is heard loudly – and crudely – in what we learn of his usury, fornication, and other 'lewd, pestiferous, and dissentious pranks' (*1H.VI* III.i.15), and in the guilty conscience that racks him on his deathbed.

Humphrey is a critic of popish ways, along with his other good qualities. When Winchester maintains that Henry V succeeded because the Church prayed for him, the duke rejoins that on the contrary the Church must have prayed for his death, because it likes only feeble princes whom it can overawe (*1H.VI* I.i). Relations between Church and State are in the forefront in *King John*, a drama with a background of Protestant admiration for John as a champion of England against Rome. John intends from the start to make the rich abbeys pay for his French expedition (I.i.48–9). Pandulph the papal legate is a dignified and fearless churchman, but he is totally blind to all interests other than those of the First Estate, and expects peace and war to be made at his nod. In return John talks pointedly of the corruptions of the Church under the 'usurped authority' of a meddling Italian priest, and makes use of 'the free breath of a sacred king' to declare himself 'supreme head' of his own Church (III.i.147 ff.). In *Richard III* the roles are reversed when the Cardinal-Archbishop of Canterbury, after expressing horror at Crook-back's purpose of violating rights of sanctuary, gives way weakly to *raison d'état* (III.i.37 ff.).

At a lower level than the political, the first two plays contain anti-popery of a more knockabout species. A bogus miracle is exposed and punished by the shrewd Humphrey; this is in line with polemics of Shakespeare's day, where Catholics were accused of concocting miracles. A graver impression is created by the episode of the ambitious Duchess Elinor hiring necromancers to raise a spirit so that she can consult the powers of darkness about her plottings; two of them are priests. It seems to be left to the audience to consider this spirit another hoax, or an authentic 'fiend' from hell, as it calls itself – though, like Macbeth's, a 'juggling' fiend.

A stringent test, either of religious sentiment or of human fibre and courage, is the approach of death. Such courage, one of Shakespeare's most highly esteemed virtues, could be displayed by many sorts of people; there is a curious affinity between some words of two men very far apart in all else. 'A man can die but once', says Falstaff's recruit Feeble, the woman's tailor (*2H.IV* III.ii.34). 'Cowards die many times', says Julius Caesar. It should be noticed that Shakespeare's wolfish feudalists are sheltered from religious fears by their unquestioning confidence that they have been born with first-class tickets to heaven, as part of their aristocratic entitlement. Talbot and his son will die together on the battlefield, he proclaims, 'And soul with soul from France to Heaven fly' (*1H.VI* IV.v.55) – stopping at no intermediate point like Purgatory. Margaret bids farewell to her fellow-captives with a promise to meet them again 'in sweet Jerusalem' (*3H.VI* V.v.7–8). Some change is appearing when York dies committing himself into God's hands, and his son Edward, before rushing back into battle, prays quite earnestly that the 'brazen gates of heaven' will open to his 'sinful soul' (*3H.VI* I.iv; V.iii).

There is no sign that such pious sentiments have any influence on the speakers' behaviour. Possibly the writer may be hinting that their heaven is as illusory as their expectation of reaching it. Some other crime-stained feudalists of Shakespeare's first generation, facing more lingering deaths, reveal lively apprehensions of what lies before them. Edward IV, in his later years, is a prey to superstitious fears, which his brother Richard knows how to profit by. On his deathbed he reminds his jarring courtiers of God's watchful eye. Buckingham, on his way to execution, dreads the wrath of the 'high All-seer'. Some spectators may have pursued him in fancy into a lurid place of burning; but what seems to be meant is rather that guilty men make their own doom, that punishment follows crime as a necessity, a shadow, of man's life among his fellows.

When Henry V, in solemn tones, unmasks the English traitors, we see a consecration of nationalism. State and people, as well as monarch, are now anointed. An extension is in progress of a privileged class's assurance of preferential treatment in the next world as in this, to a favoured nation's conviction of having God on its side, of Englishmen being – as the guns of the Commonwealth were before long to shout to the world – the new Chosen People. They are sublimely sure that heaven looks with partisan sympathy on their wars with the French. 'The battles of the Lord of hosts he fought', says Winchester, a dubious witness, of Henry V (*1H.VI* I.i.31). 'God is our fortress', says Talbot (II.i.26). 'Baleful sorcery', 'the help of hell', can win the enemy only an occasional success, and even they may glimpse the truth that God is an English deity (II.i). King John, in France with his army, announces himself as 'God's wrathful agent' (II.i.87).

Such catchphrases abound, but practically the only Christian we can identify in these plays is Henry VI. Shakespeare must have had in mind the cult of Henry as a saint; pilgrimages to his tomb in Windsor chapel long continued. Piety is no asset to him as a ruler. Friend and foe are at one in holding that 'church-like humours fit not for a crown', as York derisively comments (*1H.VI* I.i.242 ff.). His wife despises him as a besotted collector of relics, images, beads (*2H.VI* I.iii.53 ff.). This seems to have been Shakespeare's own picture of him at first; but king and playwright grow and develop together, and Henry's piety evolves from mere religiosity to a true Christian morality and resignation. He brings a gleam of light into a prison world. Winchester's tormented death inspires him to a moral that might serve for many other occasions in Shakespeare: 'Forbear to judge, for we are sinners all' (*2H.VI* III.iii.31). His dying words are of forgiveness for his murderer, Crookback. Against them we can weigh a summary of the political creed of the realists, the words of Richard of York, with Somerset's blood on his sword: 'Priests pray for enemies, but princes kill' (*2H.VI* V.ii.71).

His son Crookback, at the opposite pole from Henry VI, is the gladiator who knows best how to make religion serve his turn. He boasts to us of his finesse in dissembling and deception, with bits of Scripture to cloak his 'naked villainy' (*R.III* I.iii.334–8). His order for his brother's murder follows without a pause. Yet he proves, after all, too clever by half. Machiavelli, as Shakespeare may want us to realize, is not a safe guide to practical politics. Richard alienates nearly all those about him and, worst of all, ends with waning energy and confidence even in himself. He is as much a failure as Henry VI, for opposite reasons. Henry deemed himself heaven's 'unworthy deputy' (*2H.VI* III.ii.385–6); Henry V will know how to win a reputation as its very worthy deputy. But the inability of monarchy and morality to form a natural blend was one that Shakespeare could not sweep out of sight.

'Shakespeare regarded human history', one sanguine reader pronounces, 'as a progressive revelation of God's judgments upon human kind' (Winstanley 54). Many of his – or rather his characters' – sayings may seem to corroborate this. Margaret tells us that the 'heavens are just' (*3H.VI* III.iii.77), but there is little sign of it in the economy of things here below. Later on we hear her exclaim 'O upright, just, and true-disposing God', as she finds 'the course of justice' doing its work; but all this means no more than that she rejoices to see some of her enemies sharing her own misfortunes (*R.III* III.iv.55, 105). We may feel more ready to listen to Henry VI when he hails Warwick as the 'instrument' – a Shakespearian word – of his deliverance, and God as its 'author' (*3H.VI* IV.vi.18).

On the whole it is extremely hard to discover any consistent attempt by Shakespeare to interpret the flux of events as directed by an over-riding Providence. There may be cause to surmise that he would have liked to believe in the existence of some such guardian power, but this is no proof that he did believe in it. Religion in the Histories is a terrestrial phenomenon, sometimes ethical and good, more often political and bad. We are not moving – as, for instance, in Massinger's plays – in a realm of miracles, with a trap door into heaven continually opening. The few supernatural solicitings that occur aim frankly at stage effect, like the triple sun that the Yorkist princes see in the sky, an omen of returning fortune, or the ghosts that appear on the night before Bosworth.

For the popular mind, such aberrations of Nature were easier to digest than most of the official creed. No divine aid is expected or begged for by the peasant rebels of Kent, no disapproval feared. Shakespeare's was a questioning era, and he must have been at least as quick as his neighbours to detect the hollowness of many conventional views of world history offered them from the pulpit. Even about the meaning of the supreme fact, death, doubts must have been widespread. We may be little surprised at Richard III talking of it as 'the blind cave of eternal night' (V.iii.62); but women show no more sign of religious feeling than men. Edward IV's virtuous widow uses identically pagan words about her consort's departure 'To his new kingdom of ne'er-changing night' (R.III II.ii.46).

Her brother-in-law Clarence, mewed up in the Tower, has a fevered dream of death; it is lent a classical setting by Charon and the Styx, with 'a legion of foul fiends' to add a Christian touch, but what the sleeper feels he is on the brink of is 'the kingdom of perpetual night', or annihilation (R.III I.iv.45 ff.). Justice Shallow is struck by the thought of an old acquaintance dying, but his maundering reflections are mixed up with livestock prices (2H.IV III.ii.30 ff.). Perhaps Shakespeare is showing us the common sense, however muddled, of the average man. John of Gaunt on his deathbed is another who thinks of death as an 'endless night'. But with Richard II and the crisis of monarchy, and divine right as its refuge, things are changing, and religion is frequently, if sometimes awkwardly, invoked. Gaunt himself finds an excuse for not avenging a brother's death by trusting the matter to God, all the more because the culprit was His 'deputy anointed' (I.ii). To have divine right made a cloak for murder casts grave doubt on it, and the widow's expostulations bring out the contradiction.

Younger men, Richard especially, now have a more positive view of religion and what it can do for them. Before the abortive trial by battle Mowbray has gone to the confessional (in exile he turns crusader); his opponent's pledge that his 'divine soul' will 'answer it in heaven' makes a fitting response (I.iii). Old men helpless amid the press of events and the crumbling of their world resign themselves to heavenly designs they cannot understand. York, left in charge of the government, may be shuffling off responsibility, but there is sometimes in his words a note of the indistinct but deep trust in some kind of Providence that is often heard in later plays. Richard's misfortunes must have been permitted by God 'for some strong purpose', and his 'high will' cannot be gainsaid (V.ii).

This contrasts with the outlook of the men of action, who know what they want, strive to get it, and look to God to assist them. Heaven will indeed protect a true king, the loyal Bishop of Carlisle admonishes Richard, but only if he avails himself of the earthly means that it affords him (III.ii). An honest conservative, the bishop opposes his deposition, and then joins with the Abbot of Westminster and other conspirators in a plot to assassinate Bolingbroke. He is sentenced by the new king to no worse than retirement, out of respect for his character and 'high sparks of honour' (V.vi). Spectators must have seen a likeness between this plot and the Catholic murder plots known or suspected in their own time.

Richard suffers from a belief that the ceremony of anointment, more magical than religious, authorizes him to draw on heaven for unlimited succour. He lapses easily into despair, none the less, which may be attributable to a lurking awareness of the absurdity of such a claim, as well as to an unstable nature. In the remarkable scene of his return from Ireland, he can soar on the wings of divine right into fine poetry; but it is plain to those hearing him that he is retreating into a fool's paradise. Dashed by news that his Welsh forces have dispersed, he clings again to the mystique of royalty: 'Is not the King's name twenty thousand names?' – but very soon he is drooping once more (III.ii). It is the same when he has to confront Bolingbroke. He demands proof that 'the hand of God' has dismissed him from his 'stewardship', and threatens divine vengeance that will strike, indiscriminately, generations yet unborn; but defiance soon gives way to tame submission (III.iii).

In the deposition scene (IV.i), the finest in the play, Richard is a pathetic, scarcely a tragic, figure, because he is conscious only of his own fall, not of how much harm he has done his subjects; he can admit his 'weaved-up follies', but the deposing of a king is a sin far more deeply 'damned in the book of Heaven'. He does at least realize that what he is being forced to relinquish is a 'heavy weight'; the 'unwieldy sceptre' is beyond his strength. And this is the real curse that his successors are dooming themselves to: no man can be equal to the burden of kingship. In prison Richard's mind runs much on the 'small needle's eye' that separates worldly success from spiritual truth, and the discrepancies in Scripture that 'set the Word itself against the Word' (V.v.13–14) – a phrase used differently a little before by the Duchess of York, pleading for her son. Richard's meditation on Christianity is one of very few in Shakespeare; he has a good many briefer ones on religion in general.

In the later Histories, men who are moving with the times are ready at least to show a proper respect for religion, while those of the time departing are indifferent. Falstaff is fond of religious tags, in a humorous way, and recommends his friends to 'repent at idle times', but he has forgotten what the inside of a church looks like (*2H.IV* II.ii.127; *1H.IV* III.iii.7–8). Mistress Quickly has an involuntary acquaintance with her parish clergyman, Master Dumbe (*2H.IV* II.iv.80 ff.). Hotspur calls not on God but on Bellona, and Mars 'up to his ears in blood'; he dies uttering his finest words, as men do on Shakespeare's battlefields, but there is no relish of salvation in them.

Meanwhile the House of Lancaster is learning what stars to steer by. Bolingbroke repulses Richard's murderer, unrewarded, and vows a pilgrimage to the Holy Land as expiation (*R.II* V.vi). Sundry allusions to crusading are scattered about, as if an idea were floating in Shakespeare's mind, as it did in various others', of Europe sinking its differences and combining against the Turks. Gaunt recalls the part played by Englishmen in crusades; his son's first words in *Henry IV Part 1*, like his last in *Richard II*, are of the Holy Land. His practical concern is always with civil wars that may break out; a crusade may serve as prophylactic. All this is for the public ear, part of a new political style. Similarly before Shrewsbury he claims God's favour 'as our cause is just' (V.i.120) – a solemnity at once capped by Falstaff's soliloquy on Honour. After the battle Henry taxes Worcester with not having delivered his offer of pardon to his fellow-rebels 'like a Christian' (V.v.9). Yet under stress of continual anxiety Henry really is falling under the sway of religion, though to him it is another shadow much more than a comfort. His troubled conscience makes him fearful of a 'secret doom', and of his thoughtless son as 'the rod of heaven' sent to punish his transgression (*1H.IV* III.ii.6, 10).

His younger son John of Lancaster, that 'young sober-blooded boy' (*2H.IV* IV.iii.84), who may be taken as a first sketch of Octavian, renders God the credit for his morally very questionable tripping up of the next set of rebels (IV.ii.121). From Prince Hal we can already catch the accents of Henry V when he promises his father amendment 'in the name of God', not forgetting to put the blame on others – 'God forgive them' – who have turned the king's thoughts against him (*1H.IV* III.ii.129 ff.). In *Henry V* divine favour in battle takes the place of divine right, and the cry is 'God for Harry, England and St George': heaven is expected to side now with a nation and its leader, not with an egotistic individual like Richard II.

If religion is to serve its due purpose, relations between Church and State must be on a due footing. Prince John rebukes the Archbishop of York for stirring up civil strife instead of keeping to the work that has won him respect as a priest deep in 'the books of God', 'the speaker in His parliament' (*2H.IV* IV.ii.15 ff.). In *Henry V* the Archbishop of Canterbury plays his part to perfection; he is a true fire-eating imperialist, like a long line of prelates and royal chaplains after him. The interests of both parties are served; though some auditors must surely have felt that Canterbury's call to the king to unwind his bloody flag, and win his rights 'with blood and sword and fire' (I.ii.10, 131), was not quite the way for a Christian, even an archbishop, to talk.

Henry is a worthy pupil. He is not a hypocrite; religion is genuinely a part of him, filling up any inconvenient gaps in his philosophy or personality. Perturbed before Agincourt by the thought of his father's usurpation, he seems to be trying to 'bargain with his God like a pedlar' (Ellis-Fermor 47), as he reminds heaven of the two chantries he has founded to say prayers for Richard's soul, and his other acts of contrition (IV.i.291 ff.). They were likely to strike Shakespeare's hearers more as Romish superstition than as true piety. But there is a prophetically Cromwellian ring in his ultimatum to the French, calling on them 'in the bowels of the Lord' to surrender to his will; and his summons to Harfleur brings in Satan, Leviathan and Herod.

Indeed, the hero's religiosity is overwhelming. Leaving aside casual ejaculations, he is heard calling on heaven no fewer than thirty-three times – fourteen times in the great fourth Act alone. Hotspur as well as Falstaff would have laughed at all this. Shakespeare must have done the same at times, and sometimes seems to invite us to join him – most openly when Henry threatens with capital punishment anyone in the army who brags of the victory at Agincourt, instead of giving the glory to God, and Fluellen pipes up: 'Is it not lawful, an please your majesty, to tell how many is killed?' (IV.viii.115 ff.). But Henry has to quiet an uneasy conscience, as well as to impress others. He complains of his soldiers wanting to put the blame for everything on him; he himself, as Shakespeare must want us to notice, is just as eager to put the responsibility for his war and all its sufferings on God.

Women and the Family

In the feudal world family counted for more than individual, man for far more than woman. In the early Histories fathers and sons are close, as we see with Talbot and his son perishing together in battle. York can take pride in his sons' heroic fighting, and their attempts to rescue him (*3H.VI* I.iv.7 ff.). Fraternal ties, too, may be warm. Dying on the battle-field, Warwick calls out for his brother, only to learn that his brother has died calling out for him (*3H.VI* V.ii.33 ff.); a use of parallelism that Shakespeare was fond of in his years of apprenticeship.

In a disintegrating society the family is a surviving stronghold, but one that cannot for long resist the general breakdown, especially as the leading theme of these plays is dynastic schism. In *Richard III* the family collapses, undermined by individual ambition and the same thirst for power which formerly held it together. Clarence has deserted his new party to return to the bosom of the Yorkist family, and ends by being murdered by his two brothers. Their mother recites a threnody over its ruin when she looks back over Richard Crookback's life of crime, and lays her curse on him (*R.III* IV.iv.116 ff.). There is no recovery of the bond between father and son. Three of the five kings after Edward IV are childless, and another, John, practically so. What we are left with is discord, taking various forms, between the generations. It is not the familiar rift, as in *Romeo and Juliet*, between ardent youth and crabbed age. In both *Richard II* and *Henry IV* it is more a matter of age and caution being flouted by reckless, lawless youth. Falstaff laughs at them both. It is hard to believe that he himself was ever a member of any family – his offhand allusion to his 'brothers and sisters' notwithstanding (*2H.IV* II.ii.131).

Hotspur's outburst at his father's absence from Shrewsbury is not one of filial respect (*1H.IV* IV.i). He was not too entirely headstrong to refuse to consider terms, but his uncle Worcester, from self-regarding motives, conceals the royal offer of pardon from him (IV.iii.107 ff.; V.ii.1 ff.). Henry's bitterness against his truant son breaks out at times almost in the accents of Lear. He has been led to suspect the Prince of Wales of wanting him out of the way – even, it would seem, of being ready to murder him (*1H.IV* III.ii.121 ff.; V.iv.48 ff.); the prince's action in saving his life in the battle removes this suspicion only for a while. His long tirade about sons turning against the fathers who have toiled all their lives for them seems to range beyond a personal situation to a general social malaise, not surprising in an epoch like the Elizabethan, over family properties and inheritance, and the impatience of the rising generation to see the last of its parents. Henry foresees an England turning after his death into 'a wilderness again,/Peopled with wolves' (*2H.IV* IV.v.136–7).

Most of the women who play a part in the historical events Shakespeare is concerned with are either bad – at least over-ambitious – or helpless, from weakness or from having suffered defeat. Joan of Arc is the great exception; but as a mysterious, half-legendary character she cannot be very clearly pictured. In her earlier appearances she is treated with commendable respect, as if genuinely inspired, certainly brave and able to breathe courage into others. The French nobles are an unimpressive lot; it is she who is the voice of France. Through her Shakespeare makes amends for a prevalent tone of jingoism by showing patriotism as not an English monopoly, and English triumphs as having to be paid for by French sufferings. It is only after defeat that she is made to invoke infernal assistance. In her final scene there is a jumble of good writing and very sad stuff, surely not both by Shakespeare. But this play was being written at the height of the European witch-hunt; actors may well have felt that it would be good for business to have some demons and a whiff of black magic. On the whole Joan comes off well. Possibly a memory of her was afloat in Shakespeare's mind when he wrote of Frenchwomen mocking their nobles for their failure to throw back the invasion of Henry V (*H.V* III.v.27 ff.).

A masculine tribe of ladies of rank, hard and resolute, formed in Shakespeare's mind before his Portias and Rosalinds dawned there – naturally enough, because for the spitfires he had history to counsel him; the enchantresses had to be conjured up out of his own imagination. It was only in times of disorder that women could push their way to the front, and then only if they were as good fighters as the men. Power struggles distort their natures equally with men's. They give way far more readily to hatred than to love, and pour it out in floods of angry words. Queen Margaret boxes Duchess Elinor's ear, pretending to mistake her for a servant; the duchess threatens to scratch the queen's face (*2H.VI* I.iii.73 ff., 136 ff.). King John's mother and her daughter-in-law Constance abuse each other like a pair of fishwives, each casting doubt on the other's morals, and the Bastard and Austria join in, until King Philip interrupts with 'Women and fools, break off' (II.i.122 ff.). We can fairly guess that Shakespeare enjoys letting some of his great ones behave in so undignified a style, and knows that some of his spectators will enjoy it. The briefly seen French princess Bona, heedlessly jilted by Edward IV, is as furiously avid for revenge as Margaret could be (*3H.VI* III.iii.212–13).

Shakespeare's fighting-women belong to the earlier Histories, the times of chronic civil war. So too do the active partnerships between women and men, which have very few counterparts in Shakespeare from then on: Joan's with the Dauphin, Margaret's with Suffolk, who is also her lover, and then with Warwick; Queen Elinor's with her son John. Duchess Elinor wants to forge an alliance with her husband, Humphrey; she is a forerunner of Lady Macbeth, 'a woman of invincible spirit', ready to climb to power on 'headless necks' (*2H.VI* I.iii.6–7, ii.65). With no backing from the duke, all she can do is to turn to infernal arts; and her spirit-raiser, the priest Hum, is taking money from her enemies to betray her. She has forgotten that her world is one of greed and faithlessness. Like its male denizens when they come to grief, she bears her disgrace with dignity rather than remorse.

Margaret, much younger at the outset, has a much longer career. Shakespeare takes care to give her convincing motives. She is set going by her liaison with Suffolk and her resentment at being looked down on as the dowerless daughter of a beggarly French princeling (*2H.VI* I.iii.75 ff.). Unexpectedly become a queen, she is a beggar on horseback, overbearing and bent on holding sway. She is able and resourceful, but her intrigues fatally weaken the Lancastrian dynasty. She is in her way a devoted mother, who would have let the soldiers toss her on their pikes rather than surrender her son's right to the succession, as Henry has done (*3H.VI* I.i.244); but this makes her all the more ferocious. In such ruthless times men might like to think of women as their own opposites, as York does before his death when he protests that women ought to be all that Margaret, that 'she-wolf of France', is not – 'soft, mild, pitiful and flexible' (*3H.VI* I.iv.111, 141).

It would seem that while Shakespeare found humour, even clowning, compatible with the dignity of history, he felt otherwise about love, and reserved it for his Comedies. It is an unflattering comment on the *belle passion* that practically the only woman to fall in love is the adulteress (one of extremely few in Shakespeare) and murderess, Margaret. Suffolk – a married man, though we hear nothing of his wife – inveigles Henry into a politically disastrous marriage with her, so that she will be in England and available to him too. He argues adroitly that even a royal marriage should rest on free choice, not on dowry-haggling fit only for 'worthless peasants':

> For what is wedlock forcèd but a hell,
> An age of discord and continual strife?
> (*1H.VI* V.v.62–3)

– a progressive sentiment that Shakespeare was to repeat in many worthier contexts. Before long Margaret is angrily contrasting her manly admirer Suffolk with her feebly religious husband, fit only for the Church (*2H.VI* I.iii.40 ff.). Passionate feeling between her and her lover is fully revealed only at the moment of his banishment and their leave-taking, a dialogue rising at times to true poetry.

The obsessive Elizabethan thought of female misconduct and bastardy is not long in showing itself in these plays, where the feudal ambience gave it a special pungency. Legitimate transmission of estates, rank, power from father to son would be jeopardized if women were allowed to range at will. A king's consort guilty of tainting the royal blood risked being sent to the stake. In the prevailing atmosphere of male mistrust Elizabeth's ostentatious role of Virgin Queen took on an added lustre. Suffolk, himself a queen's seducer, in his heated altercation with Warwick insults him by declaring that his mother must have been in bed with some 'untutored churl' (*2H.VI* III.ii.210 ff.). In lighter vein Falstaff, impersonating Henry IV in the act of reprimanding his son, grumbles: 'That thou are my son, I have partly thy mother's word ...' (*1H.IV* II.iv.442–3). Henry V at Harfleur calls on his men to give warrant of their mothers' virtue by displaying courage equal to their fathers'. All this lends further meaning to the task Shakespeare set himself in other plays: of restoring marriage, on modern foundations – an endeavour that brought him close to the more enlightened Puritans. In *King John* he allows one great exception to his principle of marital fidelity (he may, for all we know, have made other exceptions in his own favour): the Bastard does not hesitate to accuse his mother of having been a royal mistress, and she has few qualms about confessing it (I.i). He is the play's hero, whereas the Bastard of Orleans in *Henry VI Part 1* is a decidedly more unpleasant Frenchman than the Dauphin.

It can at least be said for the brawling barons that they were too busy with their feuds to have much time for amorous dalliance, and Shakespeare was not inclined to drag Cupid in by the hair, in Hollywood style. Edward IV's philandering draws unfavourable comment; and after his death, when his brother Richard sends Buckingham to harangue the citizens and throw discredit on him, and his young sons with him, a predatory and 'bestial appetite' for women of all sorts is one of the accusations he proposes (*R.III* III.v.79 ff.). Women's light-minded readiness to yield is pilloried in Act I Scene ii, the scene of Richard's *tour de force* in persuading Anne to marry him, by dint of flattery laid on with the trowel, over the bier of her first husband, Henry VI's son Edward, whom Richard has killed. To compose such a dialogue Shakespeare must have had moods of misogyny, which he could work off in dramatic form.

All this deepens the impression of a moribund society whose blight has spread to its inmost point, the family. Men are growing wickeder, women weaker, morally as well as practically. Edward's wife Elizabeth, a matron of modest rank with grown-up sons when he met her, was virtuous enough to refuse to be his mistress; but the marriage was foolish as well as freakish. *Richard III* is loud with the outcries of aggrieved women who are always denouncing their enemies with little, if any, sign of regret for their own misdeeds, or of feeling for what their rival factions have cost the country. In this blindness we may see evidence of the inability of the old order to turn over a new leaf, grow self-critical, reform itself from within. A new dynasty is required, a New Monarchy, to open the way for radical changes in the national life – including the Reformation.

From the point of view of women's more active sphere *King John*, that outer planet among the Histories, comes before *Richard III* and their reduction to nullity, though it may point to this as imminent. Blanch, a youthful princess who is made a political shuttlecock, is an unlucky waif amid the clash of arms. Shakespeare bestows on her 'beauty, education, blood' (*KJ* II.i.493), a triad of the qualities his heroines require. As regards marriage, she defers very demurely to her guardian's fiat. There is no room in the Histories, where young ladies are part of the politicians' stock in trade, for the emancipated outlook of the Comedy heroines. But there are touches of pathos, and a feeling of the curse of war, when she laments the renewal of bloodshed on her wedding day, and her painfully divided loyalties (III.i.300 ff.).

The two women of action here, John's mother and his sister-in-law Constance, are both involved in business of the same kind as Margaret, but less independently, with more need of men to do their work. Hence they are less active in crime, but their aims are not of a sort to appeal much to us – or to Shakespeare, judging by the quality of what he gives them to say. In the Histories men want the throne, and revenge for their fathers; women want to get or keep the throne for their sons, and their maternal attachment has bitter fruits for others. Elinor's spirited 'I am a soldier' is promising (I.i.150), but it is only in the first Act that she is given her head, and after the third she disappears and dies. She has some pricks of conscience about John's usurpation; whether they become sharper and, like Lady Macbeth's guilt, bring on her decline and death, is left to our guesswork. John feels unmanned by the loss of her, but her influence has been no more wholesome than Volumnia's over Coriolanus; she is 'An Até stirring him to blood and strife' (II.i.63).

Constance dies at the same time, 'in a frenzy' (IV.ii.122); again, we learn of this only as news from afar. Her death can more obviously be ascribed to the frustration of her hopes. Her 'War! War! No peace!' (III.i.113) sounds too bloodthirsty, and her abuse of Austria for deserting her cause comes close to Billingsgate. In later years Shakespeare learned more about aristocratic manners, and his ladies in distress learn more self-control. But in the later Histories women of the ruling class have lost all political ambition and influence, and gained very little in exchange. Their world is changing; they have only a marginal member-ship of it. Women are more visible and audible now lower down in society, in Eastcheap, although with no gain in respectability such as ordinary men win in the army of Henry V.

Richard II's queen is a devoted wife, who has done nothing to check his follies and, at the first sign of trouble, shares his facile slide into despair. Henry IV has no consort living, Hal no mother. Lady Percy is the only woman of rank who stands out now. Her partnership with Hotspur is a patchy one. As with a good many other characters, Shakespeare seems to have begun without a clear plan for her, and to have been content to let her grow under his hand. She starts with a long speech in 'heroic' vein – an appeal to her husband, very like Portia's to Brutus, to admit her into his confidence. Hotspur, very unlike Brutus, brings things down to a jocular level, with disparaging talk about a woman's lack of wisdom and inability to keep secrets. This reduces her at once to mere pettish complaint; she is in no awe of him and calls him, with some warrant, a 'mad-headed ape' (*1H.IV* II.iii.109 ff.). He can relax in her company, and crack jokes with a rather barrack-room flavour, but he quits her without a word. We hear nothing more of her until after his death, when she recaptures the heroic vision and pays a long, eloquent tribute to his memory. It includes a personal trait that Shakespeare would not have noticed earlier: his way of 'speaking thick', which admirers imitated (*2H.IV* II.iii.24).

Romantic love comes back, but it is kept to an ironical minimum. Mortimer and his wife are deeply in love, but he knows no Welsh and she no English; we are being shown how to be happy though married. Henry V's bride has learned little English; as she is virtually the captive of his bow and spear, and he knows her answer in advance, his blunt mode of laying siege serves well enough. Her mother supplies whatever else is needed with a pious adage about 'God, the best maker of all marriages' (*H.V* V.ii.356). This one has been arranged by the god Mars.

Our first information about Henry as Prince Hal is that he is going to carry a prostitute's glove as a favour in a tournament at Oxford (*R.II* V.iii.16 ff.). (We hear at the same time that he has not been seen by his father for three months; and as this is just after Richard's deposition, it may be that Shakespeare was looking ahead and providing his future hero with an alibi, proof that he had no hand in the business of usurpation.) But this unsavoury kind of prank is not repeated. Shakespeare may laugh at masculine Honour; he is never frivolous about the 'honour' of women. We never have reason to suspect Falstaff of making use of women to lead the prince astray. With Falstaff himself they do not seem to have been the worst part of his life, and we can take it as humorous exaggeration when Hal talks of him as a wencher, or of finding 'memorandums of bawdy-houses' filling his pocket (*1H.IV* I.ii.7 ff.; III.iii.158). In his own mock-defence of his character Falstaff denies being a 'whoremaster', which Hal has not accused him of (II.iv.459–61).

At any rate now, in old age, all that he wants from women is money. There is a rich tailor's wife whom he thinks of as a source of supply, and he has been promising marriage every week for years to an old Mistress Ursula (*2H.IV* I.ii.43 ff., 236–8). He has been cajoling Mistress Quickly in the same way, and she is indignant at being made 'an ass and a beast', while he has piled up a debt of a hundred marks (II.i.29 ff.). She is determined to have him arrested; the way he talks her round has a ludicrous resemblance to Crookback talking Anne round. Women's retaliation is to come with the *Merry Wives*, towards which much in *Henry IV Part 2* points the way. When Sir John and Doll Tearsheet are together Shakespeare keeps the scene free from either grossness or sentimentality. They are both old, and old associates, and there is some rough goodwill between them (*2H.IV* II.iii). Shallow, that other old acquaintance for whom Falstaff feels only contempt, is much fonder of recalling the *bona robas* of their frolicsome days when – Falstaff remembers – he was as 'lecherous as a monkey'. But all this belongs to a fading past, and Jane Nightwork too has grown 'old, old' (III.ii). One witness gives us a darker moment of Falstaff on his deathbed babbling of women, as well as of green fields, and calling them 'devils incarnate' (*H.V* II.iii.30).

Past and Present

Every genuine poet is a teacher, Shakespeare in the highest degree; the Histories may be called his 'Mirror for Magistrates' and, still more, for the public. There could be little to learn from the past if the past had not much in common with the present; England's social structure had altered in two centuries much less in reality than in appearance. He was giving his audience a mixture of the far-off and exotic, an extinct species of feudal barons in dinosaur armour, with the here and now. Many scenes of the plays are laid in London; a London audience was watching events in its own city, with the grim Tower, its fortress, close by the theatre.

Countless topical allusions have been unearthed, or guessed at, in Shakespeare's plays, and sometimes – if not very often – they have real significance. This may be so especially in the field of foreign affairs, where the writer might feel more free to point to parallels. It would be cheering for English folk to be told that the French are 'a fickle and wavering nation' (*1H.VI* IV.i.148), and some will have recalled these words in 1593 when England's ally, Henry of Navarre, much to Elizabeth's disgust, turned Catholic, on the plea that 'Paris is worth a Mass'. (It would be equally cheering for higher-class spectators to be assured that the discontented poor were a fickle and wavering class.) Anti-French speeches in *Henry V* might easily translate themselves in listeners' minds into anti-Spanish invective, as they have in this century into anti-German. In 1584 William of Orange, the father of Dutch freedom, was assassinated, on Spanish instigation; Shakespeare's King John is poisoned by a monk; Catholic plots to kill Elizabeth lent reality to Henry V's warning: 'Treason and murder ever kept together' (II.ii.106).

Charlie Chaplin, as a son of the people, used to disclaim any taste for Shakespeare, on the ground that he was concerned only with crowns and coronets, instead of with ordinary men and women (275). Walt Whitman the great democrat began with a similar mistrust, but came round to finding Shakespeare's 'distinctiveness and glory' more in the Histories than in any of his other works (34, 57, 109–12); their panorama of feudalism, with its 'towering spirit of ruthless and gigantic caste', arrogance, cruelty, was designed, he believed, to sap what remained of its fabric in men's minds. Certainly the Wars of the Roses are shown not as a magnanimous contest whose protagonists we can admire, but as what one of them calls 'base and envious discord' (*1H.VI* III.i.194). We see great men brawling, plotting mischief, hurling abuse at one another, hiring assassins. Most of them come to a deservedly bad end. It needs no great stretch of fancy to imagine a good part of the audience rejoicing at the spectacle of a ruling class tearing itself to pieces, its ringleaders falling in battle or being marched off to the block. Richard III's mocking spirit, contempt for any rules of conduct, and boundless egotism are not an aberration from the feudal type, but its naked self stripped of pretensions. Whatever Shakespeare may have thought about the 'mob', it can be said for him that he was giving commoners a liberal education with his unsparing criticism of both high and low: above all, by letting Demos hear what his masters really thought about him.

Henry IV is not so much a continuing drama as a study of politics and society; it shows both in a parlous condition, and with no regenerative principle coming to light. The old world is left to serve as butt for Falstaff's wit; like him it has misspent its days, and is feeling intimations of mortality. To enable men of position to go on living their more or less worthless life there has to be a league among them at the expense of their inferiors, who are sent into the world to be made use of by them, like animals. Falstaff also makes use of Shallow, or his purse; in return Shallow hopes that Falstaff will be useful to him, as 'a friend i' the court' (*2H.IV* V.i). It may be a question whether the men in power when this play came out would be pleased to see a JP's little weaknesses exhibited, or would have preferred them hushed up. This, in any case, is not an England for the poor and friendless to be happy in. Falstaff and Shallow are both callously indifferent to the wretched conscripts' feelings. 'Mouldy, it is time you were spent', Falstaff answers brutally when the poor man protests that his 'old dame' will be left helpless. 'Spent!' he echoes pathetically; the Justice shuts him up (*2H.IV* III.ii.15 ff.). When the beggar who has pretended a miraculous cure from blindness is arrested, his wife urges that 'we did it for pure need'; Duke Humphrey's reply, very much in the spirit of Tudor social legislation, is to order them to be whipped through the country back to their place of origin (*2H.VI* II.i). On occasion the poor can think of revenge, as the grandees always do. The wicked Earl of Suffolk's declaration of his disdain for all plebeians is promptly followed by the Cade rebels' declaration of war against all patricians (*2H.VI* IV.i; IV.ii).

Shakespeare was very conscious of an accelerating social mobility all around him: many families rising in the scale, many sinking. Suffolk's captors may be taken as specimens of a large impoverished section of the gentry class and its dependants. Individuals of this sort could be more useful for melodramatic purposes than poor men from lower down. Tyrrel is recommended to Crookback, for his worst purposes, as 'a discontented gentleman/Whose humble means match not his haughty spirit' (*R.III* IV.ii). In more jocular terms Falstaff carps at 'these coster-monger times' when youth and talent like his are neglected; he wants hanging for theft abolished (*2H.IV* I.ii.166 ff.).

It is with the Bastard, his wits sharpened by his ambivalent social position, that awareness of a new state of things breaks in most rudely. He has much satire to bestow on new men and manners, a social life full of pretence, flattery, dissimulation. (As a raw youth from the country he cannot have seen much of it yet: it is Shakespeare who is ventrilo-quizing.) It behoves a man who wants to get on, and not be thought old-fashioned, 'a bastard to the time', to cultivate a haughty air, learn the vices in vogue, and be ready to supply others with what they want – 'Sweet, sweet, sweet poison for the age's tooth' (*KJ* I.i.184 ff.). His great monologue on 'Commodity, the bias of the world', covering both self-interest and material gain, strikes the keynote of his view of contemporary life, even if it is not very germane to the business of the play. Its assumption is that society is naturally well-regulated, like a bowl 'Made to run even upon even ground', but is now being disordered by unbridled greed and pursuit of profit (II.i.574 ff.).

Richard Crookback is another mouthpiece for the jeremiad about upstarts disturbing the fixed gradation of ranks – 'the world is grown so bad ...' (*R.III* I.iii.69 ff.). Margaret follows her antagonist with abuse of the family of Edward IV's wife as climbers, nobodies (I.iii.253 ff.). What is wrong, for all these conservatives, is the blurring of lines of distinction that are needful to a hierarchical society. Their concept of order is not simply one of obedience to political authority, but includes the solidity of the social fabric underlying this. It includes also what mattered most to Shakespeare – the moral order, in the sense of acceptance of rules of conduct appropriate to status, as the code of Honour was to nobility. All this had a good deal in common with the orthodox Hindu horror, enshrined in the *Gita*, of any mixing up of castes, as fatal to the right working of the universe.

Falstaff is incensed at purse-proud tradesmen with their 'high shoes' and 'bunches of keys' (*2H.IV* I.ii.36–8), precursors of the coming masters of England. We catch a fleeting sight of muffled shapes in the back-ground when the thief Gadshill assures his accomplice that they can count on protection from notables, not only 'Trojans' (like Prince Hal) but 'burgomasters and great onyers' (*1H.IV* II.i.74 ff.), the latter probably revenue officials; the idea conjured up is of a shadowy network of corruption and profiteering. Shakespeare had grown more and more critical of the old order, but he was not enamoured of the new one coming on the scene, whose uglier aspects would catch the eye more prominently than its better qualities.

In *The Comedy of Errors* mention of Ireland makes Dromio think of bogs; of Scotland, barrenness (III.i). This may have been about as much as an average Londoner, as well as Syracusan, knew about them; but an Elizabethan politician needed to know a good deal more, and from the Histories a playgoer could learn at least a little more. Though Shakespeare's concern was always primarily with England, as time went on he took increasing account of the other regions of the British Isles. No scenes in these plays are set in Scotland or Ireland; *Richard II* has a short one in Wales, *Henry IV Part 1* a longer one. But during the civil wars forces from these countries make repeated appearances, besides others at times from the Continent. York's scheme of going to Ireland as regent and then using his army to capture power at home (*2H.VI* III.i.341 ff.) sounds remarkably like a forecast of one of the schemes of which Strafford was to be accused in 1641. Shakespeare's account is garbled: in fact York made no move for months after his return, and it was then with a large force from the Welsh borders that he marched on London.

Hotspur's plot brings Douglas and his Scottish levies into England, and a Welsh contingent is expected to join them, though it fails to do so. That England is to be partitioned is a warning of the perils of continuing division within the British Isles. In *Henry IV Part 2* we hear of the king facing a threefold threat from the northern conspirators, the Welsh, and the French; and Northumberland, after seeking shelter in Scotland, eventually rejoins his friends in England with a Scottish force. Early in *Henry V* there are uncomplimentary references to 'the weasel Scot', a 'giddy neighbour' who may molest the North while the army is away in France (I.ii.136 ff.). Shakespeare may be telling his hearers that to have King James on the throne will permanently remove the old peril of a war on two fronts.

The two outstanding Celts in the Histories, Glendower and Fluellen, are both Welsh. Stratford was not very far from the Welsh border, and Shakespeare must have known Welsh folk there. In *Henry IV Part 1* Welshwomen have mutilated the bodies of the slain after a battle (I.i. 43 ff.): Wales, at least in the old days, is made to seem a land of savages, like Ireland in Elizabethan propaganda. But the Tudors made much of their Welsh descent and mythology, to compensate for deficiencies elsewhere in their pedigree, and Welsh fighting-men helped them to the throne at Bosworth. Shakespeare has to keep thinking of two epochs, past and present, and to remind us that there is now a Wales civilized by English influence and rule. Glendower turns out to be a polished, well-read 'gentleman', proud of his English as well as Welsh culture (III.i.163 ff.).

Henry IV, however, has to make him out an ogre, 'the great magician, damned Glendower' (I.iii.83), and he himself, convinced that he is no ordinary human being, is as proud as Prospero of his magical powers and 'deep experiments' (III.i). Shakespeare's countrymen, themselves super-stitious enough, may well have credited Welshmen with uncanny gifts, such as men of the hills have often been thought to possess. Glendower's wonderful arts seem to have no practical utility: we see them at work only when he summons musicians from 'a thousand leagues' away to perform for his guests. The three Englishmen show no sign of being either impressed or incredulous, or surprised at his having no players nearer at hand; but Hotspur is tactlessly sceptical about Glendower's talk of the portents that heralded his birth. Hotspur's chase after Honour is fantastical enough, but in matters like this he is an embodiment of sturdy English common sense – a legend then in its first stages, to which the poet was contributing.

Here and often elsewhere Shakespeare may be leaving those who want to believe in magic free to do so, and the more rational to join him in scoffing. He may be hinting at the bad practical effects superstition can have when he twice shows it interfering with army operations. Earlier on, when he was still only Bolingbroke, Henry was expecting to have to fight Glendower, and Richard's party was counting on Welsh support; but the Welsh forces that collected were scared by ominous signs, like withered trees and shooting stars (R.II II.iv; III.i). We can sympathize with Hotspur's attitude to mumbo-jumbo when we learn that Glendower has failed to keep the rendezvous at Shrewsbury because 'o'er-ruled by prophecies' (IV.iv.16–18). This does not come from Holinshed, and looks like an invention of Shakespeare.

Ireland had been thought of for centuries as a place whose inhabitants – or those 'beyond the pale' or boundary of the English settlement – were hopeless barbarians. Spenser served there for some years, and was one of those who argued that extermination was the only treatment for them (Coughlin). 'We must supplant those rough rug-headed kerns', Richard II declares when preparing for his expedition: Ireland has no snakes; human beings are its 'venom' (II.i.156 ff.). But Shakespeare hints at something better, incorporation of Ireland as a partner in a coming union of the British Isles. His quartet of officers in Henry V's army includes a Captain Macmorris, a sapper. What kind of Irishman he is is left unspecified; he may be of mixed stock, like his name, or belong to one of the other three main sorts of Shakepeare's day – native Celtic, Catholic 'old English', and more recent Protestant settlers. Macmorris is sensitive on the subject, and takes offence at an innocent remark from Fluellen about his 'nation'. 'What ish my nation? Who talks of my nation?' (III.ii.119–21). Nationality was becoming a ticklish question over much of Europe, and for Irishmen more so than most.

Shakespeare's relapse in *Henry V* into raucous jingoism has been a stumbling-block to many since Hazlitt, but it was the only way open to him of broadening the horizon from English to 'British'. Having in *Henry IV* seen the British Isles in turmoil, in *Henry V* we are suddenly given an opposite picture of all these lands – of spokesmen from each, at least, as forerunners – drawn together under English leadership in a common purpose. The effect is patchy: Shakespeare was having to overcome hastily a yawning gap between real and ideal, just as he was when trying to make nobility and soldiery in his army feel like brothers. Macmorris and Captain Jamy the Scot appear only during the siege of Harfleur; he may have found them and their dialects harder to handle than his Welshman. Nevertheless, the play can in some ways be seen pointing along the highroad of later British history.

Gower, the English officer, reproves Pistol for jeering at a Welshman (*H.V* V.i) – a habit, no doubt, of many of Shakespeare's Londoners. Fluellen, like Glendower, is a blend – though a more endearing one – of the admirable and the laughable, and helps to give the play the light relief it badly needs. As Henry knows, Fluellen is brave, and when roused 'hot as gunpowder' (IV.vii.176–7) – traits belonging, very probably, to a Welsh stereotype. So, perhaps, with the frugality and simplicity of his offering Williams a shilling, to mend his worn boots: ''tis a good silling, I warrant you' (IV.vii.70 ff.). He is a gentleman, but puts on no airs. When he brags of Welshmen having served in older wars in France, Henry responds, with his ready affability, 'I am Welsh, you know, good countryman' (IV.vii.96 ff.). He has, at any rate, been Prince of Wales. One of the four men of note in his army who lose their lives at Agincourt is a Welshman, Sir Davy Gam.

The lesson of all this is that the peoples of the British Isles ought to form an 'incorporate league', as England and France at the end of the play are to do, but with more permanence. It does not seem to have struck the poet or anyone else that the Celtic languages would be an obstacle to union. So far as Ireland was concerned, the Ulster rebellion was already falsifying the play's amiable hopes. It was crushed in 1601, in spite of a Spanish force coming to its aid; the outcome was a brutal colonial occupation destined to last for three centuries.

Shakespeare's Henry V declares that he has been looking to France as his true kingdom, with England merely his temporary camp (I.ii.272 ff.). At Edinburgh James VI was pining for London as the capital where he would reign in splendour, instead of in the squalid penury of his own city. His desire was to be sovereign of a united Britain, like his legendary predecessors Brutus of Troy and King Arthur (Thomas 495–6). In this aspiration he was to fail. Many less foreseeable things lay concealed in a future close at hand. The revolution against his son was to break out first in Scotland. In the ensuing Civil Wars, all the Celtic regions were to be on the royalist side: evidence that the monarchy belonged, like the Celts as they were then, to the past.

History itself was soon becoming a battleground. Thanks in good measure to Shakespeare, the Wars of the Roses were far from having been forgotten, and the thought of a new outbreak on similar lines could still beset people's minds. When hostilities broke out in 1642 'the political nation had been, for over a decade, obsessed with medieval precedent and its gothic past', writes Adamson (93): his study suggests that many echoes of conflicts long gone by can be heard in this later contest. Englishmen were, as often happens, walking into the future backwards. A good deal of the old England still survived, and the schism of the 1640s divided the nobility, and to a very considerable extent the gentry, as the red and white roses had done. At bottom the differences were far greater. In the English camp before Agincourt, Bates and Williams derided Henry's invitation to find fault with the king if he deserted them: 'you may as well go about to turn the sun to ice with fanning his face with a peacock's feather'. Half a century later their grandsons, soldiers of Cromwell's New Model Army, were ready not to fan the king's face but to cut off his head with the crown on it.

PART III

Experiments

1

Tragedies

Sandwiched between the two series of plays of the 1590s, those where lordship and honour are on trial and those where love and loyalty are under scrutiny, we are faced with an assortment of compositions little connected with one another, and varying very much in interest. They may all be called experiments, some of them not to be taken up again later. They are decidedly 'serious', rather than light-hearted, and from this point of view have more affinity with the Histories than with the comedies – except for *The Merchant of Venice*, not very distant from them in date. Two are tragedies, the two long poems are both tragical, many of the short ones are in a sombre key. So far as this can be taken as testimony to habitual moods of their creator, at least in the middle years of the decade, to which they mostly belong, these moods would seem to have been far from sanguine.

Shakespeare came to the theatre soon after Tragedy had won an established place there. His own involvement in it was cautious. He had two early tries, but in general was content in the 1590s with the tragic themes supplied by his Histories. Even in his maturity, his tragic subjects were to be largely historical, and thus firmly linked with the world's affairs as well as those of individuals.

Titus Andronicus (1594?)

This first attempt is anomalous in having only a pseudo-historical location, although it can be called 'intensely academic' (Frye, *Fools* 47), with a heavy debt to Seneca for emotionalism of a peculiar, not very 'Shakespearian' kind. It was published in 1594 as a 'Most Lamentable Romaine Tragedie'; it is indeed lamentable enough in many ways, sensational beyond its two models – Kyd's *Spanish Tragedy* and Marlowe's *Jew of Malta*. Yet there has been of late more willingness than formerly to think it – or most of it – genuine early Shakespeare, in spite of its wild and whirling story and grotesque horrors: a change of opinion which must owe something to our own prodigiously grown appetite for the sensational. An attempt has been made to extend Shakespearian author-ship to the play *Edmund Ironside*, on the strength of parallels between the two (Sams 34–7, etc.). These are indeed striking; but such a species of melodrama could quickly gather, like our crime film, a common stock of devices and phrases, available to all. 'Nothing could be too bloody and horrible for an Elizabethan audience' (Wright and LaMar). *Titus Andron-icus* was extremely popular both on the stage and with readers, for whom it was often republished. They listened to fire-and-brimstone sermons, and by pulpit and pamphlet were plied with gruesome warnings about Satan's agents, the witches in their midst.

Shakespeare was not an eighteenth-century rationalist, but he may fairly be supposed to have taken this nonsense with a pinch of salt. He was helped by not being conventionally religious; he was, moreover, a great humorist, and fond of burlesque. Some critics have been unable to resist the temptation to see him laughing in his sleeve during some of the scenes. One such is Act II Scene iv, where Titus's brother Marcus, finding his mutilated niece Lavinia in the woods, instead of attending to her delivers an interminable tirade. Still, the versification – there is very little prose – is not in general bad, and a good many graphic touches catch the ear. In the opening scene Titus's words of farewell to his fallen sons, left now to the peace of 'silence and eternal sleep', recall the 'eternal night' of the Histories. Tamora's praise of countryside charms (II.iii) is quite poetical.

There are no breathing characters, only passions personified, though one or two, if not fully human, may be called humanoid. The plot is all revenge and reprisal. Aaron the Moor is clearly modelled on Marlowe's diabolical Barabbas the Jew, but as Dover Wilson says has far more vitality: his engagingly robust enjoyment of his crimes gives him a kinship with Richard III (edn *Tit.A.* lxii–iv). He is certainly the play's 'most entertaining and most individual character (Brower 28). Like the rest of Shakespeare's brood of villains, he loves to advertise his villainy. As paramour of Tamora, captured queen of the Goths and soon consort of the new emperor Saturninus, he has done remarkably well for himself, and his hopes soar still higher. It is not clear, therefore, why he is soon declaring to Tamora: 'Blood and revenge are hammering in my head' (II.iii.39). But melodrama has no place for contented villains.

Tamora's enemies are censorious about her taking a lover of so swart a hue – 'Spotted, detested' – or, as Lavinia says, 'raven-coloured' (II.iii. 72 ff.). In his study of Shakespeare's aliens and outsiders, Fiedler attributes to him ambivalent feelings about race and colour, and associates Aaron with the more hostile of these (140). He may well be right; yet Aaron, so far from appearing soured by consciousness of his colour, as Crookback is by his deformity, can seem quite proud of it (IV.ii.111 ff.). Like Ruddigore he makes a point of committing a crime daily. His pranks are much like those that witches and wizards were accused of, and the Devil often revealed himself in the shape of a black man. One of Aaron's diversions is setting fire to barns and haystacks at night (V.i.139). His sole redeeming touch is his bold defence of his bastard infant by Tamora, which she wants destroyed for fear that its dusky skin will betray her (IV.ii). Shakespeare gives us few pictures of parental fondness like this. Sentenced to a cruel death, Aaron, like Iago, goes to his doom unflinching.

Tamora is intelligent, self-reliant, witty, entitled to plume herself on her talent for fascinating others (IV.iv.95 ff.). She is inhumanly cruel and treacherous; nearest to her in the Histories is Margaret. Titus is a stage Roman, of interest as a highly coloured picture of how Englishmen conceived heroic Romans, with their ramrod spines. At the outset this inflexible patriot and patriarch has only four sons left, having lost the other twenty-one in the service of his country; he now takes offence at one of the survivors, and kills him. Shakespeare may have felt that a certain respect was due to such monolithic figures, carved out of granite, so much the opposite of his doubters and hesitaters. Yet at the end Titus is calling in an army of Goths to punish the persecutors of his family, like that later militarist Coriolanus calling in the Volscians to punish Rome for his banishment. Nationalism has always abounded in such contradictions.

As to the Roman citizenry, Shakespeare, on his first encounter with them, can hardly be said to flatter. In the disputed succession they give a perfunctory approval to the winning candidate, Saturninus. He, however, does not regard 'the giddy men of Rome' (IV.iv.93) as negligible, and does not trust them: he keeps his ear to the ground by going about incognito, and it is his awareness of public disgust that makes him despair of resisting the Goths. But it seems that Rome's liberation can be expected only from foreign intervention. Titus has learned from the way he and his family are treated that the city is no more than a 'wilderness of tigers' (III.i.54).

Shakespearian plays often contain a network of associated thoughts or features, and *Titus* is no exception. A taste for long stretches of 'railing', or abuse and complaint, so intrusive in the early Histories, shows here too. Titus promising to read to Lavinia 'sad stories' of old days (III.ii.87–8) has been noticed as resembling the 'sad stories' Richard II asks for. There is a hint of a future tragic vision of life when Marcus tries to soothe his tormented brother, though forced to confess that the spectacle of life on this earth is enough 'To stir a mutiny in the mildest thoughts …' (IV.i.90–92).

Romeo and Juliet (1594–96)

Romeo and Juliet marks an immense advance, though it still shows many signs of its author's nonage. Rhymed couplets are frequent; they may suit a speech like the Friar's opening one, of sententious moralizing, in Act II Scene iii well enough. Mediocre writing is not hard to find, with fine lines or touches breaking in. Still awkward, as in the earlier Histories, with women in emotional states, Shakespeare was too ready to fall back on the word-play that the drama opens with and too often returns to. Juliet quibbles over words when she is supposed to be desperately afraid that her Romeo is dead (III.ii), and passes from this to a piece of artificial rhetoric.

Their story, from Italian sources, was well known and popular before Shakespeare touched it. It had a strongly dramatic shape to recommend it to him. He turned it into a plot that is not always convincing in detail, though a defect of this kind cannot have disturbed him unduly. Romeo's first thought after the marriage ought to have been to remove his bride from her father's house, as Othello did Desdemona, and from Verona. She was ready to follow him 'throughout the world' (II.ii.148), and he is well furnished with money when we see him later at Mantua. Altogether, the practical side of this romance is managed as fatally as the darkest stars could have wished. There is, besides, a lingering of the fondness for horrors that Shakespeare, at this time of his life, may have shared with his audience. Of course the feud demands sacrifices, but the vault of the Capulets is left crammed with corpses. Shakespeare could see the ridiculous side of such a piling up: it is impossible to miss its likeness to the guileless drama enacted by Bottom and his friends. 'Eyes, look your last!' exclaims Romeo, over Juliet's supposedly dead body (V.iii.112). 'Eyes, do you see?' Pyramus, or Bottom, exclaims over that of his Thisbe. Whether or not the author was caricaturing himself, he was capable of seeing life in one mood as tragedy, in another as farce.

Whatever frailties there may be in the plot, Shakespeare succeeds in making it a succession of antithetical moods, contrasting revelations of human life. Tragedy is still only a part of this life, not its whole, as it comes to be later on. Light and darkness supply the leading imagery (Spurgeon 310 ff., App. 4). In the opening scene a sunrise, a favourite sight with Shakespeare, is conjured up and contrasted with sombre night and the 'artificial night' of Romeo's room, curtained against the 'worshipped sun'. In the play's first half there is a strong element of light-hearted jollity, youthful high spirits. Of the two opposing themes, hatred and love, the first is guyed at the start by the comic brawling of the servitors; the second by the clowning jocularity of the musicians just after Juliet's 'death' (IV.v.96 ff.) – and by much else. Jest and earnest fit into one pattern, instead of merely alternating to make a 'tragicomedy'.

Youthful aristocratic gaiety and plebeian humour, better drawn than in most of the Comedies, are needed to give us a poignant sense of how enjoyable life might be in Verona if it were not for the feud, the intrusion of evil from some alien realm, or from a dead past. All tragedy teaches this in a way, but few tragedies bring the lesson so close as this one does. Mercutio, that magnetic invention of Shakespeare's own, makes fun of love, and laughs at the absurdities of duelling too, until he is killed fighting a duel himself. His death marks a focal point in the drama, after which its colour changes abruptly.

Tragedy involves collision between man and fate, as well as between men: 'fate' being our symbol for the complexity of factors, human or other, which so often seem leagued to thwart us. For Elizabethans, as all over their Europe, fate exercised its will through the stars, and this was no mere metaphor. This play's Prologue announces 'star-crossed lovers', and Romeo's last speech is about the 'inauspicious stars' whose yoke he is about to shake off. Gloomy dreams and presentiments multiply the fate-laden shadows. A doubt falls across Romeo's mind as he prepares to enter the hall of the Capulets (I.iv.106 ff.). Juliet, taking leave of him after their wedding night, has 'an ill-divining soul', and seems to see him a corpse (III.v.54).

Man is caught in a web of causes that to him (if not to religious clairvoyance) appear irrational. They must seem all the more so in a society riddled with inexplicable change, compared with the relatively static setting of the French classical theatre. It is only when two epochs, rival values, are in conflict that tragedy like Shakespeare's can be born. In sublunary terms, the human sensation of being confronted by a hostile universe means that men or women are singly confronted by an uncongenial community and its laws. In this play individual right asserts itself on two historical planes. An older generation of nobility claims a charter to carry on private warfare, without regard to public order and in defiance of the authority now vested in absolute monarchy. Secondly, a younger generation of the same class, infected (in London, if not in Verona) by the thinking of newer middle classes, claims liberty for each to choose his or her partner in life.

Old and young are both rebels, but the old want to tyrannize over the young, as the State seeks to tyrannize over them. For the young, love also means rejection of a family quarrel, another appendage of the old order. These lovers (unlike their mentor, Friar Lawrence) have no thoughts to spare for the good that their union may do by ending the feud: they are wrapped up in themselves, and pursue their own aim in a fashion liable to inflame family relations still further. Nevertheless, they are, in their own way, rebelling against the past's morbid hold over the present. They belong to an era which is beginning to regard each person as a separate human being, not as one limb of a family tree.

Towards partial assent to such views Shakespeare's England was moving. Juliet's father, old Capulet, is as enlightened in this way as one of his upbringing could be, and likes to think of himself as an excellent parent to his only child. He tells her suitor Paris that he must woo her and win her affections, not simply have her handed over to him. Juliet, for her part, is not at all averse to marriage, and assures her mother that she will do her best to like Paris. He is perfectly eligible, though uninteresting; he has a title, and 'fair demesnes', and other good points (III.v.179 ff.), and he is truly in love with her. Juliet's readiness at first to consider him favourably is the counterpart to Romeo's calf love for Rosalind.

It is only after falling in love with Romeo that Juliet feels she is being kept in bondage by her parents. It may be allowed that her refusal to marry Paris, so soon after her promise of docility (III.v), is brusque and tactless; and there is something of Desdemona's cavalier treatment of her father in the way she suddenly turns her back on kith and kin. Capulet, to be sure, is a hasty, capricious, unreasonable old fellow; he has to disgust us with his harshness, in order to ensure that our sympathies will remain firmly with Juliet.

To keep the love story from dragging, it is put into a very condensed form. Hero and heroine are on the stage together – alive – in only four scenes, and most of these meetings are quite brief. They fall in love in the twinkling of eighteen lines of conversation in a crowded ballroom. Romeo's previous self-pitying sighs are blown away: he is transformed into a new man, ready for action, and the play is lifted on to a new level. Equally, from a girl Juliet turns into a woman, though in fact, as her nurse insists on telling us in prolix detail, she is a little under fourteen years of age (I.iii.17 ff.). Girls of the Tudor aristocracy might sometimes be married very young, for reasons connected with property or family influence; but the average age of marriage in ordinary families was quite high – for women, about twenty-four.

In a home-bred girl ten years younger than this, Juliet's modish manner of speech, high principles, heroic conduct, are of course perfectly unbelievable. Shakespeare could not have been unconscious of this; he had daughters of his own, aged (in 1595) ten and twelve. It would have cost him nothing to give Juliet half a dozen extra years. More easily still, he could have left it to each of us to guess her age. None of his Comedy heroines is a child. But Juliet, like Miranda in *The Tempest* (who, however, has nothing to do, and little to say), is only in part a person; in part she is an emblem of a new era, a new dispensation, and Shakespeare cannot fully blend this second function with a flesh-and-blood personality.

Juliet is an idea, a new spirit of romantic love. When she and Romeo first meet, their words combine to make a sonnet: a stylized kind of wooing, even if sanctioned by the conventions of a masked ball, but it helps to convey the required sense of a youth and maiden hypnotized by the magic of life, becoming its half-conscious train-bearers. This is carried still further by Romeo's face being concealed by a mask; Tybalt detects him only by his voice. Such a love has a ritualized, almost mystic quality, as the pair themselves feel; she talks of his 'divine perfection', and he feels that in her love he will be 'new baptized' (II.ii). It is the only time that Shakespeare invests mortal love with such a sacramental atmosphere, or bestows on it, through his Friar, the special blessing of religion.

Love at first sight – or first hearing, in Juliet's case – spares Shakespeare and us the embarrassment of lovemaking on the stage, which can scarcely ever be convincing, and of which he was always chary. He again saves himself trouble by the device of letting Romeo hear Juliet confess her love in a soliloquy (II.ii). She is only slightly abashed at finding herself overheard. She believes in frankness, not in coy concealment, and thinks open love is more likely to last. This openness soon leads her to make it clear to Romeo (as Miranda does to Ferdinand) that if he wants her he must marry her, even though their union may have to be kept secret from her family. Old-style feudal marriage belongs to the past, but matrimony remains sacred as the bedrock of social behaviour and stability, one of the indispensable continuations between old world and new.

On these terms Juliet is quite ready to welcome her nurse's counsel – 'Go, girl, seek happy nights' (I.iii.107). She deems 'true love acted simple modesty'; and the highly poetical opening of the leave-taking scene (III.v) throws a romantic glow over the wedding night just past. But as Shakespeare was fond of reminding us, there are diverse kinds of love, and different points of view about it. The Capulet servants have their own wenches, and are going to have them in while the ball is in progress. Plebeian paganism has a splendid incarnation in the nurse, who is everything old, earthy, unromantic, though also truly devoted to her Juliet. Like Annabella's nurse in Ford's tragedy 'Tis Pity She's a Whore, she represents a hearty humanity of the masses along with indifference to both abstract morality and high-flown idealism.

At the other extreme is the unreal, affected pose of the gentlemanly amorist. Mercutio's light-hearted banter, with a spicing of indelicacy, has an easy target in Romeo's languid infatuation with Rosalind. His posturing is as silly as the clumsy word-play that he and Benvolio regale each other with, much as the servitors in the opening scene do. It may be that Shakespeare is reminding us, as he does in his early Comedies, that master and man are, after all, not so far apart. (The rank breath of the mob often disgusts him; but it has not escaped Mercutio that a high-born lady's breath may be tainted by too much eating of sweets [I.iv.75–6].)

Mercutio's talk of 'vain fantasy', 'more inconstant than the wind' (I.iv.98 ff.), prepares us for Romeo's instant fall out of one love into another. But the play raises more serious questions about this second one, which we cannot be meant to overlook. At first Juliet has a sensible feeling that they should let their love ripen, not be in too much haste; but the next minute she is pressing for an immediate wedding (II.ii). Romeo's wild talk of suicide when he learns of his banishment sounds to the Friar like that of a hysteric or a madman (III.iii.108 ff.). He has already reflected, with foreboding, that 'Such violent delights have violent ends' (II.vi.9); which in one way is the play's moral. Only the unnatural atmosphere created by the family vendetta could make so desperate a passion seem natural, even inevitable.

We take sides with the rebel lovers against parental obstruction, and with the government against the brawling nobles. Escalus is a ruler with plenary power, unlike some in the Comedies; evidently in Verona such authority is needed, but it is not always effective. Though he is masterful and dignified, Escalus is conscious that he has not been strict enough. To pardon murder is false mercy, he declares after the deaths of Mercutio and Tybalt: from now on he will be 'deaf to pleading and excuses' (III.i.191). Feuds like Verona's were still endemic and troublesome in late-sixteenth-century Scotland, and not unknown in Wales. Some Englishmen would be aware that France was much plagued with duelling, the more individualistic sequel to the family feud, and that Henri IV was reproached with granting pardons too easily.

It is from this point of view that the Prologue summarizes the play's theme. Hatred and love are bound up together, the lovers a necessary sacrifice for the peace to be restored. More conspicuously than anything else could do, the feud advertises the obsolescence that overtakes old customs and values. Whatever hints there may be of a 'tragic flaw' in the love of Romeo and Juliet, the real flaw lies in society and its falsities. We never hear how the quarrel began. No one in either family is bent on keeping it going, except the bully Tybalt. Neither hero nor heroine feels the slightest interest in it. We are watching a case – in Marx's words – of the past weighing like a nightmare on the brains of the living.

In the first minutes of the play the feud is erupting afresh, in the caricature style of servitors brandishing their weapons at one another. We are being shown its absurdity, though also, as Coleridge said, the touching fidelity of these underlings, or what he quaintly calls their *ourishness* (102). For them, as for some retainers in the Histories, their combativeness brings a breath of excitement into their lives, and a feeling that they too are men of spirit – despite some nervous tremors – like their betters, with a part to play in the annals of two great families. All they earn by their loyal zeal is Tybalt's contempt for them as 'heartless hinds', or cowardly nobodies (I.i.64).

Such a scuffle looks all the more futile, though deadly, when old Capulet calls for his sword, and he and Montague struggle to get at each other while their wives hold them back. It adds another impression of an outworn past that Escalus talks of 'Verona's ancient citizens' having to be called out to part the rioters with their 'old' hands and weapons – as if there were no longer any young men in the city, except a few hotheads. Old age haunts the play, as it does the latter part of *Henry IV*, and the generations have no better tie than the moth-eaten feud. Capulet and his cousin have a strong likeness to Justice Shallow and Silence, especially when Capulet looks fatuously back on a time when he too could whisper in ladies' ears, ''Tis gone, 'tis gone, 'tis gone ...' (I.v.17 ff.). The Friar is old, as a priest should be; the nurse frets Juliet, impatiently expecting her with a message, into crying out that old people are like corpses, 'Unwieldy, slow, heavy' (II.v).

It has been noticed that Capulet does not always succeed in appearing the head of an ancient house he is supposed to be (Byrne 189). Shakespeare was not yet as much conversant with aristocratic manners as he came to be. When all the servants are out of the house, Capulet runs off on an errand himself; he jokes with the ladies at his ball about their corns (I.v.17 ff.). He takes credit for long and painful labour to secure a good match for Juliet (III.v.176 ff.); as he is rich and she is lovely, there would seem little need of this, unless he is looking very high. As the Friar says to him, and might have said to many a rich burgher of London, ''twas your heaven she should be advanced'. Paris is a count, or 'earl', as well as a kinsman of the prince; so that among Juliet's merits we must reckon her rejection of a splendid promotion. Her parents make an unamiable pair. We may take them for an illustration of what the old-style marriage system may lead to. Lady Capulet is clearly a good deal the younger – about thirty, if we pin Shakespeare to his dates (IV.iv.11–12); we are free to think of her as blighted by premature union with a much older man. She has no fellow-feeling, all the same, for her daughter, until she thinks Juliet dead; she shows her disposition by coolly telling Juliet that she means to have Romeo, as her nephew Tybalt's slayer, secretly poisoned (III.v.88 ff.).

Tybalt is a bold swordsman, prompt to imperil his not very useful life, but also one of those 'fantasticoes' or 'fashion-mongers' who so annoy Mercutio with their martial airs and jargon (II.iv.28 ff.). These are a parallel to Romeo's early amorous foppery, and Mercutio dislikes both; it is not always the old ways that are bad, or the new good. In the first scene

Benvolio is trying to quieten the servants, but immediately engages Tybalt when he is called a 'coward', an insult only blood can wipe off. Later on, Mercutio draws his sword against Tybalt simply because he is outraged by Romeo's refusal to do so. He dies with 'A plague o' both your houses', twice over (III.i.90, 105). But neither house called on him to fight; he rushed into combat on his own impulse, and his dying reproach should be addressed to the code of honour of his class. This code, or creed, was to haunt European life and literature for another three centuries (Kiernan, *Duel*). Aggression, writers like Walter Scott saw, was wrong, but what should a man do if he was challenged by an aggressor? There could be no way out of this blind alley until history had moved a long way further forward. Here was one of the earthquake tremors that Shakespeare was conscious of in his society, one that neither he nor it would know how to exorcize.

Like the gentleman's honour, romantic love had to be exposed to the touchstone of peril in order to justify its claims. Love and danger must go together, for heroine and hero alike. Romeo has to risk his life for their one night together. His grand claim on us is the self-control and moral courage that enable him to reject Tybalt's challenge, but we are also compelled to admire him when he fights Tybalt after Mercutio has taken up the quarrel for him and lost his life. If he did not do this he would forfeit our respect and his own, and his right to Juliet – though it is, fatefully, her cousin whom he is obliged to kill.

His creator must have intended us to see him as growing, developing by stages, until when he learns of Juliet's supposed death he can be content with nine quiet words – 'Is it e'en so? Then I defy you, stars!' (V.i.24) – in place of his former torrential outpourings. He is resolved at once on suicide, and acts with prompt energy. In the tomb he is as 'savage-wild', 'inexorable', as Hamlet in one of his furious fits; he turns on the meddlesome 'boy' Paris as if he now feels himself to be much the older of the two (V.iii). The tragic hero is whirled along by a fate with which his whole being comes to be bound up; 'fate' meaning all that men are called on by their human, but also social, condition to do and suffer.

Juliet is willing to look up to her husband as her 'lord', but seems to grow and learn self-command more quickly than he does. 'My dismal scene I needs must act alone', she says before drinking the Friar's potion (IV.iii.19); the star-crossed have to undergo their ordeal in solitude. These two prove their love by each choosing death rather than life without the other. Rationally, this is frenzy; we are moved by it because we can be rescued for a while from our torpid earthbound existence by the spectacle of any passion strong enough to engross itself so completely in an object outside itself.

No one in the play has a thought to spare for the ban that all

Churches laid on suicide and in principle, at least, on duelling; the air we breathe is a pagan one. Mercutio's irreverent joke about parsons dreaming of tithes would be taken by the audience as a hit at Anglican worldliness (I.iv.79–81). It comes not long after an allusion to heretics being burned, which would remind hearers of Rome and Spain and their cruelties (I.ii.94). Lawrence is one of those 'friars', of an Order founded by Shakespeare, whose vague designation allows them to live and serve on their own, respected anchorites who have turned their backs on the world – including, apparently, the Church. His 'ancient ears' (II.iii.74) accentuate his air of a straggler from an older time; so too do his words about old age and its sleep-banishing anxieties. He is a learned man, able to talk of both philosophy and botany. He belongs, moreover, to a Shakespearian series of thoughtful men who try to guide and improve human affairs; distantly, at least, he can be compared with the Duke in *Measure for Measure*, and with Prospero. His practical wisdom does not match his good intentions.

His religion is a dim vision of the mysterious, possibly benign Providence that seems to have floated at times through Shakespeare's mind; it served him poetically, if no more. Lawrence's warning about 'the Heavens' and 'their high will' (IV.v.94–5) is very much in the poet's later vein; so is his exhortation to Juliet, over Romeo's dead body, to 'bear this work of heaven with patience' (V.iii.260–61). Her own cry of distress when she is ordered to marry Paris – 'Is there no pity sitting in the clouds' (III.v.196) – is one of many such appeals in Shakespeare to an indistinct protector; they suggest a traditional deity fading into myth. The answer, so far as the events of this play can tell us, is No; human beings must look to themselves alone for salvation.

The place often occupied in Shakespearian drama by war is here taken by the feud; it may occur to us that if one of these is foolish, the other may be so too. Images of gunpowder exploding are reminders of this other (III.iii.132–3; V.i.64–5). Violent deaths are needed to bring the feud to an end, sacrifices to lift a lingering curse. Few are left of the rival families, and we are not much interested in the reconciliation between two doddering seniors. A truer reconciliation has taken place among the dead, when Paris begs with his dying breath to be laid beside Juliet, and Romeo does as he asks, and himself in his last words asks forgiveness of his 'cousin' Tybalt (V.iii.73, 101). But the weight of the play falls not so much on this as on the theme of crime and punishment. Men who kill others, to honour their family scutcheons, are criminals. 'See what a scourge is laid upon your hate', says the prince to the two old men who have lost their children, reproaching himself again with his inadequate severity (V.iii.292, 308). It may have occurred to Shakespeare that some day men might learn to renounce wider-reaching hatreds, of nation or religion.

Juliet pictures love as a kind of 'wealth' (II.vi.34), and Romeo's last words are spoken when he is about to meet 'engrossing Death': death is the great monopolist, the all-swallowing maw. Apart from such mercantile images, there is scarcely any shadow of a 'social problem' – of the fact that while Verona has been divided by a family quarrel, it and the world have been more deeply divided by wealth and poverty. In the play's first scene the lovelorn Romeo asks idly 'Where shall we dine?' (I.i.172). He and his associates have never had to ask: How can we get something to eat? He has resolved on suicide when the thought seems to come to him that while gentlemen kill one another, starvation cuts short the lives of the poor.

He pauses in the street at Mantua, recalling in detail an apothecary's shop he has seen there, and its owner, both miserably poverty-stricken. This unexpected speech is not put in, as suggested by some editors, to give the man time to appear at his door, for Romeo calls him only at the end of it, and he appears at once. Its dramatic purpose – to tell us why he will be willing to break the law by selling poison – could be achieved in a very few words. Romeo goes on to urge that his poverty and hunger, 'need and oppression', justify him in breaking any law. Receiving the poison, he comments that the gold he is giving in return is a far worse and more destructive one (V.i). Earlier he has talked casually of 'saint-seducing gold' (I.i.213): now he sounds like Timon. His own misfortunes, it seems, have brought him to feel and pity those of others. There is no reason why a Mantuan druggist should be reduced to such an extremity; in Romeo's mind the starveling he is buying peace from must stand for all suffering humanity.

2

Poems

Venus and Adonis (1593)

Closure of the theatres during part of 1592–3, because of the plague, is enough to account for Shakespeare's turning to another field, and composing his only two long poems. *Venus and Adonis* was published in the spring of 1593, and the next year *Lucrece*, a title later turned by a shrewd publisher into *The Rape of Lucrece*. Shakespeare had caught the eye of a youthful nobleman, the Earl of Southampton, intelligent enough to appreciate good writers and rich enough to scatter largesse among them. In 1593 he was nineteen. Both poems were dedicated to him, the second in noticeably more familiar terms.

Their author's choice of subjects must have been influenced by the taste of such connoisseurs in Renaissance Europe. From the Induction to *The Taming of the Shrew* we gain some idea of a typical collection of paintings. 'Venus rising from the sea' was a favourite theme, and Venus in love with a young man might make an equally attractive poem. It and *Lucrece* both had the merit of being classical stories, and thus displaying Shakespeare as no ignoramus despite his profession and lack of college education. The two form a pair, each concerned with physical desire, first female and then male, as if Shakespeare was preoccupied with the perilous violence of this passion. Venus lavishes blandishments on a handsome but frigid youth; Tarquin makes no attempt to seduce a virtuous married woman, but resorts at once to threats.

Most of *Venus and Adonis* takes place in sunlight, all of it in the open air. One of its best features is the lyrical freshness of its response, for instance in a sudden splendid passage about the dawn (853 ff.). On the other hand, Nature is given a blood-smeared look by masculine ardour for hunting. A long description comes in of a hare trying to escape, and of dogs injured by the boar they have been set on, until the boar, or Nature, takes its revenge by killing and mangling the sportsman, Adonis. Lucrece is compared to 'the poor frighted deer', not knowing which way to flee its pursuers (1149–50). Men are turning into beasts of prey, she

reflects: other animals may be less savage. Venus and Adonis are each
reduced metaphorically to animals, when he is first invited to feed or
graze on her body, and then to play the stallion; his horse sets an example
by bolting in chase of a mare.

Classical myths of amours between deities and mortal beings may be
supposed to have flattered Renaissance man's sense of being only a little
lower than the angels, loudly though theologians might proclaim that he
was very little higher than the devils. But not seldom in the long-drawn-
out wrangle between goddess and obdurate youth, Shakespeare seems
close to the border of absurdity, possibly by intention. It ends on a note
of bathos when Adonis runs away and 'Leaves love upon her back deeply
distress'd' (814). She is left to lament, groaning or singing, until she takes
alarm at the thought of Adonis in danger in the hunt, and at last
discovers his dead body. Shakespeare must surely have smiled as he made
her think of the goring tusks as the boar's kisses, and of how she, if
endowed with such teeth, would have kissed Adonis to death (111 ff.).

Yet there is a strain of something more romantic or ideal in her
infatuation. Early on in the story she descants in higher style on her
voyagings through the air; her declaration that 'Love is a spirit all
compact of fire,/Not gross to sink' (149–50) is prophetic of Cleopatra's 'I
am fire and air'. For dead Adonis's sake she lays a curse on love, which
henceforth is always to bring more grief and folly than joy (1135 ff.); she
means to go into retirement on her island of Paphos, though Shakespeare
can scarcely have meant to convert the goddess of love into a celibate.
She has expressed for him the anti-ascetic bent of the Renaissance, and
repudiated those 'Love-lacking vestals and self-living nuns' (752) who
are pitied in *A Midsummer Night's Dream*.

Still, the Middle Ages could not be simply left behind, and pagan
innocence or freedom from shame recaptured; love and all its regalia
would have to be attained by painful pilgrimage. Something like this was
to form a good part of the thinking of Shakespeare the dramatist. Before
breaking away from his temptress, Adonis launches into a sermon –
which sounds far beyond his years or attainments – about the gulf
between true love and lust; he has listened to warnings about the risks of
indulgence; Venus should not call what she feels love, 'for love to heaven
is fled' (793: he forgets that heaven is where his visitor lives). Venus is
given to still more inappropriate speech-making, as characters in the
plays so often are. Myth and life impinge often and oddly. She wanders
into a complicated commercial metaphor about kisses and rates of
interest. From her picture of the hunted hare she draws a human parallel,
as Jaques in *As You Like It* does from the wounded deer: those in
misfortune are trampled on, not succoured (707–8). When she comes on
Adonis's bleeding hounds, and is frightened by the sight into guessing

that he must have been killed, Venus compares herself to 'the world's poor people', long perturbed by 'apparitions, signs and prodigies', inspiring 'dreadful prophecies' (925 ff.). The poet may well be thinking of the uneasiness with which Englishmen awaited the death of Elizabeth, now only ten years away; but there seems no reason for Venus to be perturbed over it. Her most improbable plea to Adonis is that he ought to breed children to propagate his good looks (163 ff.). In his early sonnets Shakespeare was preaching on the same text to a young man baulking at marriage. This parallel makes it all the more credible that the young man of the sonnets was the patron to whom the poem was dedicated.

Lucrece (1594)

By contrast, the second poem unfolds its story indoors, most of the time shrouded in darkness. It makes for tragedy in a far more meaningful way: death comes not from a boar's tusks but from the wickedness of man. Yet it has not seemed to most readers to mark much of a poetic advance. Saintsbury even judged it inferior to *Venus and Adonis*, except as a 'school exercise' ('Poems' 228). Hawkins commented on how little is made of the political or heroic elements of the tale, with the result that the effect in the main is 'pathetic, not tragic' (158). In a work primarily addressed to courtly readers, Shakespeare may have thought it undesirable to strike too radical a note. Levi takes the poem as a study of 'the breakdown of society' (88), and this is what it might have been: sex can serve as a seismograph, and Lucrece's fate could be a register both of exploitation of the weak by the strong, and of fission within a dominant class. Little of this emerges, however. It has been observed that *Lucrece* is too nearly akin to *Titus Adronicus* in its 'fascinated contemplation' of desire and bloodshed; its conception of tragedy is youthfully crude (Prince xxxvii). In Elizabethan England the idea of rape, like the spectacle of bear-baiting, might pander to sadistic instincts. Marlowe's Tamburlaine had a special relish for wholesale massacres of virgins.

Venus and Adonis employed a simple six-line stanza, popular with Tudor writers of narrative verse. In *Lucrece* the stanza is a weightier one of seven lines, more difficult because one rhyme is repeated three times. As Thomas Gray pointed out in detail in his commentary on Lydgate, Elizabethan poets were already suffering from some of the problems, the shrinking number of available rhymes, brought about by shifts of pronunciation since Chaucer (370–72). Shakespeare was too impatient a writer, too much an *improvisatore*, to be an expert rhymer. We can fancy him thinking of himself when his Lucrece hesitates over how to begin her letter because so many thoughts 'Throng her inventions', like a press

of people at the door each trying to get in first (1301–2). Rhyme was a
hobble, as often in the Sonnets too. 'Evil' and 'devil' partner each other
with tiresome regularity. Syntax is sometimes distorted, meaning
obscured.

Lucrece is considerably longer than its predecessor, and moves so
slowly that in spite of its central episode it cannot be called a dramatic
poem. At every turn the story is clogged with strained conceits. Readers
must have enjoyed these complications as something to exercise their
minds on. Venus was voluble, but Lucrece is far more so, no doubt with
better excuse. Everything her eyes fall on, in her desperate grief, 'too
much talk affords' (1106). Her long plea to Tarquin to spare her is a
declamation with little emotional force, like so many woebegone
speeches in the early Histories. Left alone, she pours out her tormented
feelings in a soliloquy of 273 lines, encrusted with every sort of polished
ornamentation. With 'this cursed crimeful night' (970) she comes close
to the eloquence parodied by Pyramus and Thisbe in *A Midsummer
Night's Dream.*

Lucrece and her husband Collatinus are an ideal couple, though not
an equal one. Women are necessarily weaker. She feels some self-
reproach at not having offered any active resistance to Tarquin. She was
intimidated by his threat to kill her, but we are reminded that he had
also threatened her with disgrace. Women, with their 'waxen' minds (the
term recurs in *Twelfth Night*), ought not to be blamed for failings that are
really the fault of men (1237 ff.). None the less, Lucrece has strength to
face what she deems her duty of suicide. It is a duty because she belongs
to her husband, and her body, his treasured possession, has been
'poisoned' or 'corrupted' by Tarquin's act. Unlike her Christian sister
Juliet, she debates with herself the moral issue of suicide (1153.f.). For her
it raises the question of body and soul, so prominent in Christian
thought and handled here in what may seem a deliberately scholastic
manner. This settled, she can feel once more 'mistress' of her fate. Her
husband and friends try – not very urgently – to dissuade her; the knife
frees her soul from its 'polluted prison', though not before she has
exacted a pledge of vengeance on Tarquin, invoking the knight's duty to
right women's wrongs (1688 ff.). Christian and Roman ideas jostle
together. Collatinus is disappointingly inert, and it is left to Lucrece's
father to take the lead.

Tarquin has nothing romantic about him and feels no more than
animal passion, against which 'reason' is feeble (243). Except in his goal,
he has a marked resemblance to Macbeth – nowhere more so than when
he wrestles beforehand with his conscience, or rather with prudence
(190 ff.). A kind of false pride drives both men on. Tarquin tells himself that
only weaklings are awed by 'a painted cloth', and that his scruples are

really nothing but unworthy fear. 'Thoughts are but dreams', until they are turned into actions. A great deal of Shakespeare is condensed into these conflicting impulses. The crime is soon committed – in darkness, so we are not compelled to watch (as we would be in a modern film rendering) – and quickly followed by a revulsion of feeling, shame and self-disgust. Uncontrollable until gratified, lust is then only 'a bankrout beggar' (703 ff.). Shakespeare's horror of 'lust in action' and what it ends in is the true subject of the poem, as it is of Sonnet 129. Religious associations are insistent. Under such a load of sin the soul is a 'princess' overthrown by 'foul insurrection' (719 ff.).

This is not a political poem, as it could have been, but it has political and social overtones. Its villain is a prince (or king – Shakespeare is hazy) and this, it is reiterated, does not cover up his sin but makes it far more heinous. 'Kings like gods should govern everything' – including, it is implied, themselves – Lucrece protests; their transgressions cannot be concealed (602). As often in Shakespeare's plays, the principle of monarchy is extolled, but its representative is a very unworthy one. From such unworthiness common people have to suffer. Lucrece, like Romeo, is one of Shakespeare's people who are led by their own misfortunes to think about those of others, 'The poor, lame, blind, halt', and those groaning under oppression: 'Justice is feasting while the widow weeps...' (902, 907).

As in *Venus and Adonis*, things of long ago and far away run together with English realities. Imagery distils an atmosphere of a highly commercialized society, such as England was acutely conscious of being because the process was overtaking it so rapidly. As Tarquin hesitates outside Lucrece's chamber the same perils, rocks and storms and pirates, come into his mind as into Antonio's in *The Merchant of Venice* (335–6). Trafficking for wealth seems to lurk close under the surface of the story, as if Shakespeare felt that mankind in his time – he himself along with the rest – was in danger of losing its soul for gain. Rape of a married woman is a trespass against her rightful 'owner' (412–13). Collatine, shocked by his wife's tale of woe, is 'the hopeless merchant of this loss' (1660). She laments her own shattered happiness as a cancelled contract (934–5).

There are trains of thought here that were becoming habitual with Shakespeare. One is his puzzle about how a goodly exterior can hide a vicious disposition (1528 ff.). Most besetting of all is the obsession with Time, more often than not as the enemy of everything mankind can make of its world. Time is 'injurious', a robber and destroyer, as so often in the sonnets Shakespeare was writing; we may guess him to be feeling that he had not made enough of his life so far, that age was going to overtake him unawares. In one extended passage he seems for a while to take a more comforting view: 'Time's glory' is to perform good works, to end old quarrels for instance (925 ff.). Lucrece prays to Time to curse Tarquin (967). But Shakespeare was overwhelmed by it, unable to come to terms with it; he could only throw round it a tumultuous riot of images.

At many points linkages can be noticed between the poem and various of the plays, besides *Macbeth*. Lucrece's words about a prince's duty to be 'the glass, the school, the book' for others to learn from (615–16) are a rougher version of Ophelia's tribute to Hamlet. We are told less about Collatine than about the groom who carries Lucrece's message to him, a humble honest fellow, a 'pattern of the worn-out age' (1345 ff.), of honester times gone by. Richard II's faithful groom, and old Adam in *As You Like It*, were men of the same mould. Life in London might well set Shakespeare brooding on the corrosion of the human family by selfish competition; there was much of the past he wanted to rescue, as well as much he wanted to abolish.

Whether or not he took the legend of British descent from Troy as seriously as many did, the very elaborate and irrelevant description of the painting of the siege of Troy in Lucrece's house would be enough to reveal a keen interest in the subject, in advance of *Troilus and Cressida*. It may remind us, too, of Venus's dire predictions of the future in store for love: among its curses will be an 'unsavoury end', jealousy, and responsibility for wars (1135 ff.). Shakespeare was to write plays exhibiting all three. It is a grey light that the two poems throw on the human condition as he was seeing it.

They were applauded, and frequently reprinted. Nevertheless, their author showed no further interest in literary reputation. He had won success by adapting himself to a very artificial fashion of writing, and can scarcely have felt pleased for long with what he had achieved. Hazlitt may go too far in saying that these poems were 'as glittering, and as cold', as a couple of ice-houses; but he was right in saying that Shakespeare's imagination could find freedom only in drama (*Characters* 263–6). Whatever dramatic qualities the poems have they owe to the clash of unyielding wills, such as always thrilled him when he was composing for the stage. In narrative verse, to be read at leisure, he was too free to luxuriate in language for its own sake. He was redeemed from this temptation – not all at once – by the theatre, whose demands compelled him to get on with his tale, instead of overflowing into the stagnant waters of commentary on it. Intuition must have taught him that only in the theatre could his genius be at home. He was of too independent a mind to sink into reliance on private patronage, more fickle than the many-headed audience. We may suppose that during 1593–4 he was also sketching his next plays, or gathering inspiration for them.

3

Sonnets

In 1609 a collection of 154 sonnets ascribed to Shakespeare was published. In literary merit they range from very high to distinctly low; from every other point of view they are enveloped in more than the usual Shakespearian uncertainties. Shakespeare may have authorized their publication, though Dover Wilson is very probably right in guessing that the editor upset him by including some he would not have wished to appear (*Sonnets* 17–18). Murry (93) and Levi (94) are among those who doubt whether the poet gave any such approval. His and many other men's sonnets must have circulated privately, in handwritten copies. Francis Meres wrote in 1598 about his 'sugar'd sonnets among his private friends'.

A brief vogue of sonneteering, inaugurated by the appearance of Sidney's collection in 1591, was over by 1600. It may be safe to suppose that Shakespeare was taking part from the time when his long poems were written, and went on through the 1590s and even after. The judicious Tucker attributes them to 1592–1601, with a few later additions (xxv; cf. Ellrodt 43–4; Burto 195). Some have a depth of feeling and maturity of language akin to those of the 'problem plays' and tragedies. Shakespeare may well have found, in what began for him as a literary or social exercise, a means of relieving his mind of painful feelings, the 'perilous stuff that weighs upon the heart' which Macbeth's doctor could not cure.

He was not, at any rate, following the conventional plan of an epistolary wooing of a lady, real or imaginary, though he might often be said to be wooing a patron. It would have been out of place for a young writer of no social standing to address amorous poems to a lady, and ridiculous to address sonnets to a woman of his own station. Later on he could follow custom by finding, or inventing, a faithless siren to reproach. His Sonnets were exceptional, too, in not forming a unitary sequence; as a whole they do not fall into any logical order. There is a sequence of seventeen at the beginning, and what look like fragments of other groups; some come in pairs, like Nos 27–8.

He could not have taken long to discover that sonneteering had a ridiculous side, more in tune with Romeo's first love than with his second, and that it attracted some very silly writers. One of these is the Armado of *Love's Labour's Lost*, where a crop of poetasters put their feelings into fourteen lines. Longaville's sonnet, a poor one, is indited to a 'goddess' (IV.iii.58 ff.), as a great many others of the time were. Women were assumed to be as greedy for flattery as monarchs; though one at least in this play had the sense (as Queen Elizabeth often did not) to dismiss an outpouring of it as 'a huge translation of hypocrisy' (V.ii.50–51), and one man has the sense to deride a fashion 'which makes flesh a deity,/A green goose a goddess' (IV.iii.73–4). The king's effort with his pen (III.iv.24 ff.) has the mixed quality of many of Shakespeare's own, where fine images from Nature are spoiled by laborious love-conceits.

Sonnets belonged, in fact, to a vast literary hobby or industry of Renaissance Europe, and it was inevitable that Shakespeare, like the rest, should sometimes be repeating things that others had said, or rehearsing stock sentiments, long since stale. Sidney Lee's examination shows this in relentless detail. It was a familiar pose of scribblers to lament their grey hairs, whether they had many or few (Lee, *Life* 155); they had to sound lugubrious. The idea so tediously propounded in Shakespeare's first seventeen pieces – that a handsome young man ought to marry and enrich the world with progeny in his own image – was a commonplace (185). As Philip Sidney commented in his *Defence of Poesy*, poets were lavish in guaranteeing immortality to their patrons: somewhat impertinently, Samuel Butler remarked – a nobleman with a distinguished career open to him might not want to be told that his fame would depend on some versifier's rhymes (79–80). Poets, like preachers, denounced lust, as Shakespeare did in Sonnet 129. But Lee, as some have felt, pushed his inquisition too far, allowing too little for what Shakespeare added. Thoughts in No. 53 may well derive from Neo-Platonism (Lee, *Life* 180), but the imaginative leap from archaic metaphysics to the magical opening lines cannot be measured. No. 119 borrows two striking words for its fine opening from the now long-forgotten Barnabe Barnes; but to borrow and transfigure was something Shakespeare was always doing.

Some of the feeling in the Sonnets *must* be real; the sketchy episodical framework may or may not be, and the best argument for its reality is that if the Fair Man and the Dark Lady were inventions, Shakespeare could have been expected to produce better ones. Tucker felt that with some pieces at least, like No. 90, it would be 'almost a wicked scepticism to doubt that he is speaking genuinely for himself' (xxxiii; cf. xxxv–vi). To Auden all the sonnets, apart from the initial set, sounded like 'naked autobiographical confession' (xxxiv). Lee, on the other hand, much less impressionable, could detect 'a strain of personal emotion' only here and there (Lee, *Life* 168). This seems self-evidently wrong. Yet it seems also that even in these brief poems, where, if anywhere, we might hope to come face to face with the living Shakespeare, he is still often wearing a mask, or leaving his meaning to be fully understood by a few intimates only.

The hour had not yet struck for a poet to reveal all his feelings to a public audience, or even to a private circle. What he said might be more like a 'dramatic monologue' by Browning than self-disclosure. It cannot be accidental that the 1590s saw both the private vogue of the sonnet and the coming of age of the public drama; the one was an elitist shadow of the other. Shakespeare was one of the middle-class writers who were advancing towards realism – that is, realistic exploration of human feeling, whether in a naturalistic setting or not. As a sonneteer he could not always be sure of his footing; hence many awkwardnesses and imperfections. It has been noticed that he wavers between addressing his patron familiarly, as 'thou', and formally, as 'you' – a dilemma from which the revolution was soon to free writers by abolishing 'thou' and 'thee': one of its few contributions to equality.

How much of Shakespeare himself went into a sonnet can best be judged from its quality; but the finest ones are apt to be the most enigmatic. A possibility cannot perhaps be ruled out that Shakespeare felt some physical attraction towards men, as well as a stronger one towards women. In this and other contexts, real feeling may be disguised under conventional husks. If he, like others, affected an air of being older, more decrepit, than his real age, it is possible that he often did feel like this under the strain of an exhausting life. He may have been about thirty when the Sonnets were begun, with scarcely twenty years of active life ahead. In youth he had been imprudent; in London his private life may have been at times as tempestuous as he says. In spite of this he grew into a saving man, a shrewd investor, a citizen in good standing. Tensions between two sides of his nature – inherited, perhaps, from parents with discordant temperaments as well as different social backgrounds – may sometimes have been painfully acute.

In spite of his success in the theatre, he may have felt his profession as a burden when he contrasted it, as he must have done, with the easy, graceful idleness of his aristocratic young acquaintances. Embitterments of this kind are less likely to be fabricated than disappointments in love. A soldier renowned for many victories can be disgraced by one failure (No. 25): Shakespeare may be reflecting on how precarious a trade his must be, and No. 29 looks like mortification at some such reverse. In No. 110 he is stung by the thought of having made himself 'a motley to the view', or played the clown to amuse people; as a witty companion he must have been in demand – sometimes in circles where he, like Hamlet, might be fooled to the top of his bent. In the next sonnet he is soured by the ill-fortune that has left him to earn his bread by 'public means which public manners breeds'.

Unpromising though their theme is, the first Sonnets are not deficient in poetry. Perhaps in writing them – about 1593–4 – the poet was often thinking of his own son, rather than of the son he was urging his young patron to set about begetting, and looking forward to having grandsons to follow him. Some words of No. 13 – 'dear my love you know/You had a father …' – would suit this reading; like such a phrase for his patron as 'lovely boy', they suggest paternal more than any other feeling. If so, Hamnet's death in 1596 cut short such hopes; the New Place bought the next year at Stratford would go to others, like Macbeth's crown, 'no son of mine succeeding'.

Whatever their credibility in detail, the amatory sonnets reveal at least turbulent sensations. Shakespeare was living apart from his wife, and a substitute relationship of any wholesome kind would be hard to achieve. Actors were greatly admired, by women, no doubt, even more than by men; and he could put on a surly defiance of opinion, in-difference to the 'rank thoughts' of others about his 'sportive blood' and 'frailties'. 'No, I am that I am …' (No. 121). True, he was writing comedies, among other things, and we have stray testimonies to a light-hearted social life among his peers. He cannot always have been looking forward to his exit from 'this vile world', as in No. 71. But the dark moods, it must be thought, were black enough.

Everyone with a pen has written about Time, but Shakespeare said far too much about it for there to be any doubt of its poignant meanings for him; and it rarely failed to inspire him. It is a salient theme of fourteen sonnets, three of them in the opening set. As in *Lucrece*, Time is most often a negative force, an enemy: it is 'injurious' (No. 85), 'devouring' (No. 86). He is running a race against Time, or swimming against a tide of change he dislikes. For men and women of that era, religion helped to sharpen consciousness of Time – the morbid consciousness of the isolated soul much more than any spirit of social effort and confidence. One of its key-words was 'eternity', which throws a huge shadow over the Sonnets.

Time brings death and oblivion; but Nos 18–19 move to another hackneyed but more congenial idea: that of the poet's verses conferring immortality. It is, of course, his own literary immortality that the poet is interested in, whatever he may profess to be saying. Ambition to survive in fame was one of the Renaissance legacies from Antiquity; one of the splendid sonnets (No. 55) – 'Not marble, nor the gilded monuments/Of princes …' – is an imitation of a Horatian ode (III.30). Horace's prophetic claim for himself and his work had come true; Shakespeare's might too.

With No. 77 he sends his friend the gift of a blank commonplace book, recommending him to record his thoughts in it as they arise, and thus save them from being swept away by Time. It is an interesting sidelight on his creative processes when he adds that thoughts thus rendered visible take on a fresh vitality. One must wonder whether he carried a scribbling-pad himself, and jotted ideas down as they occurred to him – some of them to be stuck in wherever there might be a nook for them in poem or play.

All the sonnets on fame run between Nos 18 and 83 in the published order; if we can trust this so far, it may be that afterwards Shakespeare came to feel that his reputation was assured. Or it may be that his interest in it dwindled. Writers unappreciated by their contemporaries have often turned away in quest of the approval of generations unborn. He could not content himself with this kind of ghostly intercourse with his fellows; he needed a more flesh-and-blood interchange, and found it in the theatre. Perhaps it was because there were no more pressing calls from the theatre, after he retired, to rouse him to activity, that he failed to revise his plays for the First Folio.

Most of his sonnets would have found few readers in later days if they had been written by anyone else. There is much monotonous repetition. An inspired 106 and 108 follow on a batch of mostly dull apologies for silence. Quality throughout is very uneven. This may not always matter when we are looking for signs of Shakespeare's ordinary interest in the social life round him; it matters much more when we ask which poems can be taken to disclose the poet's most poignant sensations. Few can doubt that poetry of the highest order is, in Shelley's words, 'Struck from the inmost fountains of the brain.'

Landor judged none of the sonnets first-rate. Auden, who quoted and dissented from this dictum, considered that forty-nine were 'excellent throughout', while many others had good lines (xxiv). My own count adds up to fifteen in the first class (Nos 29, 30, 53, 57, 64–6, 107, 110–11, 116, 129–30, 146); forty-nine others with flashes of poetry. Those that can be felt to record Shakespeare's own responses to his environment were part of the complex historical process that was heightening men's sense of their own individuality and, at the same time, of the uniqueness of each relationship between one individual and another. Religion had given them their first preoccupation with the self; now they were ready to throw off its swaddling clothes.

What may be called the official or 'court' culture was as elaborate and showy as a courtier's costume. In his sonnets as in his long poems, Shakespeare was submitting to its artificialities, its conceits and verbal capers and quibblings (e.g. Nos 24, 46), devoid of any real meaning.

Sonneteering must be an easy way to work off a tepid sensation of love, Elizabeth Bennet in *Pride and Prejudice* once remarked. The namby-pamby Dauphin in *Henry V* has written a sonnet in praise of his horse. From feeling obliged, early on, to write so stiltedly, Shakespeare may well have had fits of self-doubt. In No. 55 he is triumphant; in No. 72 he is ashamed of 'that which I bring forth', 'things nothing worth'. Through all this he was a professional writer in the making, working his way towards a diction far more lucid and direct than most amateurs attained. Sidney's sonnet-manner is often tortuously rhyme-cramped. Moreover, Shakespeare was discovering, like Milton not much later, how greatly the sonnet was capable of being improved and expanded.

With the court style went a flavour of the humbug or insincerity that infected the court itself and all the higher walks of life. Shakespeare's sonnets of absence and separation are, for want of a worthy occasion, among his most fulsome and overstrained. Some of his compliments have a distasteful streak of servility, whatever conventions he was obeying. Usually the closer he comes to boot-licking, the further he is from poetry. In some of his sonnets addressed to a man, the tone might suggest an association then considered improper, but in Elizabethan usage the word 'love' was elastic enough to cover a wide span of meanings. The dedication of *Lucrece* begins with the author's 'love' for his patron, meaning no more than warm attachment. 'My sweet boy', 'my heart', Falstaff calls out to Hal, in the street (*1H.IV* V.iv.44, 48).

If all artists have, like Heine, two souls in one breast, this may have been more acutely so with Shakespeare than with most. In the long poems the court culture was predominant; in the Sonnets we see it wrestling with newer ways of thinking and behaving; and in the later, harshly realistic ones, the newer ways prevail. In Nos 40 and 95 (both containing the word 'lascivious') we have a picture of vice gilded by aristocratic graces which might easily, for a while, charm an impressionable young man from the country. Shakespeare points out quite clearly the blurring of right and wrong that this entailed – with little show of repulsion, but his moral sense must have gone on working to throw off the alien element. Yet high culture is always a fusion, a compound. Shakespeare was not abandoning old standards but seeking to bring them into a more durable amalgam, fit for a coming age, and thereby at the same time to ennoble the standards of a social order now emerging.

General reflections on life are the staple of the finest sonnets; the persons they are supposed to be addressed to are brought in in deference to a prescribed pattern. There is an evolving style, and 'Shakespeare is moving nearer to Donne than to Spenser' (Ellrodt 43). In Donne's 'metaphysical' style a true fusion of cultures could not be brought about; it was more a mixing up of ideas of professional middle-class scholars and writers with those of a sceptical courtier type: the two agreed in rejecting the fulsome, overblown emotionalism of court poetry. Such a convergence can come about more easily on the artistic plane than on the political one of class interests, but it was too intellectually contrived to be fully congenial to Shakespeare. His imagery continued to belong to the perennial world of nature, and of social relations.

Sonnets 1 to 17 were addressed to a young man, apparently of high station, who may have been – as Tucker, among others, thought (xxxvii ff.) – William Herbert, third Earl of Pembroke, to whom the First Folio was dedicated; but he was only fourteen in 1594, and a more probable candidate is the Earl of Southampton, to whom Shakespeare dedicated his two long poems. Wranglings about the rival claimants may never end, since as one critic remarks both sides have to depend a good deal on plausible assumptions (Booth 547–8). Their arguments have been reviewed lately by Wait (ch. 1) and Calvert (Section 2). On the whole Southampton seems to have the better case; A.L. Rowse in 1984 deemed this perfectly obvious. With equal confidence he identified the 'Dark Lady' as Emilia Lanier, orphan daughter of an Italian court musician, and herself a poetess as well as an 'outspoken feminist' (Sonnets x, xix ff.).

Southampton was a youth of adventurous or freakish spirit, whether or not capable of serious thinking; a Catholic, a ward of the great Lord Burghley, he got into trouble in 1598 by a clandestine marriage. The same man may have been the recipient of some or all of the later sonnets to an aristocratic patron, a close but not always reliable friend. What these poems tell us is perplexingly hard to unravel. We can see which poems or lines are good, but can only guess at where their sap, or inspiration, was drawn from. Some may have been deliberately indistinct. Anything like a political allusion, even one not meant for the press, would have to be muffled. As actors, with royal patronage, Shakespeare and his colleagues were, in their way, public figures, and it behoved them to watch their steps. He may not have taken due note of this at first. An aging queen would scarcely have enjoyed reading No. 7, where twelve lines are about how the sun is revered while 'his sacred majesty' is young and fresh, but when he feebly declines towards his setting people withdraw their 'homage' and 'look another way'. Shakespeare may have run some risk of being compromised by his connection with Southampton when the latter's friend and leader, the Earl of Essex, was executed after his attempted rising in 1601, and Southampton, who was implicated, narrowly escaped the same fate.

Instead he was sent to the Tower; the 'confined doom' of No. 107 can plausibly be related to this. A separation lamented in No. 97 is compared to a bleak winter; it breathes real feeling, or at least has real eloquence, and may be taken for an expression of sympathy. A number of sonnets,

mature in style, are unusual in their political images or cryptic allusions
to events – like 'the blow of thralled discontent' in No. 124, which
suggests a conspiracy, or the 'suborned informer' of No. 125. They give
us the mood of Elizabeth's last years, when fears were mounting about
what would happen when she died. Everything was, in fact, being
arranged in advance by the politicians, but, as Samuel Butler admits,
'with the utmost secrecy' (140); the public could not know that there was
little to fear. The 'mortal moon' and her 'eclipse' (No. 107) have usually
been taken to refer either to the queen's survival of her 'climacteric', at
the age of sixty-three, in the autumn of 1596, or to her death in 1603.
The later date seems preferable because the now-promised 'olives of
endless age', or enduring peace, fit the undisturbed succession of James I
– which, among other things, brought Southampton's release. In 1603 all
the poets made play, as Lee says, with eclipses and olives (*Life*, 227). A
Shakespeare character had anticipated them when he reported to Henry
IV that a rebellion was over, and 'Peace puts forth her olive everywhere'
(*2H.IV* IV.iv.87).

The 'Dark Lady' items sound realistic in a very different way, though
their subject may have been either one woman or a conflation of several.
They begin with a satire on cosmetics (No. 127), a commonplace topic
but seeming with Shakespeare more closely linked to disapproval of the
rich, who bought and used them, and of the moral cosmetics of pretence
and insincerity. There is more farce than tragedy in the situation that
develops, as a writer of comedies cannot have failed to perceive. With
some indecencies thrown in, it becomes a sort of *conte drôlatique*. The
woman is compared – in a homely reminiscence of country life, the
longest extended image of the collection – to a housewife chasing a
runaway hen (the rival) while her child (the poet) runs after her
(No. 143). More serious, and morbid, is the fact that he cannot help
wanting this woman, whom he knows to be worthless and promiscuous.
Here the tone (Nos 137–8) is strikingly 'modern', and suggestive of an
experienced man in middle life taking leave of such adventures – or of
Antony trying to shake off his subjection to Cleopatra. Through a
shifting medley of moods and feelings, we reach the earthy opposite of
the romantic love that floats like a perfume through the Comedies. Why
it is always haunted there by incredulous questionings, we can better
understand in the light of these unromantic sensations recorded in the
Sonnets.

In No. 152 we have the sole allusion to the poet being a married man
who is breaking his vows. This seems to lead back to a group of a dozen
sonnets on the theme of remorse, which have a more genuinely personal
ring than any of the others. They point to a gloomy scene of unfaith-
fulness, folly, debauchery. Penitents have often, of course, found a

perverse satisfaction in holding themselves up as 'the chief of sinners'. Virtuous sonneteers could denounce lust in order to set their own perfect love in a brighter lustre. But the dark shape of 'lust in action' in No. 129, 'murd'rous, bloody ... savage', can have grown only out of sombre experiences, whether they belonged to fantasy or to reality.

In Nos 146 and 151 there is the standard Christian antithesis of body and spirit. Similarly, Sidney wrote of the soul suffering infections from 'the dungeon of the body', and two of his best sonnets are a renunciation of both desire and love (111, 167–8). The words of No. 147 about 'reason' as the 'physician' trying to rescue him from the 'fever' of a mad passion have a startling likeness to Iago's words about our 'reason' being a bit to curb our raging lusts. As so often in Shakespeare, Christian ethical feeling – here, medieval asceticism – outlives dogmatic teaching. All the reflections in the Sonnets on Time, age, death, are entirely pagan. There is no infernal blaze in No. 13 to warm 'death's eternal cold'.

True love, or close friendship, is a refuge from the ravages of Time – a consolation, as the two very fine sonnets 29 and 30 say, for all life's crosses and disappointments. Another, No. 116, on love as the one immutable thing in human life, is a declaration of romantic love fortified by Christian fidelity; it is embedded among the poems of remorse. Its opening, 'the marriage of true minds', is contradicted by what follows, the 'alteration' that may affect one but not the other. There is nothing 'private' in the lines, until at the end the poet offers his own faith as pledge of the truth of his words. Nos 123–4 repeat the challenge.

No. 109 concentrates an impulse that seems to lurk hereabouts in the Sonnets: a wish to reassure someone he has been absent from that he still thinks of him or her as his closest and dearest, and that any 'stain' of 'frailties' he has contracted can and will be washed away. Here can be felt the most wholesome expression of deep attachment, romantic but not facile, anywhere in the Sonnets. The poet is turning back, in revulsion from the idols he has gone roving after, to a straightforward, un-pretentious, well-tested affection. We cannot doubt that he means what he says, even if we may need to remind ourselves that though poetry can tell truth, it is never likely to tell the whole truth and nothing but the truth – a task, perhaps, impossible in any human speech.

The overture he is holding out would be most fittingly made to a neglected or ill-used wife; something like this occurs in some of Shakespeare's latest plays. If Anne Hathaway must regretfully be considered ineligible, the best alternative would be some woman Shake-speare has got to know in London and has formed a close bond of trust and fondness with. She would not belong to fashionable circles, or to the factions hinted at in No. 124, but would have enough intelligence and education to understand him; she would be younger than him, but not over-young; attractive, though not ravishing – No. 21, an early, simpler version of No. 130, avers that he loves his lady as much as he could love anyone, though he will not indulge, like others, in ridiculous hyperbole. In lines like these we may discern a serious relationship, such as he wanted love and marriage between 'true minds' to develop into. No. 110 speaks only of a 'friend', but it works up to a prayer for welcome back to a 'pure and most most loving breast' – surely a woman's. Conceivably in No. 116 it is not himself, but this woman he is turning back to, who is credited with the unshaken fidelity of a 'true mind'.

A writer's choice of imagery is revealing in many ways. Often the best part of a Shakespearian sonnet consists of its 'asides', or metaphors sprouting from generalities, while the concluding couplet, ostensibly the point of the poem, may have nothing to add. Many of these flowerings come from Nature, but they may be entwined with observation of social life. 'Summer's lease hath all too short a date' (No. 18): the word 'lease' is ubiquitous, and a reminder that short leases of land were weapons in the hands of those many landowners who were busy ejecting superfluous tenants. Mercantile phraseology is remarkably prevalent. The nervous poet fears that his patron, growing conscious of his defects, will hold an 'audit' and decide to dismiss him (No. 40). It is not 'forbidden usury', No. 6 says, to advance money to borrowers who 'pay the willing loan'.

Through all the romanticism runs this train of associations with property, law, trade, money. Subtle influences of a commercializing society were seeping into literature, as into every other sphere. Shakespeare's mind turns nostalgically to 'days long since, before these last so bad' (No. 67). This may be partly a pose, but like most Englishmen he was still at the stage of looking back, instead of forward, in search of happier times. The litany of social evils in No. 66 makes clear what were the corruptions, old or new, that weighed on his mind. An evident thread joins it to Hamlet's catalogue, and runs on to Lear. His complaint is never of human life in itself, as either painful or meaningless: it is of the man-made evils that dehumanize it. They might well make him crave for a firm human attachment, a haven the contented mind has less need of.

Four consecutive sonnets where he communes with his Muse (Nos 58–61) are concerned with literature, and reflect his awareness of rapid changes of taste and an author's need to go on supplying novelties if he is to keep his footing. Clearly he did not take kindly to all the new modes, and the 'time-bettering days' of No. 82 sound ironical. In another group, Nos 79–86, he is faced with rival versifiers, outstripping him in the patron's favour by their 'gross painting', or flattery. No flattery could be grosser than some of his own, but it seldom extends to more than a young man's looks. In No. 86, the best of this set, he pays enigmatic tribute to one competitor, whose superior talent has paralysed his inventive faculties. Many have thought Chapman to be indicated (e.g. Tucker 163; Harrison 121). But as against Shakespeare's despondent air, the travel sonnets point to absences at Stratford that may have been resented by a patron or other fashionable acquaintances who wanted him always dancing attendance on them.

Here, once again, we can think of instinct calling him back to the theatre, where he was on his own ground. Even if his audience might sometimes, like a private patron, oblige him to write against the grain, this could seem to him less humiliating. In any case, the theatre was far more bracing. From a nobleman's mansion to the Globe was all the distance between a feudal climate and a modern one. In the Sonnets Shakespeare usually seems to be experiencing life passively – inclined, like a Richard II, to luxuriate in regrets. When he indulges in 'sweet silent thought' (No. 30) it is to call to mind the pangs he has undergone, the friends he has lost. By contrast, with the stage in view he is always dramatic; even when some of his people seem to lose themselves in discursive talk, it is under the sway of a strong dramatic situation. The theatre was his salvation from introspection, the sonnet his means of sinking back into a mood that was 'sweet' because it was solitary.

Like the long poems, the Sonnets have many echoes in the plays, where events may sometimes be seen as crystallizing sensations earlier clothed in rhyme. Rumour, as Prologue to *Henry IV Part 2*, talks of 'Making the wind my post-horse'. In Sonnet 51 the poet talks of how he will post homeward, spurring 'though mounted on the wind'. Such verbal repetitions abound in Shakespeare, but a more significant link between the sonnets and *Henry IV* is a certain congeniality between the poet and the fat knight. Ludicrous as this may seem, all Shakespeare's greater characters must be projections of his own relations with life, at one angle or another; and England's foremost comic writer and foremost comic character could not be without some special kinship. Falstaff is endowed with a double portion of his creator's wit and humour. He too makes himself a motley to the view (No. 110) and suffers from bouts of disgust with himself and the company he keeps. He can be thought of as one of Shakespeare's many purgations, freeing him from uncomfortable thoughts by transferring them into another skin.

'I am old, I am old', Falstaff can lament on his behalf, as it were ahead of time; and the Chief Justice dilates on how aged and decrepit Sir John has grown (*2H.IV* II.iv.270; I.ii). In the judge's eyes he is a perverter of youth, who haunts Prince Hal 'like his ill angel' (I.ii); Falstaff plays on the expression, as Shakespeare does in Sonnet 144. If Falstaff is painfully conscious of advancing age, so is the sovereign whom he antics, and Henry's laments over his debility, 'this bare withered trunk' (IV.v.229), have the same note as Sonnet 73, with its winter scene of bare leafless trees. All three men feel chill winds blowing over them; king and poet feel them also blowing over their England. It is out of such confluxes of personal and social that poetry is generated. At the end, when Hal, now king, rebukes Falstaff as an old 'fool and jester' (V.iv.49), we may hear Shakespeare rebuking himself, as he does in some sonnets, for sacrificing self-respect to amuse young idlers; he must have had sour premonitions of decline into a superannuated jester. The jealousy he felt of another poet–flatterer has its analogy in Falstaff's comic outburst against Poins, who is in a way his rival as the prince's companion (II.iv.238 ff.).

By the time Falstaff was taking shape, some of the sonnet agitations must have been subsiding into recollections ready to be transposed into a comic key. 'A proper gentlewoman', Doll Tearsheet is sardonically called, but we hear that she is as common as the road from St Albans (II.ii.166–7). Shakespeare's faithless mistress may be a lady, but she is 'the wide world's common place' (Sonnet 137). 'I am meat for your master', Doll offends Pistol by telling him haughtily (II.iv.120–21); we can fancy a Dark Lady giving Shakespeare some such snub – but also placating him with something like Doll's assurance to Falstaff: 'I love thee better than I love e'er a scurvy boy of them all' (II.iv.271).

In *Henry IV Part 2* the archbishop's explanation of his party's rebellion is that England is full of 'rank minds sick of happiness', and has had to take to civil war as a cure (IV.i). As a political statement or excuse this is (as pointed out earlier) very lame, not to say unintelligible. It becomes easier to comprehend how Shakespeare's mind is working when we read Sonnet 118 and find the same logic applied to his own affairs. He has grown 'sick of welfare', 'rank of goodness', with his true love, and has turned away to worse company like a man swallowing a bitter purge. If there really was a good woman whom he loved but neglected, we are reading his apology.

PART IV

The Comedies

1

The Comic Realm

In the 1590s, while Shakespeare in his Histories was letting his tongue 'tang arguments of state', as Malvolio meant to (*TN* III.iv.73–4), he was also writing a series of romantic comedies, prefaced by one or two farces. This was one mark of his exceptionality: most other playwrights were sticking to sterner themes, like war (Gurr, *Playgoing* 137). He must have felt a need to escape from these at intervals, into milder realms. Romantic comedy was not his own invention; he had an important predecessor here in John Lyly, as in history he had Marlowe. Lyly was the man who 'set a standard, and shaped a model', more artistic than the popular mode of Peele, Greene, Nashe, more natural than the Italian Commedia dell'Arte with its stereotyped characters (Bradbrook, *Comedy* 61 ff.). His mode was not an offspring of the regular professional theatre; he was writing, in the 1570s and 1580s, for performances by the boys of the Chapel Royal and St Paul's choirs. As a novelist he brought into fashion a fantastically ornate style of writing, which can be seen imitated but also made fun of in *Love's Labour's Lost*; two of this play's characters are in part copies from Lyly.

It cannot be said that Shakespeare was adding much artistry of construction to the model he took over. Rules or formulae had little meaning for him. The nearest he came to well-rounded symmetry may have been in *A Midsummer Night's Dream*, where mankind is laid under a spell, relieved of responsibility for its actions. On the other hand, nearly all these plays are full of precious metal that only loose construction and free indulgence in fantasy could have allowed Shakespeare to store them with. This feature of the Comedies goes with a shift of the centre of gravity from Adam to Eve. 'Shakespeare has no heroes,' said Ruskin, 'he has only heroines' (116). This is scarcely true of the whole corpus of his work, but it comes close to the truth of the Comedies. Their world is a feminine one, instead of aggressively virile. Men were making havoc of their world, and neglecting to repair and renovate it; in a kind of humorous despair with them, when Shakespeare wrote comedy he made

them abdicate, and leave things to women. In the Histories women were
fish out of water, either bad or helpless. In the Comedies they can be
perfectly natural, and often able to direct events. As a rule (*The Merchant
of Venice*, in various ways, stands by itself) their success is limited to their
own circles; they are not new brooms with a mission to sweep out the
Augean stables that men have made of life, though they can do much to
create a new atmosphere, a new hope.

It suited Shakespeare's design to choose exotic settings for all the
Comedies except *The Merry Wives of Windsor*. Four of them are set in
Italy, but he was not going there, like so many dramatists, in search of
tyrants, poisoners, or suchlike figures of melodrama. Things may often
look very English, but room is allowed for a free play of fantasy, deriving
from old traditions of storytelling, fairy-tale, magic. In a sense we are
being transported into the past; yet as Gurr says, to conservatives of his
day Shakespeare's heroines and their views on marriage could appear 'an
alarming novelty' (Gurr, *Playgoing* 149). As in the Histories, he has less to
do with the respectable citizenry than with those above and below; his
stage is for the gentry with their cultivated wit, and for common folk
with their broader humour. It is in keeping with this that the setting is
seldom urban. Illyria has a seaport, but a nameless one, which we visit in
only a few scenes.

Shakespeare's method gave him licence to depict humanity without
photographic realism. His own society was changing rapidly; he himself
was part of a ferment of change. His characters often break away or are
swept away from their moorings and undergo unforeseen experiences
among new landmarks, like the heroines who disguise themselves as
men in order to be – or to discover – themselves. There could be no
occasion here, as in the Histories, for patriotic attitudes, and he could
talk of Englishmen and foreigners with equal freedom. Fanciful land-
scapes lent an 'insulating agent' to social criticism (Byrne 209). 'I am a
great eater of beef and I believe that does harm to my wit', says Sir
Andrew Aguecheek in *Twelfth Night* (I.iii.87–8). He is an Illyrian, but too
much eating of meat was a bad habit of Englishmen who could afford it.
There is a cut at French manners in Berowne's jibe about Boyet as an
affected fop, a 'monsieur the nice' (*LLL* V.ii.315 ff.) – and at French
morals in Dr Caius's complacent assertion that in his country husbands
are free of the vice of jealousy (*MWW* III.iii.164–5). If it was a current
notion that 'Germans are honest men' (*MWW* IV.v.66), they may be said
to come off best. England, at any rate, is being shown as part of Europe.

From Europe Shakespeare is free to let fancy roam still further afield.
One of Portia's would-be husbands is a Moroccan prince, like Othello
very conscious of his colour and given to a high strain of eloquence. He
boasts of having slain a Sophy, or Shah of Persia, with his scimitar, and

talks of other suitors hastening to Venice from as far away as 'the Hyrcanian deserts' and 'wide Arabia' (*MV* II.vii.41–2). Fairies are above any colour prejudice: Titania is quarrelling with Oberon over an Indian boy whose mother was a bosom friend of hers. Lysander, by contrast, repulses Hermia as a 'tawny Tartar' (*MND* III.ii.263), and Claudio, in *Much Ado about Nothing*, thinks of a dark-complexioned woman as an 'Ethiope' (V.iv.38). Horizons continue to expand as time goes on. There is a new map of the Indies; and Sir Toby hails Maria as 'my metal of India', or gold (*TN* III.ii.76–8; II.iv.15). Curiosity extended to China, still known by its old name of Cathay, and 'Cataian' was already a synonym for *cheat* (*TN* II.iii.78; *MWW* II.i.130) – an illustration of how quick we are to form a bad opinion of outsiders. 'Vapians passing the equinoctial of Queubus', in a jester's nonsense-talk (*TN* II.ii.25–6), may be taken for a skit on the often garbled or far-fetched reports of explorers.

Two plays, *Love's Labour's Lost* and *As You Like It*, are not so much dramas as conversation pieces, or exercises in talking, with only a pretence of plot. Shakespeare was savouring his own passion for words, and for reflections on life – tastes evidently shared by many theatregoers. Absorption in words could spill over into the Histories. Bardolph and Justice Shallow have a droll debate about the word 'accommodate', and Shallow remarks that 'good phrases are surely ... very commendable' (*2H.IV* III.ii.68 ff.); Mistress Quickly is as full of malapropisms as Dogberry. Shakespeare's unwillingness to be penned into any conventional limits shows above all in the irruption of the comic genius into history with Falstaff, and that of something akin to the tragic into comedy with Shylock. Romantic love first appears in full glow in a tragedy, *Romeo and Juliet*. In the Comedies it never makes itself altogether at home: it is there, so to speak, on probation. Shakespeare was learning too much about life to be credulous. He looked on at his people's doings with a half-sceptical detachment. With him reality was invading a romantic realm 'guarded like a dream' (Raleigh 193). In the late Histories he failed to revive the Heroic, or faith in it; in the late Comedies he failed to breathe fresh life into the romantic. It was time for them both to give way to other kinds of drama, other voyages of discovery.

2

The Plays

The Taming of the Shrew (c. 1590)

Troublesome wives have been a staple of male gossip and mythology; they had a place on the early English stage in miracle plays. Shakespeare's shrew is a caricature specimen. He makes it as hard as possible for us to feel any sympathy for her. She begins by threatening to hit someone on the head with a stool. She ties up her younger sister Bianca, and strikes her when she protests at being treated like 'a bondmaid and a slave' (II.i.2). Next we have Hortensio, disguised as a music teacher, complaining that she has broken his lute over his head (II.i). In her first encounter with Petruchio she gives him a box on the ear. What the play is about, in short, is not simply a man bullying a woman, but a bullying woman subdued by a male bully.

Petruchio is a caricature of an ordinary domineering male. 'She is my goods, my chattels – my horse, my ox, my ass' (III.ii.328) – his man-of-property attitude to a wife only magnifies what men in many lands and times have really thought. He has a boorish temper, as we hear from Grumio, his 'ancient, trusty, pleasant servant', when Petruchio angrily wrings his ear for not understanding an order (I.ii). At his wedding he knocks the priest down, presumably as a warning to Katherina of what she may expect. There is nothing whatever in his behaviour to her to give him any claim on her respect.

Folk-tales seem to demand a 'moral' (Bethell 112), and this farce ends with one – Katherina's 'beautiful speech', as a Victorian editor called it (Marshall 316), announcing her abject surrender and unquestioning obedience. Shakespeare underlines its comic incongruities by making her talk of how husbands care for their wives, their 'painful labour both by sea and land': as his audience was well aware, nothing could be further from the thoughts of the dowry-hunting idlers who haunt these plays. The real moral is that this is how husbands ought to behave, not how they do behave. Shakespeare's joke is aimed at fossilized conservatism in every sphere. When Katherina talks of the oaf Petruchio as her 'lord', 'king', 'sovereign', Shakespeare is ridiculing not merely husbands who take themselves too seriously, but monarchs as well. Some of his English kings will soon be learning to make speeches about their painful toil for the welfare of their subjects.

Amazingly, as late as 1968 another editor was echoing Katherina's nonsense by expatiating solemnly on 'the submission of wife to husband as a law of nature', and declaring that this pair are now true lovers (Hibbard, *Taming* 7). Shakespeare had to be made a pillar of Order in the domestic as well as the political realm. Later still, in 1986, a commentator has managed to see Katherina's subjugation as the first step towards Petruchio's conversion from 'obstinate perversity', and her own emergence as 'a true winner in the perennial battle' (Bryant 113). Most surprising of all is a feminist writer's discovery in the *dénouement* of 'a harmonious synthesis' of masculine and feminine (French 85). The same writer holds that Shakespeare never shook off a conviction of a 'natural and ineradicable' inequality, amounting to 'a class difference', between men and women (84).

The Comedy of Errors (c. 1590-93)

Farcical as it is, this piece gives the lie to Katherina's new gospel by portraying an overbearing and unfaithful husband and a resentful wife. It has much more ingenuity of plot, and a serious meaning which shows every now and then amid the slapstick. There is for once a distinct atmosphere of a commercial city, and there is more than a whiff of topical reference. In the lively opening account of hostilities between two governments arising from a trade war and bans on foreign goods, the Syracusans are said to be 'seditious' (I.i.12), or engaged in rebellion against Ephesus: when the play was written, the Dutch were in revolt against Spain, and during the long conflict bans were imposed by Madrid on Dutch seaborne trade (see Israel). 'Guilders' are mentioned as a Syracusan coin, and as useful currency for Eastern trade (I.i.8; IV.i.4). Baldwin's study of the play (*William Shakespeare Adapts a Hanging*) unearths a network of allusion to the Anglo–Spanish war and the anti-popery alarms of the late 1580s.

There is plenty of indignant feminism in the play, but women are not yet in the foreground. Their chief representative, the Abbess, does no more than preside over a cobbled-up 'happy ending', happiest in a fairy-tale family reunion. There is no meeting of minds between Antonio of Ephesus and his ill-used Adriana: he is not reproved by his virtuous mother the Abbess, and in the last scene his wife is scarcely allowed to open her mouth, while his 'courtesan' receives from him a promised diamond (paid for with Adriana's money). There is no prospect of the

Dromio twins being freed from slavery as a reward for long service, and allowed to make new lives together.

Love's Labour's Lost (c. 1595)

This may have been the first comedy that was completely Shakespeare's own. It has a plot made up by him, which does him no great credit; but the piece is to be judged less on its story than on its dialogue. Because it is so much his own, it may be safer than it is in most cases to look for traces of the author's own feelings. Parallels with the Sonnets are many. There is much more rhyming than in any other play. The opening theme of Fame as guardian against the ravages of Time is another reminder of the Sonnets, which share with it the imagery of 'scythe' and 'brazen tombs'. But the gaiety of this play may warrant a surmise that some, at any rate, of Shakespeare's sonnèt-tears were of less than scalding temperature.

The court of Navarre might be mistaken for an English country house. There is no town in sight, but a park and a dairy are not wanting, together with the usual appurtenances of a village: curate and school-master and constable. The young king, who converses so familiarly with his circle, might be a squire who has arranged a reading-party with his college friends. It has always been thought that there are numerous topical or personal allusions. Armado's name obviously recalls the Armada, and to have an absurd Spaniard to laugh at, full of gentlemanly pretensions but lacking a shirt, would tickle any English patriot. Spain had a multitude of shabby-genteel *hidalgos*; but Armado looks much less like a haughty Castilian than a skipping Mounseer, that already cherish-ed figure of fun.

In the Histories all the competitors are avid for power. In the Comedies personal distinction, fame, is the goal of ambition. Navarre's first words to his friends are about 'fame', 'honour', just as if Hotspur were speaking: they too will be 'conquerors', though by other means. Supported by rigorous self-mastery, self-denial, they will make their little country 'the wonder of the world'. We can smile both at this parody of national conceit, and at the anachronistic ideal of asceticism. A choice between learning and love, Athena and Aphrodite, was a topic of student songs going back to the twelfth century (Waddell 199). Renais-sance culture sought to combine the two: a gentleman should be, as Shakespeare repeats in many contexts, courtier and soldier and scholar all in one. Underlying this was the ideal of a fusion of the good qualities of different educated classes. Navarre's bookish scheme is a turning backward; he can think only of arid scholarship for the sake of scholar-ship. He wants, as the sensible Berowne says, to pore over 'Things hid and barred ... from common sense', and vouched for only by 'base authority from others' books' (I.i.57, 87). Berowne is giving an airy version of the Baconian doctrine of knowledge as useful information, to be won or tested by experiment. He stands for the march of mind, against musty scholasticism.

Denied the company of women, these scholars are to have for light relief that of Armado, who has 'a mint of phrases in his brain', and comes out with so many 'high-born words', 'fire-new words', that one can even 'love to hear him lie' when he tells his tall tales of Spanish chivalry (I.i.165 ff.). This might seem poor fare for young men of spirit, but in England language was taking on a very unusual importance, and was viewed with a respect that makes its immense literary harvest less hard to comprehend. England was growing, and English was coming into its own; it was no more than two generations since a gentleman was expected to be able to converse fluently in Latin, as Queen Elizabeth could. Lovers of English, from Shakespeare down, were learning it and helping it to develop simultaneously; and this verbal fever seems to have been shared in some measure by all ranks. A shimmering rainbow of words overarched the sky, announcing the departure of the medieval Deluge. Homage to language could link all men – and women – of education; and, further, the amalgamation of gentry and middle class, or their best elements, into a new elite. These two components could be closer in that period of social flux than they were to be later on, when the dividing lines of a new social pattern had hardened, with forms of speech for cement.

The language itself was at a special stage in its development, not unconnected with the interaction of social strata, and making possible the unique Elizabethan richness of imagery (Weimann, *Structure* 227). When Holofernes the schoolmaster, after turning over on his tongue four other adjectives, hits on *peregrinate* as the *mot juste* for Armado, Nathaniel the curate whips out his notebook to jot down this 'most singular and choice epithet' (V.i.14–15). Nathaniel counts himself blessed in his freedom from the 'monster Ignorance'; it elevates him above poor Dull the constable, who is 'only an animal' (IV.ii.27). Even Costard the clown is ready to try his tongue on a new hard word. These humble 'intellectuals' of Navarre are the opposites of Jack Cade's men in Kent, so vehemently convinced that all learning is their enemy. But studied modes of speech have their snares: they can lend themselves to affectation, and to verbiage in place of thinking. Wit may too easily be used to wound others. Armado's contempt for the vernacular which he mangles – the 'base and obscure vulgar' – goes with his gentlemanly seduction of a girl of humble station, whom he has talked of meaning to marry (IV.i.60 ff.).

Shakespeare was making fun of all this preciosity, but also revelling in 'the great feast of languages' that was going on (V.i.38–9). He was busy piling up his prodigious vocabulary; he never ceased to be a venturesome experimenter. We can see him, under the name of Holofernes, imping the wings of his own exuberant genius, at present far richer than his knowledge of the world – 'a foolish extravagant spirit, full of forms, figures, shapes, objects, ideas, apprehensions, motions, revolutions ... (IV.ii.72–3).

The blending of social qualities that he seems to look forward to, refinement with solidity, has an accompaniment in complementary endowments of men and women. Berowne and the princess have much in common. He is the sensible, plain-spoken member of the male quartet; it is he who leads the way back to rational acceptance of life and humanity. On her side the princess has always been sensible as well as charming, a mild preceptress to her ladies. At the end she gives them a lead in the right way to treat their impatient suitors. She has all Shakespeare's suspicion of light-spoken vows. 'Your oath I will not trust', she tells the king candidly, and imposes on him a year's probation in 'some forlorn and naked hermitage' (V.ii.784 ff.). We could wish that she had thought of something more constructive for him to do. Her ladies insist, each in turn, on the same twelve months of waiting; only Berowne is given a useful task: to visit the sick and try to amuse 'groaning wretches' with his wit. The play seems to hold out the promise of a sequel; but Shakespeare may not have found it as easy as his lovers to believe that love could survive the ordeal of twelve months' separation, to say nothing of hermitage or hospital.

The Two Gentlemen of Verona (c. 1593-94)

Shakespeare's Comedies contain little in the way of adventure, or deeds of derring-do. He had enough of that in the Histories. The *Two Gentlemen* is unusual in its descent into melodrama, of an absurdity suggestive of modern pantomine or operetta. Valentine, the hero, is compelled by threats from a company of Italian *banditti* – two of them named Moses and Valerius – to become their 'king' or 'general' (IV.i). Some of the brigands are gentlemen, banished for 'petty crimes' of youth like homicide; they all scorn 'such vile base practices' as robbery of women or the poor. This sounds like a comic version of Robin Hood, who is referred to with his 'fat friar'. Altogether the piece has so much resemblance to Gilbert and Sullivan as to suggest reflections on a permanent strain of English humour, running through the centuries.

In Act V the operetta style takes full control. Proteus has rescued Silvia, who rejects him and reproaches him for deserting his true love, Julia (who is hanging about disguised as a man). He is about to ravish her when her true love Valentine enters, and denounces him as a false friend: Proteus's disloyalty upsets him far more than Silvia's plight. 'Such is a friend now' – all friendship has decayed (V.iv.63); but Valentine lives up to its claim himself by forgiving Proteus and handing Silvia over to him. She makes no comment; it defied even Shakespeare to think of something appropriate for her to say. There was a cult in his day of extravagant friendship, as well as one of hyperbolical love; he was equally ready to burlesque either of them.

The two young women deserve a much better fate than to be cast away in such company. Shakespeare evidently enjoyed painting – or sketching – their portraits, as well as inventing freakish adventures for them. Julia's constancy shines the more brightly in contrast with Proteus's prompt transfer of his affections from her to Silvia, the Duke's daughter. For a princess, Silvia has unconventionally free-and-easy manners, and her vitality and sprightliness put her too among the chosen band of Shakespearian heroines. One of their essential qualifications is virtue, and Silvia can even be called 'holy' (IV.ii.5, 41). Rather than submit to an odious marriage she takes flight, is captured by the bandits, and faces this fresh trial with courage; her cry 'O Valentine, this I endure for thee!' (V.iii.15) is in the accents of Imogen. In his first Comedies Shakespeare had pilloried brutish behaviour in husbands; in the more serious strands of this play, men are again shown in a bad – or at least flickering – light, while women and their love are exposed to slings and arrows.

A Midsummer Night's Dream (1596)

In this second of the few plays Shakespeare seems to have made up for himself – an experiment he soon tired of – he was helped with his intricately interwoven plot by the fairyland magic he had at his command. It is only early on that all the human beings are acting on their own volition, and have to be provided with motives. The play is romantic by virtue of its poetry and atmosphere, the perfume of the moonlit woods; most of its human beings contribute little but noisy discord. When the forest is left behind, only faint memories of its happenings survive, a fading revelation of the chaotic underworld of human behaviour, normally kept out of sight.

Theseus has, as he says, wooed Hippolyta with his sword (I.i.16), as Henry V wins his French princess. He is a forerunner of Henry also in his shrewd, common-sense outlook; the plain-speaking, plain-dealing man of action belonged to a species that Shakespeare was drawn to by a sort of attraction of opposites. Whether from good nature or from policy, this Duke of Athens sees (like Henry again) that common folk ought to be given their due, and kept in good humour; whereas his courtiers and bride look down on the hard-handed artisans and their performance with pitying disdain. These plebeians are all very loyal subjects, breathing a reverence to their ruler which in England was entering its twilight. They are ridiculous only because they are out of their proper orbit; Shakespeare finds vital sparks in them, and Bottom is a more sturdily interesting person than either of the pasteboard young gentlemen.

The first part of Spenser's *Faerie Queene* had come out in 1590, and Shakespeare may be suspected of setting up against its 'Gloriana' another fairy queen, stripped of ideal embellishments. Gloriana was also Queen Elizabeth, and if our author was making fun of Spenser's laborious epic he may have judged it tactful to make clear that his Titania was *not* Elizabeth by inserting a poetical tribute to his sovereign (II.i.155 ff.), as well as providing Titania with a consort. Fairyland's royal pair are more convincing than the human lovers; their quarrel is a commentary on the fragility of wedded love. Titania accuses her lord of sundry strayings, and of Hippolyta having been his 'buskined mistress' and 'warrior love'; he retorts by taxing her with a past connection with Theseus (II.i.71 ff.). 'What fools these mortals be!' Puck exclaims, but the taunt might be returned. Between the two there is no gleam of affection; presumably they have been married a very long time. In the end Titania has to submit, though she is tricked into surrender, not browbeaten like Katherina the Shrew. Puck may be supposed to personify the freakish effects of accident on human affairs. He is Oberon's jester as well as factotum, and Shakespeare's mouthpiece for some strictures on human manners. He is happiest when things 'befall preposterously' (III.ii.120): 'a shrewd and knavish sprite', fond of practical jokes and mischief (II.i.33).

When things begin Hermia and Lysander are lovers, but Helen has been jilted by Demetrius – formerly, as he confesses, betrothed to her, but now determined to have Hermia instead. He has no qualms about getting her savage father to threaten her, as by law he can, with death or a nunnery if she refuses him. Conduct like this ought surely to exclude any man from the benefits of a happy ending, but Shakespeare has no qualms about letting him off. Helena, faithful like Julia of Verona to her unworthy favourite, goes to the woods in pursuit of him, and in the hope of pleasing him betrays her bosom friend Hermia. Of the four only Hermia comes out tolerably well, and the moral seems to be that love, in male hearts at least, is haphazard, unstable, and egotistic. For Lysander, with the magic drops in his eyes, his Hermia becomes a 'Vile thing' (III.ii.260). Demetrius tells Hermia he would like to throw her lover's carcass to his dogs (III.ii.64).

Shakespeare may have been trying to teach men a lesson in self-restraint; but the women, as rivals, display the same venom. Romantic love is called into question more light-heartedly when the magic drops throw Titania into love with Bottom, despite the ass's head that Puck has clapped on him; and she declares her passion 'On the first view' (III.i). Bottom and his friends may be bungling actors, but their play reduces tragical love to farce. Altogether, in this play love 'comes in such a questionable shape' that we must wonder, as very often, what Shake-speare really thought of it. He may never actually have been able to make up his own mind.

The Merchant of Venice (1596-98)

'Is the *Merchant of Venice* a Problem play?' asks Salingar (*Dramatic Form* ch. 2). W. Cohen speaks of 'the difficulty of transforming the play into a paraphrasable meaning of any kind' (195). Shakespeare could not make 'an intellectually coherent whole' of it, concludes Murry (192). It stands out, in fact, as one of the clearest cases where Shakespeare's story can be taken only as a refracted picture of social cracks or tensions, class animosities, in his England, because it is impossible to make sense of it in any other way.

No other comedy by Shakespeare, except of course *A Midsummer Night's Dream*, contains anything so fabulous as the casket scene, or the pound of flesh, many versions of which were afloat in Europe; Sinsheimer cites one from Serbia (79). The casket test is given a moral as well as supernatural colouring when Nerissa tells us that Portia's dying father was inspired to knowledge of how to ensure her happiness (I.ii.26 ff.). Portia herself does not feel that she owes him any thanks for it.

There is much good and varied prose in the first three Acts, much less in the rest. This partly corresponds with a mixing up of realism and fantasy, which no doubt strikes us more than it did the first audiences. When reality turns into Shylock, the discordance becomes extreme for us. Hatred of Jews had been kept alive in England by religious pro-paganda ever since their expulsion three centuries before, but this gave them an aspect more demonic than simply wicked, and to an ordinary Elizabethan – at any rate, before he saw this play – Shylock would be a kind of Caliban-monster. To us, without Shylock his Venice would be an uninteresting place, and after his downfall the play is over; Act V is only lyrical poetry and a mildly amusing joke.

Poetic drama may be possible – indeed, credible – only when its events are free to float on the tides of imagination, not chained to terra firma. But contradictions and improbabilities are multiplied here beyond bounds. It is unbelievable that a wealthy philanthropist like Antonio should find himself, all of a sudden, both friendless and penniless. Has he no house to sell, or mortgage? Shakespeare has to leave him a blurred, ambiguous figure, to deter us from asking such questions. Bassanio goes off to Belmont without telling him about the caskets, and passes the three months before the bond falls due in enjoying Portia's company and hospitality. He is only a few hours' distance away, yet these two devoted friends never think of letting each other know how things are going with them.

Lancelot Gobbo, again, must be Shylock's apprentice, not house-servant; otherwise it would be pointless for his master to complain of his being 'Snail-slow in profit', and Lancelot would not be so hesitant about running away (and incurring penalties by breaking his contract). We are asked to suppose that this wealthy Jewish businessman's entire establish-ment consists of his daughter and one obviously incompetent assistant – a Christian. Portia wants to dazzle her husband and his friend by rendering them a wonderful service, but Italy must be very short of lawyers if a young lady can learn overnight to do better than any of them. Her appearance in court makes effective theatre, however, and that is enough for Shakespeare.

Portia is a lady residing outside Venice, in a sphere of her own, which heightens her magnetism as a being above and beyond the everyday world. Morocco extols her as a 'shrine', a 'saint', drawing pilgrims from far and wide (II.vii). We do not know how she has come to acquire so magnificent a reputation, at her age. But Shakespeare has embarked on a story which threatens to burst the bounds of comedy; aggressively male passions are seizing control, and can be thwarted only by a potent feminine spell, a heroine from a fairy-tale to play the part – in male guise – of *dea ex machina*.

To be equal to this, Portia can be a natural woman only at intervals. She has the makings of several heroines, not fully amalgamated into one personality. Her chats with Nerissa about men and their ways show a surprising knowledge of them; her jokes, especially about the missing rings (V.i), can be unexpectedly free. She is intelligent and energetic, and makes up her plan for saving Antonio out of her own head, just after assuring Bassanio that as 'an unlessoned girl' (III.ii.160) she will always depend on his counsel and guidance. These two have been learning to love each other for months, but it is typical of our author that we are not shown anything of this. Most of what they say to each other is in a formal tone; Portia has a taste for long set speeches, displays of elocution, and seems more interested in the relations between husband and wife than those between lovers. Early on she is compared to her Roman namesake, and the two owe something to the same tributary stream in Shakespeare's imagination. 'I am half yourself' (III.ii.249): each wife claims the right to know her husband's problems, to share fully in his life – a long step towards a claim of equality.

Portia is related to the leading lawyer Bellario. We do not know whether her father was a professional man, a great merchant, or a landed aristocrat. In Venice these vocations might not be far apart, as Shakespeare was probably aware. But his Bassanio is very definitely a nobleman and nothing else, who has spent more than his means by living in style, and has run up debts which only a wealthy marriage can enable him to clear off. He is regularly addressed as 'lord', and is clearly of higher rank than any of his associates. To go to Belmont with a retinue worthy of him, he needs another three thousand ducats to furnish him out. As he admits, he has nothing to offer Portia but his name. He is a gentlemanly fortune-hunter, of good carriage and well-meaning, but not nearly good enough to deserve such a prize.

Venice is somehow not as cheerful a place as it ought to be. From the start Antonio looks as world-weary as 'his grandsire cut in alabaster' (I.i.84). His depression seems to foretell shadows falling across the world of comedy. Whatever its sources, there is besides a malignity in his persecution of Shylock, and his boasting of it, that matches the Jew's own retaliatory venom. Gratiano, that amusing chatterbox, talks with unexpected gravity – and with no dramatic purpose – about the satiety that follows quickly on all happiness (II.vi.8 ff.). He is thinking of Lorenzo's coming elopement with Jessica; but his words strike a note of coming disillusion for all lovers, himself among them. At Belmont Lorenzo philosophizes about the cause of Jessica's sadness when she listens to sweet music (V.i.70 ff.).

It is not too speculative to detect in all this a morbidity generated by the unresting competitiveness of life in Venice, or rather in London. Shakespeare was living in a jungle of business greeds and worries, with luxury and poverty side by side and the hardships of the poor worsening. This play suggests many misgivings in his mind on the subject of wealth. Antonio's failure to enjoy life is needed, as well as his charities, to excuse him for being so rich. In oblique fashion Bassanio's rejection of the gold and silver caskets, his talk of the world's false shows and gauds, are a foretaste of many louder cries in later plays. They are more proper to Shakespeare, or to a Romeo about to take his own life, than to Bassanio – who, after all, has come to Belmont to look for bullion.

Shylock in his gaberdine may have a mythic aspect, but he combines it with something unpleasantly well-known to Englishmen: the sharp-clawed greed of the moneylender. To denounce this ugly reality is Antonio's mission in the play, though an incongruous one for a great capitalist. He gives expression to the misery of a multitude of hapless borrowers caught in the mantrap. Usurers were terrible figures in sixteenth-century Europe, and in some regions for long after. England was full of debtors and creditors, and many writers were denouncing the moneylenders (McVeagh 16–19). Their profits formed one strand in the complex unfolding of capitalism. Antonio despises and reviles Shylock not primarily because he is a Jew, like others in Venice, but because he wrings profit out of men's misfortunes. It is on the score of his 'moneys' and his 'usances' that Antonio has 'rated' him on the Rialto (I.iii.104–5). Shylock in turn hates Antonio not primarily as a Jew-baiter (against whom he could take legal action) but as one whose foolish benevolence, in lending money gratis to those in need, spoils the market for the usurer. This complaint is repeated five times over – three times in Act III Scene 1 alone. Antonio himself gives it as the reason why Shylock wants to destroy him (III.iii.21–4).

Merely as a moneylender with a professional grievance, Shylock would be no more than a vulgar bloodsucker. As mouthpiece of an injured people, an insulted creed, he becomes something different. Under stress of emotion he can move from his private grudge to the broader grievances of his community. It is natural for him to like to tell himself, and a co-religionist, that it is as a Jew that Antonio has harassed him. 'He hates our sacred nation' (I.iii.45) – Shylock does not forget that he belongs to a Chosen as well as ill-used People. What drives him from the narrower to the wider feeling, and sets Shakespeare's imagination working for instead of against him, is the fresh and worse injury of his daughter's elopement with Lorenzo, carrying with her a store of his jewellery and money. That he is entitled to justice against Lorenzo, as a thief, is acknowledged by the Doge, who even takes part personally in an attempt to arrest the culprit (II.viii.4–5); but the guilty pair escape to Genoa. They soon return and are sheltered from the law by Portia at Belmont; the fact that Lorenzo is an absconding criminal is quietly forgotten by all, including Shakespeare. Portia then goes off to Venice to play her role of legal expert, leaving Lorenzo – very imprudently, one must think – in charge of all her possessions.

Shylock is left to revenge himself on Antonio, who has now become for him the embodiment of all Christian injustice. 'I'll torture him', snarls Shylock (III.i.109–10). But he can now take on a tragic aspect, because he is no longer thinking only of his own grievances but identifies himself with his community, condemned to live under a 'curse' (III.i.79–80). His passionate outburst to two of the jeering Christians in Act III Scene i is, though in prose, one of the most eloquent speeches Shakespeare ever wrote. By thinking of himself as a victim of religious oppression, and as such the spokesman of a whole people, he ennobles himself and exalts the bloodthirsty reprisal he is planning – on their behalf now, as well as his own. His drama rises far above the common level of the Elizabethan 'revenge play'.

Shylock himself is not a persecuted Jew; nor have the Jews of Venice collectively any tangible grievances to complain of. They have their synagogue, and their right both to practise their religion and to make money in the city is well established. When Shylock begins to speak on behalf of a wronged people, it is only of their history at large that he can with any propriety be talking. Shakespeare must have known something about this: it was only a century since the expulsion of the Jews from Spain and Portugal. When Shylock refuses double or treble repayment of the loan, and is ready to sacrifice the money lent rather than forgo his pound of flesh, a sense of honour is chaining him to what has become for him a duty. 'I have an oath in heaven', not to be broken – 'No, not for Venice' (V.iv.225–7): words curiously akin to Prince Florizel's in *The Winter's Tale*, when ordered to renounce his love instead of, like Shylock, hate: 'Not for Bohemia!'

Yet there was still something left for Shakespeare's imaginative sympathies to supply, to expand the figure of Shylock into the towering archetypal shape that it has for us today. The time-honoured 'Chain of Being', which linked all created things into a single series from high to low (Tillyard, *World Picture*), and helped to sustain the metaphysics of Order, may not have meant much to Shakespeare; but he had something of his own in its place: easy passage from the particular to the general and from there to the universal. 'Hath not a Jew eyes? hath not a Jew hands? …' So have many other ill-fated beings, with – in Christian thinking – better claim on our interest. Shylock goes on to make himself – as Antonio has done more practically but less broadly – a champion of the oppressed. He reminds the court of how Christian Venice treats its slaves; he is the first of many Jews who, in modern times, were to speak for all humanity. He even reminds the Venetians of how they treat beasts of burden. By saying such things he is challenging the sacred and absolute rights of ownership. He is, of course, no revolutionary. He is concerned only to point out that one oppressor is as good or bad as another; that cruelty is cruelty, however respectable the perpetrator. His antagonists, Portia among them, have no reply to offer.

'A day in April never came so sweet', or well-apparelled, Portia's servant tells her, in the lyrical strain that anyone in Shakespeare can command when required – as Bassanio's messenger announcing his approach and bearing 'gifts of rich value' (II.ix.86 ff.). In this play the aristocratic mode of living is drawn with a surer hand than the poet had possessed earlier. It is a very expensive one. Bassanio's attendants are decked out in borrowed plumage. In England improvident gentlemen were being stripped of their manors by moneylenders. Antonio, a kinsman of Bassanio, is supposedly a merchant, but there is nothing mercantile about him except his argosies floating like dreams on distant waters. He has no partners, clerks, account-books, so far as we can see;

only risky ventures and creditors. His lavish offer of all his resources to a confessed spendthrift like Bassanio (I.i.153 ff.) is quixotic.

Shakespeare clearly felt, as most Tudor writers did, that a society governed by acquisitive instincts, greed for money, must be a bad one. Yet earning his bread as he did in the commercial heart of England, and at such a time, he could not want to see the clock turned back. As Bishop Hall pointed out, the shipping trade was financed mainly by loan-capital, and would be brought to a halt if no good Christian could charge or pay interest (379–80). It was desirable that overseas commerce should be romanticized, idealized, so as not to disturb the old ideal of a rationally ordered community. In the archbishop's beehive, in *Henry V*, merchants who 'venture trade abroad' have their contribution to make, though it may not be obvious what sort of bees they resemble. Antonio's management of his fortune belongs to the popular tradition of an older London where rich men poured their wealth into good works and charities.

Shylock, on the other hand, deems Antonio a 'prodigal' (III.i.42). He keeps no reserves, despite the many hazards of his business so graphically depicted by his enemy (I.iii.21 ff.). He has other anxious creditors, and finds that Jews are not the only ones who may grow 'cruel' (III.ii.317). Shylock's opinion of him is close to what real businessmen in London, the puritanizing bourgeoisie grimly in earnest about piling up money, would think of such an amateur as Antonio in their midst. Shylock in a way speaks for them too, and theatregoers unfriendly to them would easily see in him a first cousin to a hard-hearted money-grubbing Puritan. Phrases like 'my sober house', a 'thrifty mind', mark his affinities clearly; so do his miserliness, churlishness, and austere dislike of masques, feasts, 'the vile squealing' of the fife, and all such 'shallow foppery' (II.v.30–35). Fiedler has ground for seeing him as a representa-tive of puritan asceticism, Portia as less a Christian than an embodiment of Venetian hedonism (109).

It must appear contradictory to find in Shylock features both of a protester against social oppression and of a member of a grasping bourgeoisie. But in England this class was itself moving towards opposi-tion to government policies as well as court culture. Historically such a class, challenging an old regime, has always had to look for supporters by taking up – verbally, at least – the cause of the masses. Shylock is one of those greater Shakespearian characters who are too full of vitality of their own to be pressed into the service of an allegory, but who would not be great if they were not rooted in historical soil.

In England the term 'Jew' had lingered on as a piece of jocular abuse. 'If thou wilt go with me to the ale-house', says Launce to his crony Speed, 'so; if not, thou art an Hebrew, a Jew' (*TGV* II.v). 'You rogue, they

were bound, every man of them,' Falstaff affirms, 'or I am a Jew else, an
Ebrew Jew' (*1H.IV* II.iv.197–8). More crudely, Macbeth's witches have
'liver of blaspheming Jew' as an ingredient in their cauldron. Shakespeare
draws a line between the unthinking prejudice of the streets and a more
enlightened view: that a Jew ceased to be obnoxious as soon as he gave up
his bad habits. To satisfy the more conventionally minded majority of
the audience, these habits had to include creed as well as trade; and this
must now appear outrageous. But in England and all over Europe
Christians were being induced or compelled to change Churches; and
Shakespeare troubled himself little about articles of faith.

At any rate there is nothing 'racist' in the attitude of the Venetian
elite, from the Doge down. Jessica is given a ready welcome to their fold.
She is one of those makeshift characters whom Shakespeare shows in one
light or another, as dramatic convenience requires. Lorenzo calls her
'wise, fair, and true' (II.vi.56); she is wise enough to bring him a handsome
– if stolen – dowry, and has had enough education to exchange classical
allusions with her lover (V.i.1 ff.). Lancelot likes her, but he has known
poverty and is conscious of his country's overpopulated condition; he is
humorously dubious about conversions – they will raise the price of
pork, and 'we were Christians enow before; e'en as many as could well
live, one by another' (III.v.19 ff.). But Jessica's marriage is more readily
understandable if we think of her as the daughter of an English *nouveau
riche*. Marriages between middle-class heiresses and needy gentlemen
were multiplying. If Shakespeare looked towards a blending of class
qualities, he may be supposed to have approved of such unions.

There was no stage of his life when Shakespeare, as revealed in his
plays, felt himself to be living in a harmonious environment; he was too
much a social realist ever to lapse into comfortable acceptance of things
as they were. This play is a memorial to one of the times when tensions
within them pressed most sharply on his consciousness. Opposing forces
of good and evil are concentrated, more distinctly than in any other
comedy, in two figures: Portia and Shylock. Shylock gives 'a local habita-
tion and a name', fittingly alien and threatening, to disruptive forces
filtering into social life, much as Richard III sucks up into himself the
ruthless egotism of feudalism. Portia's task is to defeat and exorcize a
lurking evil that imperils Venice. This scheme of salvation fails to be
really convincing because – Shakespeare's realism compels him to admit
– good and evil, when clothed in human, social forms, cannot be so
neatly separated: they intermingle. And no moral victory can be won by
legal legerdemain. In the trial scene it is hard to dismiss Bradshaw's
objection that Portia's continually addressing Shylock as 'Jew' is 'coolly,
deliberately offensive' (25). (The Doge addresses him by name.) A
suspicion may even cross the mind that her grand speech on Mercy is

designed (by Shakespeare the showman, if not by her) to put Shylock in the wrong. By refusing to show mercy he disqualifies himself from having any title to it when his turn comes to need it – like the conspirators in *Henry V* Act II.

No other character except Falstaff, his humorous counterpart as a critic or mocker of conventional standards, can have escaped as much as the Jew does from Shakespeare's leading-strings. His creator has to rescue his play from the ruin threatened to its fabric by Shylock, and somehow send spectators home from a happy ending. Shylock's enemies have done their Christian duty by waiving the death penalty for attempted murder, and they have left him with half his capital. Christianity has demonstrated its superior virtue, and if Shylock is compelled to renounce his religion, that is a further benefit conferred upon him.

The concluding Act V is far more poetical than dramatic, and unconvincing because, as Levi says, Shylock's shadow falls across the Belmont garden (169). Another reader refers to the long passage on music, and the symbolic association for Elizabethans of music with order on a lofty plane, and points out that it is needed to smooth away the dissonances of the trial scene (Stevens). It is really a confession of failure to convince us that this charmed world of the aristocracy rests on firm foundations. Music and moonlight can lull our doubts only for the moment, and allow us to think of Portia's entry into the garden, and her words 'Let me give light' (V.i.130), though spoken in jest, as the promise of a better world. Talk of 'celestial harmony' does not come well from such a scapegrace as Lorenzo. The mischief personified in Shylock cannot end with his downfall, because it is not confined to him; in some degree it infects the whole social order. No happy ending is in prospect for the like of old Gobbo, who will still be 'exceeding poor' (II.ii.48); slaves will still be slaves, debtors will still languish in jails. A last thought may be that within half a century Jews were to be readmitted into England, and that Shakespeare's play may have had some share in bringing this about.

As You Like It (1598–99)

Discords in Shakespeare's world were kept, in his first comedies, to a mainly farcical level; in *The Merchant of Venice* they swelled up formidably, and could be overcome only by being translated into a folk-tale idiom and solution. Romantic comedy had made a limping start in *The Two Gentlemen of Verona*; it was now to enter its brief, insecure season of bloom. *As You Like It* can be read as a recoil from the violence of *The Merchant of Venice*, a continuation from the rhapsodic, but artificial, harmony of the moonlit garden. In *The Merchant of Venice* the villain was baffled; in *As You Like It* the virtuous have to run away and hide in the woods. There are two villains now for them to contend with instead of one; but in spite of their villainous bluster, these two turn out to be only men of straw.

As You Like It is Shakespeare's fantasia on the literary-pastoral style, so tenacious in its appeal to urbanized mankind. Tales of life in the greenwood carried with them legendary memories of a golden age, to which many looked back, as he sometimes did, with nostalgia, or affectionate irony. A good old duke has been in exile for years, dethroned by his brother, but neither he nor his supporters have taken any steps to restore him. They form a cheerful, carefree band, though forest life is not without hardships. This Arden is a wilderness, like many forest or fen areas in Shakespeare's England: unlike them it has wild beasts as well as sheep and shepherds, though they appear only when the prompter calls them. Doubtless the duke has been a good ruler, but even so he has benefited from the lessons of rough weather and roofless skies: they have taught him, as they are to teach Lear, that he is only a human being like the rest. Under this tutoring his followers have become his 'brothers in exile' (II.i.1), as Henry V's, in the extremity of war, are his 'band of brothers'.

As a discussion piece the play has less word-juggling than *Love's Labour's Lost*, much more sparkle and humour. Episodic scenes, of individuals or groups brimfull of their own concerns or ideas, succeed one another. In the dearth of any masculine activity in the forest there is all the more room for Rosalind, who has been forced to follow her father the duke much later into exile, to take the central place and charm us and her hearers; the fountain of her wit and joy of life can play freely. There are scoundrels and plots in the bad old world outside, but we have no need to take them seriously. *A Midsummer Night's Dream* was a play of the moonlight, as *The Merchant of Venice* ended by being; *As You Like It* belongs to daylight and sunshine and, we feel, to youth, as if an old order were getting ready to depart.

Of the two fair cousins, before their exodus from court it is Celia, heiress to the usurper, who takes the lead. It is she who proposes flight to the forest and insists on accompanying Rosalind, who adds the idea – a well-worn one with Shakespeare – of male disguise. In the woods Rosalind comes to the front. She has been used to winning approval by 'silence' and 'patience' (I.iii.78) while living at court on sufferance; she now has freedom and love to exhilarate her, as well as fresh air. Celia makes a perfect companion; it is now her turn to be more quiet and reserved, though never dull. Rosalind is intelligent, witty, charming, and quite ready to manage other people's affairs besides her own – like Portia, though the affairs are of a more trifling sort. We are easily convinced of how many fathom deep in love she is (IV.i.200–1). But there is no love-making between her and Orlando; that is left to less worthy clients of Cupid, like Touchstone. Shakespeare keeps his most likeable Comedy heroine, still garbed as a young man, lecturing to her lover on the follies of love.

Orlando has been deprived of education by a venomous elder brother, yet he has all the manners and impulses of a polished gentleman. His speech to the exiled duke is elaborately flowery (II.vii.). Shakespeare is adhering to folk-tale convention: blue blood is born with instincts that need no teachings but it helps to make Orlando an uninteresting though very respectable hero. His care for Adam, the faithful old servant who reaches the forest with him famished, does him credit; after that he has little to do beyond making up verses about Rosalind, carving her name on trees, and listening for hours to her banter without recognizing her.

These newcomers to the forest represent youth, but the only one of the duke's companions we get to know is the elderly nobleman Jaques, a misanthropist who insists on reminding us of the darker side of life which Shakespeare was unlikely to be able to forget for long. Most of the time the play is an unusually cheerful one, but there is frequent talk of 'railing', that cherished relief of stage malcontents. Celia very early proposes a railing at Fortune; Touchstone the jester does the same not much later (I.ii; II.vii); Jaques, an addict, feels impelled in one scene to rail at the first-born of Egypt; in another at the whole world and its miseries (II.v; III.ii.275). We first hear of this cross-grained, humorous philosopher, one of Shakespeare's more puzzling characters, lying under a tree and gazing at a wounded stag, whose plight inspires him to a string of comparisons with human beings injured or neglected by their fellows (II.i).

Jaques does not often seem born to be a reformer; he is content to hug his gloom and debate things endlessly, while doing nothing except that he has chosen the forest as his home. He prides himself on the travels he has made – probably the 'grand tour' – and on his deep 'rumination' over what he has seen (IV.i.17). Every profession brings its own special melancholy, he believes (IV.i.10 ff.): in other words, every kind of activity leads to disappointments, so men do well not to set themselves any goals. He enjoys meeting Touchstone, and invites Rosalind to a chat. The duke likes his company and serious conversation; Jaques, on the other hand, finds the duke 'too disputable', or argumentative (II.v).

Their chief sparring match (II.vii.46 ff.) seems related to the controversy brewing in the 1590s as to whether satire can be a wholesome social corrective, or is only a plague. Jaques feels that he could be a reformer as a satirist, if allowed full freedom of tongue to attack every sort of misbehaviour. The duke retorts that Jaques has been a libertine in his time, soiled with all the vices, and by harping on them would be spreading them wider. Jaques offers no rejoinder, and seems to accept this account of his past life. We may be hearing the Shakespeare of the Sonnets of remorse, in Jaques's disgust with the human condition. Instead of a direct answer he falls back on the stock defence of satirists: that in censuring moral ills he would not be attacking any individual reprobate. After an interruption the duke reflects on human woes, and Jaques makes his famous speech on the seven ages of man, ending in 'childishness and mere oblivion'. Arden, it seems, is no more than a little oasis in the wide wilderness of existence, like Portia's little candle 'in a naughty world' (*MV* V.i.91–2). At any rate Shakespeare must have found Jaques's gloom useful as a foil to Rosalind's high spirits.

He takes action only once, and then very properly, to prevent Touchstone from going through a bogus wedding to his shepherdess Audrey with the help of the hedge-priest Oliver Martext, whom he has somehow made her believe to be 'the vicar of the next village' (III.iii). Touchstone is a glib talker, with a love of verbal flourishes. He is Shakespeare's first professional court jester, apparently a man of breeding; out here in the forest he feels, as he says, like Ovid among the Goths (III.iii). He is devoted to his two young ladies but unsentimental about his rustic girl, and franker than most men in Shakespeare are about his physical needs. From him to Orlando, the romantic high-flier, we can see 'love' at two stages of evolution. A more laughable case of the ailment is poor Silvius's pursuit of Phebe, who, of course, is enamoured of the disguised Rosalind. All these variations effectively mimic the fashionable pastoral style.

Orlando's wicked brother Oliver and Celia's wicked father Frederick – who falls out with Oliver too – both suffer, like Richard III, from a feeling that nobody loves them, and are soured by the popularity of others. Brutal egotism brings its own penalty: a warning against individualism in its more antisocial forms. Frederick is 'rough and envious' (I.ii.229) and hates Rosalind because she outshines his daughter. Oliver cannot understand why his brother is loved, and he himself 'altogether misprised' (I.i.153 ff.). These two culprits provide Shakespeare, when he feels that enough time has gone by in amusing talk, with material for a flurry of melodramatic incidents. They are only reported, from off-stage, which may make them a shade less improbable. Magicians, like women of charm, are easily forgiven, and Shakespeare is the greatest magician of all; but even he, we must feel, sometimes tries to pull too much wool over our eyes.

In a hurry, as often, to wind up his story, he turns his offenders into a highly virtuous pair, transformed, like Bottom, in the twinkling of an eye. Forgiveness instead of revenge carries forward a leading idea from

The Merchant of Venice, but here it is scrambled together clumsily, with Orlando rescuing his brother from a lioness. 'Kindness, nobler ever than revenge' – Christianity ennobled, or grafted on to the aristocratic mode of thinking, – and 'nature', or kinship, made him risk his life for the man who had tried to kill him; and Oliver finds 'conversion' so sweet that he is a changed man (IV.iii). It is tempting to think that the audience was expected to guffaw at this, but disgusting to see Oliver rewarded on the spot with Celia, love bowling them over at first sight. A year's probation, as in *Love's Labour's Lost,* is the least that Shakespeare ought to have done to allay our indignation. Instead he bows to the convention that every young woman in a comedy must end with a husband – a notion derogatory to the new women of Shakespeare's day, by implying that marriage alone could give life any meaning for them.

Frederick is converted even more preposterously, by meeting 'an old religious man' while galloping into the forest to wreak further harm on the refugees (V.iv.157). A transfiguration as sudden as this is the spiritual parallel to love at first sight; Shakespeare may be hinting at some scepticism about both. In spite of this, the play has a trickle of biblical or other religious allusions, which Shakespeare did not take from his sources (Armstrong 111 ff.). It may be that the background of wanderings in the wilderness, and pastoral life, drew his mind back to Old Testament scenes. Still, his haste to finish things off detracts somewhat from the finale, where he – or Rosalind for him – like the detective at the end of a crime film, unravels all the tangled threads. Four couples are united; only one has the stamp of genuine love.

Much Ado about Nothing (1598)

After we emerge from the forest of Arden, comedy makes a further turn away from fantasy towards naturalism. The folk-tale species of plot is left behind; in *Much Ado* there is not even a girl dressed up as a man, and apart from the very implausible plot against Hero this is the most sturdily realistic of all. Two-thirds of the play is in prose, and Benedick, the person who along with Beatrice attracts us most, is essentially a prose-speaker, not one to think of entering a casket lottery for a wife, or to fall asleep in a woodland among the fairies. Don John is an off-the-peg villain, suited to comedy. Still, he is the cause of more mischief than the mere storm in a teacup that the title misleadingly advertises. Male jealousy was always a very grave matter with Shakespeare, whose readiness to champion the cause of women shows nowhere better than in his so often taking groundless jealousy as his target. Here it provokes a challenge to a seriously meant duel, even though, as things turn out, this is averted; in Shakespeare it is a rarity.

Benedick is given a testimonial at the outset: he has 'done good service' in the campaign just concluded; he is 'A lord to a lord, a man to a man', someone who does not stand on his rank (I.i.45). His employer Don Pedro testifies that he is 'of a noble strain, of approved valour and confirmed honesty' (II.i.355–7). His wit, however Beatrice may like to belittle it, goes beyond the verbal ping-pong of the early comedies; it has absorbed into itself a sturdy common-man vitality. There is much of Berowne in it, even a touch of Bottom. We can see here Shakespeare's amalgam of social qualities in a new and impressive form.

As a gentleman, courtier and soldier, Benedick can hardly be expected to be altogether prim and proper. Possibly Shakespeare forgot as soon as he had written them Beatrice's unexpected words about Benedick having once won her heart 'with false dice' (II.i.262–3); since Leonato and Hero, who are listening, make no comment, it may be taken that he was guilty of nothing worse than a flirtation, but the memory may have rankled in her mind. There are other hints of a fondness for the ladies, coupled with a strong aversion to marriage. Leonato jokes about this, and Don Pedro says that Benedick has 'twice or thrice cut Cupid's bow-string', or had affairs and gone off free (I.i.103; III.ii.9).

Beatrice is an orphan, though with a kindly uncle for guardian, and may have cultivated a prickly style of wit and manner, quite unlike any other Shakespearian heroine's, for protection. Her coming together with Benedick is a reversal of the overworked love at first sight. They are accustomed to carry on a 'merry war' or 'skirmish of wit' (I.i.57–9), and to encounter each other on level terms. Each is proud of being esteemed a wit, and their jokes sometimes carry a sting. Benedick is irritated at being accused of 'evermore tattling', and still more at being called 'the prince's fool', or jester (II.i). Beatrice is nettled at his saying that she steals her good things out of Boccaccio (II.i.114–15). They were among Shakespeare's best-liked characters, which shows that his audience could enjoy the spectacle of a man and woman fencing – and then loving – as equals, at least as well as it enjoyed horseplay like that of *The Taming of the Shrew*. Benedick is sturdily indifferent to witticisms from others, when he succumbs to love; they are no more than 'paper bullets of the brain' (II.iii.234).

He is confronted almost immediately by something more deadly, when he is called on to seal his love by fighting his friend Claudio and punishing his treatment of Hero. It does not occur to him – but it may now and then to us – that Beatrice is putting his life at risk in order to have justice done to her cousin. Women of the higher classes were trained to accept their men's code of honour, whose best apology was its being partly dedicated to their protection. But her abrupt and thrilling 'Kill Claudio' (IV.i.288) betokens a gathering emotional revolt of women against a morality heavily weighted in favour of men. Benedick is startled, but he has already shown his sympathy with the injured family (IV.i.243 ff.) and is quickly convinced that she is right. Next time they meet, her first question is whether he has delivered the promised challenge (V.ii), and again she shows no uneasiness over his danger, any more than Don Pedro does over either of his two followers. Dramatically, a good deal is lost; but Shakespeare must be taking care not to let his comedy get out of bounds, and turn into something different.

Hero is kept in the background; alone with her companions she can talk quite fluently; she is given two of the play's few references to Nature (III.i), which somehow seem to suit her. Her father talks lengthily to his brother about her misfortune, and his grief is genuine, but his language is stilted, with none of Shylock's tragic flashes. Claudio has little or nothing to recommend him, and no excuse but youth: he is somewhat younger than Benedick. He is interested in Hero's inheritance, and content to let the prince do his wooing for him (partly to gratify Shakespeare's love of masquerade). He parades his wit, after Hero's disgrace and supposed death, with an unfeeling jibe about the aggrieved father and uncle as 'two old men without teeth' (V.i.115). He and Benedick represent two distinct types of aristocrat, one of which Shakespeare is leaving behind as frivolous and useless. It is not merely Claudio's lack of years that makes him so; he and Don Pedro both show at their worst, and go on bantering Benedick until he dismisses their silly jokes with dignified firmness and withdraws from the prince's service. It is the play's most impressive speech, though only half a dozen lines of prose (V.i).

Once more a happy ending has to be fabricated. It is sadly incongruous in a play which, like the The Merchant of Venice in another fashion, has moved so far away from comedy. Light comedy without real emotional strain was something Shakespeare managed to keep to in The Taming of the Shrew, Love's Labour's Lost, As You Like It, and The Merry Wives of Windsor; but it did not come easily or naturally to him. All his major comedies raise 'burning moral questions', and solve them only in terms of 'theatrical ingenuity' (Salingar, Comedy 312). He gave his hearers plenty to laugh at, but unhappiness kept breaking in.

The Merry Wives of Windsor (1597)

Shakespeare's only English domestic comedy, nearly all in prose, has been too often underrated. Saintsbury was one of the few to do it justice (189); M.C. Bradbrook acknowledges it to be 'the most prosaic drama Shakespeare ever wrote', but recalls Dryden's tribute to it as the first really well made play in English (Shakespeare 75–6). Bradley found it 'very entertaining', but was disgusted by Falstaff's humiliating defeat (247–8). Falstaff is commonly thought to have shrunk in stature; it is rather that London and England and the clash of great events are reduced to Windsor and provincial intrigue. It is Falstaff's paradox that he is the supreme comic character, yet he does not belong to comedy. To be truly himself he needs a setting like that of *Henry IV*, peopled with serious personages trumpeting their strenuous messages in blank verse, for Falstaff the arch-unbeliever to direct his wit at and stand out in brilliant contrast to.

Yet much of his talk is as sparkling as ever. He is still a fat man with a lean purse; one of his best utterances is a complaint about his necessities and the shifts he is put to, which compromise his knightly 'honour' (II.ii). He resorts to a stratagem that afforded Elizabethan humorists a stock topic: a plan for getting money out of well-to-do burghers' wives by tickling their vanity. 'Money is a good soldier, sir, and will on' (II.ii.159): in one sentence a military society turns into a commercial one. Meta-phors of ships and voyages are frequent; Mrs Ford and Mrs Page are to be his East and West Indies (I.iii).

Falstaff is adopting the style of a new age when he practises economy by dismissing a pair of his disreputable hangers-on – a comic miniature of the disbanding of great feudal households in Tudor days, but also a parody of his own dismissal by Henry V. He fails to foresee that they will get their own back on him by giving away his schemes. He now has a pageboy named Robin, one more of Shakespeare's precocious juveniles, who is also playing him false. This is a society where mutual trust and loyalty are waning. Falstaff is a product of it. He has been a failure in life, poor because he chose a life of freedom from conventional bondages, a life of toping and ease and wit; he is the great 'dropout' of literature. What we are offered in this play is the spectacle of a man, vastly cleverer than we are, overreaching himself in a way that we feel we ourselves could have avoided.

We can even – unlike Bradley – rejoice at his defeat, because like his rejection by the new king his fiasco at Windsor saves his comic 'innocence' from the taint of squalid success. Worldly gear is not for him. His wonderful wit was bestowed on him for our enrichment, not for his. Alone in the world now, Falstaff does not make this a matter for pathos: he can face his situation philosophically, and fears nobody, as he tells Master Brook, 'because I know also life is a shuttle', at the mercy of accident (V.i). The play ends in harmony, more credibly than in the melodramatic comedies; everyone is ready to see his own errors, and laugh at them, or to make the best of things, and Sir John can join in the merrymaking.

It is a play, often farcical, about him, but at the same time a social study. Class relations provide the basis, mainly those between gentry and burghers – not noblemen, and not rich London merchants; this Windsor is closer to Stratford than to London. Falstaff looks down on citizens, and they look with suspicion at gentlemen on the fringes of court and fashion, like him or Fenton: a small landowner like Slender, with no frills, is more in their line. Neither class shines. Shakespeare takes few pains to polish Fenton up into an acceptable lover. Ford is foolishly jealous, Dr Caius the physician ridiculously French. The middle-class women are admirable in their way, but Mrs Page is no more sensible in wanting Dr Caius for a son-in-law than her husband, who wants the dim-witted Slender.

At the close of a comedy of manners like this, on English ground, Shakespeare can feel free to point out its lessons more directly than in his romantic comedies. He preaches against fornication in the song of the children, got up as fairies, 'Lust is but a bloody fire' – a text as ill-chosen for such singers as Adonis's lecture to Venus about lust and love. Falstaff's object was not this, but cash; but he counted on the women being desirous of an affair with him – very absurdly, as Mrs Page tells him; he himself confesses the folly of 'lust and late-walking', as something that ought to be made known 'through the realm' (V.v.139 ff.). Ford seems thoroughly cured of his silly jealousy. Young Fenton, who has married Anne Page without leave, is eloquent on the sin of all parents who force their offspring into uncongenial marriages (V.v.211 ff.).

The choice of royal Windsor for Falstaff's last appearance was a compliment to the queen, probably on the occasion of a Garter ceremony. Seemingly Elizabeth had too much sense of humour to take offence at the last scene, where Mrs Quickly, of all people, in blank verse for the first and last time in her life, calls on the 'fairies' to bless Windsor Castle and its owner, as Oberon and his retinue have blessed the palace at Athens.

Twelfth Night (1601-02)

Twelfth Night can be thought of as belonging to 1601, Shakespeare's farewell to romantic comedy when he had already really left it behind and begun moving into new territories. He uses again devices already employed with good effect; there is even an occasional return to rhyme, and nearly all the last Act is in verse, which the situation does not really require. What is new is comic, not romantic. Shakespeare's comedy framework had always been elastic, and his treatment of detail is as carefree as ever. None of his other girls disguised as men thinks of pretending to be a eunuch, and he has surely forgotten Viola's pretence of it by the time the Duke unclasps his 'secret soul' to the youth who has just entered his service, and chooses him to plead his amorous cause with Olivia (I.ii.55; I.iv.13–14). To C.L. Barber it appears that transvestism is employed here so as to 'renew in a special way our sense of the difference' between men and women (245). More recognizably, it is woven into the plot, entwined with various other strands, with greater adroitness and intricacy than in any previous play.

But Life is the great jester, or Puck, and plays tricks with human beings in order to awaken them to its realities. The Duke's infatuation has a swooning, effeminate note, like Romeo's first love: it is a pose of the idle rich, wanting to show themselves more soulful than their coarse neighbours. He and Olivia both have to be jolted into genuine feeling, taken by surprise as Romeo is when he meets Juliet. In Viola's argument with Olivia about love there is wit on both sides, Shakespeare's unfailing antidote to sentimentality (I.v.170 ff.). Neither alludes to Olivia's dead brother, for whom she has vowed seven years' mourning; Viola makes no apology for intruding on her, but simply tells her she is 'too proud'. Olivia is left musing with fatalistic resignation: 'What is decreed, must be'. Viola has just lost her own brother, but he is already forgotten, as Olivia's will soon be.

It is surprising to be told that 'Olivia is irresistible in her passion; the Duke's sensibility is charming, taking' (French 121). More unsentimentally Levin cites Johnson's view of Viola as a 'schemer', and is doubtful as to whether she is genuinely 'romantic and idealistic' (*Love* 120). She really is, but all romance has taken on by now a dream-like quality. Caught in a freakish triangle, it has reached a limit beyond which lies only farce. There is nothing in any Illyrian attachment to interest us. Olivia's vow is clearly meant to look excessive, a self-display like the young men's vow of seclusion in Navarre. When we first see her she is amusing herself with her jester; an hour later she is in love. Always unpredictable, love is now still more capricious; a wealthy noblewoman falls into the same snare as the shepherdess in Arden, a passion for a girl disguised as a youth. It belongs as much to fantasy as the drug-induced fervours of the Athenian forest; Shakespeare employs for it a suitably artificial dialogue style, with single-line exchanges, rhymed couplets, little real feeling.

Malvolio, cross-gartered and simpering, is not much more ridiculous than his betters in love. Olivia herself feels that her 'madness' and his are not far apart (III.iv.14–15). Emotion has become histrionic, or turned 'high fantastical' as the Duke calls his own love (I.i.15). Viola's twin brother Sebastian wonders whether he has gone out of his mind when he finds Olivia instantly in love with him (IV.iii.1 ff.); this follows neatly on Malvolio, who thinks her in love with *him*, protesting that he is quite sane.

Accident, coincidence, illusion, prevail. Viola speaks of the vices of 'our frail blood' (III.iv.354–5); human beings seem insubstantial creatures easily blown about by vanity or whim. 'Jove, not I, is the doer', Malvolio exclaims as he sees a brilliant future fall into his lap (III.iv.86). This (with 'Jove' for God) is conventional piety, but it is of a piece with the way the heroines resign their hopes to Fate or fortune. Viola's fictitious sister 'never told her love', but wasted away (II.iv.110 ff.). In a society bereft of orderly opinions and rational ideals, individuals are less ready for sensible planning and achievement.

Antonio the sea-captain resolves to follow Sebastian at all hazards: 'I do adore thee so' (II.i). As Shakespeare's never robust faith in romantic love wanes, he seems to turn away to friendship between men, which he had treated humorously in *The Two Gentlemen of Verona*, seriously in *The Merchant of Venice*. In the Antonio of both *The Merchant of Venice* and *Twelfth Night*, feeling is evidently stronger in the elder man. So far as the story of *Twelfth Night* is concerned, there is no real need of this character, and friendship like his sounds overblown; it invites Levin's suspicion of 'a homosexual attraction' (*Love* 142). But it gives Shakespeare a chance to upbraid Viola (mistaken for her brother) with ingratitude, and to let her protest that this is the vice she most detests (III.iv.345 ff.). It may be that the poet was working off some private sense of injury; ingratitude is a sin that recurs often in his work. Accused by the Duke of piracy – his neck in danger – Antonio, instead of defending himself, breaks into another tirade about 'Sebastian', whom he has rescued from the sea, refusing to give him back his purse (V.i.75 ff.).

Olivia can be angry enough to call her uncle Toby (such terms were loose; he may be an elder cousin) a 'ruffian', and tax him with chronic brawling (IV.i.55–7). Toby is a kinsman of Falstaff too, but not a close one. He is not a thinker, and he lives in a corner of nowhere instead of in London within earshot of the great world and its doings. We get no satire on it from him, and not much wit, but plenty of rumbustious humour; when well supplied with wine he has a hearty fondness for life, unlike the more refined characters. He too is hard up; he sponges on Olivia, and gets money out of his friend Sir Andrew by encouraging him to hope for Olivia's hand and fortune. Here is friendship of another species, a comic version of Iago's for Roderigo. Toby is no poltroon, and when he is wounded in a fight, and irritable, he lets Andrew know his candid opinion of him (V.i.105–6).

Falstaff used to promise marriage to women he got money from; Toby does better, by really marrying Maria, by way of reward for the fooling of Malvolio which is her inspiration. He thus secures an active, practical helpmate, who may put his affairs in better order. She is Olivia's 'gentlewoman' (I.v.162), not a menial servant but far below the managing young ladies before her like Portia and Rosalind. It is time for a woman of more modest station to show what she can do. High-born dames have come to feel they are hapless sports of chance; Maria does not philosophize, but she knows how to play her cards.

Malvolio, the play's newest personage, seems to be of Shakespeare's own coining. He belongs to the middling ranks and, like very many others, is a would-be entrant into the charmed circle of aristocracy. He is, we can feel sure, a reliable and competent steward; Olivia is quite on his side against Toby, and he is known to and esteemed by the Duke (V.i.378–9). He is a stickler for order and regularity, intolerant of such indulgences as noisy nocturnal revelry or bear-baiting, over which he has got Olivia's gentleman Fabian into trouble with her (II.v.8–9). In addition he gets Antonio into jail (V.i.274–5); we do not know how or why, but the fact accentuates his sour disposition.

He comes to grief because ambition and conceit make him look too high, too hastily, and sacrifice substance for shadow. His hopes may not be quite so ridiculous as the costume that Maria tricks him into donning. He is entitled to call himself a 'gentleman' (IV.ii.84); he may very probably come from some modest gentry family and, like Fabian, be one of the 'serving gentlemen' to be found in all great households. Stewards of great estates did sometimes rise high, by merit and luck. Malvolio's error is simply his failure to see through a trick, because he is blinded by inflated vanity and lack of any sense of humour. As Olivia tells him, he is 'sick of self-love' (I.v.88). In *Much Ado about Nothing* a trick was played on Beatrice and Benedick with the friendly purpose of making each think the other in love with him or her. It is a measure of the distance between that comedy, where all breathe much the same social air, and *Twelfth Night*, where classes are separating, that there a similar trick is played with very unfriendly intentions: a joke, but a cruel and malicious one. There is no pretence of reconciliation at the end, and Malvolio goes off threatening indiscriminate revenge.

He is not to be too indulgently viewed. As Maria says, he is not a genuine 'puritan' (II.iii.151 ff.), actuated by principles worthy of respect; he is simply impatient to rise in the world and then, as he tells us himself, 'wash off gross acquaintance' (II.v.165–6). Daydreaming such as he gives way to is a perennial source of mirth to others, because – as, perhaps, with all the weaknesses we laugh at – we are conscious of the same inclination in ourselves. Sir Andrew represents an opposite aspect of life in Illyria; his pursuits are eating and drinking, dancing and bear-baiting (I.iii.95). He and Toby are entertaining but disreputable; Malvolio is respectable but disagreeable. The play's best scenes combine their oddities, in comedy of a high order. But comedy itself is nearing its end. Shakespeare has been able to shuffle his resources once more into a fresh pattern, captivating but holding out no way forward. Its opposites belong to a society ready to break apart. Across dilettante posturing and vinous jollity falls the shadow of a new order. The youthful spirit so vivacious in *Love's Labour's Lost* has faded. Young ladies languish; young men for them are hard to find. The jester, who ought to spread only mirth, seems instead part of this downhill drift. Twelfth Night is the time when Christmas revelries come to an end.

Comedy Themes

Wit and Humour

Puritans of the decades after Shakespeare were too often humourless beings, as Milton was by comparison with him. When men are still groping, and see no clear way forward, they can laugh at themselves and their puzzlements; when the road seems to have been found, it is time for joking to be laid aside. Shakespeare lived when social tensions were strong enough to stimulate literature, without overpowering it. He shone in both wit and humour, an uncommon combination; perhaps above all in humour, the more democratic or 'human' faculty. His gift of laughter broadened by stages from simple forms, like punning or clowning, into something more significant, part of his commentary on the life going on round him, from Romeo overfull of sighs to Dogberry on police duty, inflated by self-importance.

Whatever its social, moralistic functions, comedy's first business has always been entertainment. This could itself be credited with wholesome properties of another sort, as it is in *The Taming of the Shrew*, where medical opinion is cited in support of the view that 'melancholy is the nurse of frenzy', while 'mirth and merriment' is health-giving and 'lengthens life' (Induction ii.127 ff.). Life, then, is to be enjoyed, not consumed in a fever of effort or ambition. When Lucentio comes to Padua to study philosophy, his manager Tranio observes that Ovid need not be altogether eclipsed by Aristotle (*TS* I.i.29 ff.). Gratiano's recommendation of carefree hilarity instead of morose gloom is in the same key (*MV* I.i.79 ff.). A star danced when Beatrice was born, and she often 'waked herself with laughing' at a silly dream of being sad (*MAAN* II.i.308 ff.).

Comedy has often meant one class laughing at another, but in some other ways it can draw the classes together in amusement at things that tickle them all. This is especially true of its simpler elements, where mankind's physical self is in question: we can all fall over buckets. Tipsiness is another leveller. Shakespeare was not much indebted to it, finding the human race comical enough even when sober. One of his few tipplers is Sir Toby Belch who, when in need of a surgeon, is indignant at learning that the man is drunk, at eight o'clock in the morning, and declares himself a hater of drunkenness (*TN* V.i.197–8). Some in the audience no doubt expected to be regaled with bawdy talk or sly improprieties; and students who have sought for these spices in Shakespeare have found them (e.g. Rowse, *Renaissance* 166; Fryer 50–56, 81).

Shakespeare started with a countryman's fondness for broad farce. It is a pointer to the continuity of our sense of funniness that he borrowed one pair of identical twins for *The Comedy of Errors* from Plautus, and Laurel and Hardy borrowed Shakespeare's two pairs for a laughable film called *Our Relations*. In Shakespeare personalities are often confused by disguises, occasionally by magic, further worsening the myopia that affects all human beings' perceptions of one another. It is the essence of farce, said Ben Travers, author of the Aldwych comedies, to display ordinary people in extravagant situations (BBC Radio 3, 27 December 1981). These spring from accident, unforeseeable disruption of our usual routine, such as lies in wait for us all. We all have lurking premonitions of it, and a dim sense that our lives have been mostly a tissue of chance happenings, more often unwelcome than not. Hercules may be beaten at dice by a nobody (*MV* II.i).

Dextrous use of words had become part of everyday life among all, high or low, who aspired to be in fashion, or to get on. As astonishing as the ability of poetry to thrive on the Elizabethan stage was the popularity of displays of verbal fencing, scarcely to be expected in large, crowded, partly unroofed theatres. Spectators must have been very attentive listeners, despite their nuts and apples. Competitions in wit would send them away ready to engage in similar bouts, and dream of scoring triumphantly off their acquaintances. 'To see this age!' the jester in *Twelfth Night* exclaims: words are always being turned inside out nowadays (III.i.11–13). Everyone wants to be thought 'an exchequer of words' (*TGV* II.iv.42–3). Viola and Toby fall as it were automatically into an exchange of punning repartee and flourishes (*TN* III.i.69 ff.).

It is an axiom among Shakespeare's young men of taste that the way to a woman's heart is through her presumed liking for wit and poetry. Silvia's rival suitors belabour one another with witticisms, some of them boyish enough (*TGV* II.iv). Sir Andrew the booby is told that he should have 'banged' his supposed rival 'Cesario' into 'dumbness' by accosting Olivia 'with some excellent jests, fire-new from the mint' (*TN* III.ii.21–3). This occurs in one of Shakespeare's most dazzling prose passages, an impromptu of a dozen lines thrown off by Fabian. He does not have much part in the play, but this speech is crammed with touches of fancy. Shakespeare's wits are self-consciously expert with their tongues, as we may guess him and his associates to have been. Benedick is mortified if one of his jokes falls flat, or so Beatrice says (*MAAN* II.i.135 ff.). With no better listener than Audrey at hand, Touchstone laments that it strikes a man dead to have his sallies falling on deaf ears (*AYLI* III.iii.5 ff.). Jaques is in a surly mood when he runs into Orlando in the forest, but cannot help being impressed by the young fellow's ready parries (III.ii.252 ff.).

It was a compliment to the ladies that they were expected to be so responsive to well-turned phrases and rhyming tributes. Shakespeare clearly believed that they could and should be educated up to this and, in addition, be able to talk intelligently themselves. All the Comedy girls have to be witty, whatever else they may be. They chat and joke among themselves in much the same strain as the men; their sense of humour is at times not much more delicate. Despite her slavish devotion to Proteus, Julia is no simpleton. The family descent Thurio prides himself on, she comments, is only 'from a gentleman to a fool' (*TGV* V.ii). It is wrong, however, Shakespeare warns us, for either man or woman to use a smart tongue to wound other people's feelings without cause. Berowne and Beatrice are censured for this, though they are never malicious in our hearing.

Beatrice is 'Lady Disdain': 'She speaks poniards, and every word stabs' (*MAAN* I.i.113; II.i.229). As her mild cousin says, her fault is to deride good qualities as much as bad, and allow no worth to 'simpleness or merit'. As soon as she is made to realize how she is 'condemn'd for pride and scorn', instead of admired, she resolves to turn over a new leaf (III.i). All comedy is concerned in some degree with persuading us to see ourselves as others see us, to be more aware of other people's existence. Benedick, like Beatrice, is willing to look into Shakespeare's mirror open-eyed. 'Happy are they that hear their detractions and can put them to mending' (II.iii.225–6) – but who, equally, are not to be swayed by frivolous mockery. 'Dost thou think I care for a satire or an epigram?' he asks Don Pedro (V.iv).

Wit and satire are not easily kept apart. Censure of individuals could easily grow into criticism, light or grave, of a class, a society, a nation. Government might be shown as a façade of sham benevolence concealing ineffectiveness and much worse. The spectacle of Dogberry and Verges instructing their watchmen (*MAAN* III.iii) is a splendid piece both of social history and of comment on authority. Especially after Falstaff's advent, Shakespeare was treating his audience to a strong dose of exposures, or hints, of things rotten in the state of England, all the more effective because Falstaff never moralizes, but is simply amused by what he sees. The country too must learn to be self-critical, and put its house in order. Public opinion was forming, grievances were finding their way into parliamentary debates whose eventual outcome would be revolutionary change. Toby and Fabian, laughing in their sleeves at Sir Andrew, invoke 'judgment and reason' as time-honoured 'grand-jurors' (*TN* III.ii.14–17).

Malvolio is not the only one who deceives himself, or is duped by others, into a false sense of importance. In the Induction to *The Taming of the Shrew* the bibulous tramp Sly, with whom a nobleman diverts himself by installing him in his own luxurious quarters, soon begins to believe that he really is a lord. Bottom, wearing his ass-head, is soon ready to fancy himself king of fairyland, and gives orders to Titania's attendants as to the manner born (IV.i). We laugh because we are being reminded that vanity can work on us all, especially when we suppose ourselves to be admired by the other sex. Shakespeare himself, Sonnet 87 seems to tell us, must have had moments of feeling, like his creatures, 'In sleep a king, but waking no such matter'.

The wit of the educated has an accompaniment of lower-class imitations, and rough-and-ready fun. At first this is stuck in here and there at random, like the long-winded bouts in *The Two Gentlemen of Verona* between the servants, Launce and Speed. Shakespeare's clowns are as fond of soliloquizing as his grand heroes and villains. Launce tells us a long tale about how his dog made a nuisance of itself under the ducal dining-table, and how to save it he took the blame on himself and submitted to a whipping. 'How many masters would do this for his servant?' (IV.i.1 ff.). There is a true, if grotesque, touch in this of the high value Shakespeare placed on fidelity; it is a plebeian version of the old attachment between lord and vassal. Another lengthy spell of drollery brings in Launce's trick of pretending to mistake one word for another – 'your old vice still', Speed remonstrates – and ends with Launce suddenly recollecting that he has an urgent message to give his companion (III.i.276 ff.).

More is to be gleaned from humour arising from the contacts between classes, their diverse attitudes to life, their opinions of themselves and of each other. Out in the country, social manners could remain little differentiated except at high altitudes. Falstaff noticed that Justice Shallow and his servants, from being continually together, had come to think and talk in just the same fashion (*2H.IV* V.I.62 ff.). Town life and sophistication hastened change, and much of Shakespeare's earlier comic dialogue arises from this. Servants often guy their masters, though social criticism is kept on a light tone. In *The Comedy of Errors* the two slaves are at least as quick-witted as their owners. We like to see our superiors, or inferiors, being made to look ridiculous, because this fortifies our own self-esteem. In *A Midsummer Night's Dream* the blunderings of the artisans performing their play, in *Love's Labour's Lost* those of the amateurish Nine Worthies, draw quizzical comments from the aristocratic spectators. Shakespeare invites us to join these in laughing at the awkward bumpkins, though not unamiably. Old Gobbo and his son in Venice both perpetrate howlers when they attempt learned words. Dogberry brings malapropisms to perfection. They are not confined to the lower orders; Slender at Windsor commits as many errors as Evans, without his excuse of being Welsh. Each onlooker could plume himself on knowing what a misused word ought to have been, or make up his mind to find out. In this light the theatre could serve as a schoolroom, as it is when Holofernes gives us a spelling lesson (*LLL* V.i.17 ff.).

It can be seen as a mark of the social tensions in *The Merchant of Venice*, the play where comedy is most in danger of breaking down, that wit has a more uneven distribution than before. The three leading men make no attempt at it. Shylock is too morose, Antonio too glum, Bassanio perhaps too exalted to descend to humour. Portia has no such inhibitions. Down below, Lancelot jokes easy-goingly with Lorenzo, his new master Bassanio's friend, until Lorenzo, with some impatience, shuts him up as a 'wit-snapper' (III.v.26 ff.). But this is virtually the end of plebeian jocularity in these plays, as if life has grown too hard for the poor to allow them any taste for it. They may amuse us, but not by intention. When he gets to Illyria, Shakespeare leaves them out.

While the stage clown is too clumsy to fit in with conventional society, the jester is too clever to want to, or to take it at face value. Each is an intruder, who keeps the world of the play from being a sealed-up, windowless one. They continue the Carnival tradition, lost to Protestant Europe, of a yearly breathing-space when rules can be thrown off, as mostly sham. Shakespeare makes use of a number of figures who in some ways resemble jesters. Puck thinks of himself as the jester of the fairy court: 'I jest to Oberon' (who seems easily pleased by practical jokes) (*MND* II.i.44). Armado's attendant Moth is far too precocious to be a credible pageboy; he and Falstaff's boy in *The Merry Wives of Windsor*, or the one in *Henry V*, have the air of 'prentice jesters, except that their wit is meant for us, not for the patrons they deride. Above all, of course, there is Falstaff himself.

Professional jesters appear only late on, in *As You Like It* and *Twelfth Night*. They belonged to a dying race, along with much else of the old feudal paraphernalia; they were escorting an old era off the stage of history. This Shakespearian pair are both in the service of ladies, who might be fonder than men of keeping old customs alive, and had more leisure to be whiled away. Their social status is indeterminate. Celia warns Touchstone, while they are still at court, and he says something disrespectful about her father, that his loose tongue may earn him a whipping (*AYLI* I.79–80) – as Lear warns his Fool. Rosalind calls him 'the clownish fool' (I.iii.130). It may look as though Shakespeare, after writing the first Act, decided to give Touchstone the more gentlemanly turn that makes him such an oddity in the forest, where he, far more than the courtiers, feels cut off from civilization. 'It is meat and drink to me to see a clown', he tells us, as he bewilders his rustic rival in Audrey's affections with a flow of long words (V.i.10). His caricature of the duelling code (V.iv) has something in common with Falstaff's derisory talk about Honour.

Feste too is a highly literate person. His nonsense talk, admired by Sir Toby, can be thought of as a parody of the pretentious diction, or the learned jargon, in vogue. Rabelais had a fondness for similar rigmarole; he was a man of the Renaissance ridiculing scholastic verbiage, and so was Shakespeare. With much less natural gaiety than Touchstone, Feste is an enigmatic person. His skirmishing with his patroness is artificial; he sometimes strikes sparks better when he is out of her house, on his own. He goes absent without leave (*TN* I.v.1 ff.); he hangs about cadging for tips; and he has Malvolio to harass him. 'Your fooling grows old, and people dislike it', Olivia warns him half-seriously, after Malvolio has spitefully asserted that he was beaten in a contest lately by 'an ordinary fool' (I.v). Such wit-contests seem to have been popular even at the alehouse level, and a jester would be expected to 'talk for victory', like Dr Johnson.

But what is coming to the front in these last plays of the series is the discord of classes and eras, more than any set-to's between individuals. Again unlike Touchstone, Feste has no warm attachment to anyone. His song at the end, though often dismissed as unShakespearian, breathes a vague disillusion, a note of failure and melancholy aided by the haunting recurrence of 'the wind and the rain'. Shakespeare may have felt at times that his own fooling was going out of fashion. He was now, in any case, taking leave of Comedy.

Men and Women

Shakespeare's understanding of human beings could help them to understand themselves; by so doing it could diminish obstacles to comprehension between men and women, and help them to see themselves as complementary parts of a whole community. In the Comedies relations between them are the chief theme, but this is not isolated from other things in life, and it has many variations. Shakespeare does not, like too many authors, rely on 'love' as a universal propellant, a fuel to bring inert natures to life. With him it is one aspect of a personality, and has connections with manners, culture, religion, class. It is often linked with social criticism, as well as emotional stirrings; we are in the company of young people often, like Yum-yum in *The Mikado*, 'very wide awake', who are feeling the currents of a new age and learning to make themselves at home in it. These plays are full of debate about marriage and love; they reflect a changing society, as the Histories mirror an evolving political system.

In the Elizabethan mind, polarized as it often was by the class structure, men's relations with women might be idealized to the point of rarefaction, or reduced to their lowest level. Shakespeare achieved a balance between ideal and terrestrial scarcely attained by any of the other writers. Like other Elizabethan poets he thought of many bad things to say about women, but he (or Romeo) was, it seems, the first to call a woman an 'angel' (Hughes 224–5). He took a hand in the current sniping at women's foibles, their cosmetics and false hair and the rest of the stock in trade of satirists and moralists. But when Viola somewhat bluntly inquires of Olivia 'if God did all' for her face, Olivia can reply ''Tis in grain ...' (*TN* I.v.240–42). 'A dangerous law against gentility', Berowne observes on a proposal to deprive women who come anywhere near the court of their tongues (*LLL* I.i.128): it will bear most hardly on gentlewomen. Still, on the whole nearly all the women of the Comedies, very unlike those of the Histories, win our esteem and affection.

Enlightened women formed, as they do today in 'developing' countries, a distinct species of 'rising middle class'. Shakespeare's 'new women' were an imaginative combination of older and newer modes of living, outlooks, values, with the liberal education that Bianca in *The Taming of the Shrew* is receiving to bind them together. They combine an aristocratic sparkle, and readiness – less aggressive than in the Histories – to take the lead, with the virtues of an upper-middle class. Wit, meaning also intelligence, forms a good part of their endowment. 'Love commonly weareth the livery of Wit', wrote Nashe (85), and if the Comedy women are claiming more equality of status, on this plane they are achieving it most quickly.

Shakespeare was at one with the middle-class writers who were upholding the sanctity of the family, with especial care for female conduct but with good behaviour incumbent on men as well. Courtly philandering is denounced in Sonnet 66, whose 'maiden virtue rudely strumpeted' would mean a poor girl ruined by a rich man; it has little place in the Comedies except to be ridiculed in the scenes of Touchstone wooing Audrey. There are no bad women. Heroines are virtuous by nature, and can be trusted on their own, beyond reach of any guardian or duenna. One of the qualities Orlando admires Rosalind for is chastity, though he can really have no assurance of it (*AYLI* III.ii.10). To meet Benedick's requirements a woman must be, among other things, 'fair', 'wise', and 'virtuous' (*MAAN* II.iii.25 ff.). Love and lust were among Shakespeare's antipodes, and his idealizing of romantic love was an attack on behaviour he must have seen most often in the upper class he was in proximity with.

More generally, it was an impulse to refine the ways in which the sexes regarded and treated each other. His young women are not expected, like their Victorian descendants, to have no eyes for male attractions. 'A good leg and a good foot', as well as money, Beatrice tells Don Pedro, are among the assets they look for (II.i.13–14). But this is a joke, and such things, when seriously meant, are apt to belong to farce. Phebe's admiring speech about 'Ganymede', the disguised Rosalind, shows that she has viewed 'him' carefully, not neglecting the shape of 'his' legs (*AYLI* III.v.119). Men could find it easy to believe that they were being appreciatively scrutinized. Mrs Page's eye 'did so course o'er my exteriors', Falstaff declares, that it seemed to scorch him like a burning-glass (*MWW* I.iii).

Shakespeare's ostensible reasons for so often sending his young ladies out into the world in male attire are not always clear; but there is an assumption in the background that women by themselves, undisguised, would not be safe. Rosalind proposes to arm herself with an axe and boar-spear (*AYLI* I.iii.114 ff.). Silvia in *The Two Gentlemen of Verona* is threatened with the fate of Lucrece. But even far short of this, it is no wonder Katherina in *The Taming of the Shrew* believes that a woman must have 'a spirit to resist, if she is not to be ill used' (III.ii.218–19). Women are subjected in the Comedies, much more than men, to all sorts of mishaps and ordeals; perhaps because in the poet's eyes they have more meaning for the human future. In flight from parental tyranny Hermia wakens up in the Athenian forest to find herself alone, deserted by her lover (*MND* II.ii). The way these unfortunates brave misfortune, and sometimes rise above it and take control of events, is a feminist manifesto by itself, a portent for the future.

Male attire can look very much like a parable of Woman's painful coming of age. Some of those who adopt it are conscious of taking a rashly bold step. Julia has qualms about her 'immodest raiment' (*TGV* V.iv.106). It seems as if Shakespeare was recognizing in women energies and aspirations at odds with the decorous seclusion they were expected to be content with. To be fully women, they must pretend to be men: a paradox in which Shakespeare may be said to compress the whole dilemma of modern womanhood and emancipation. When Portia, newly won, hails Bassanio as 'her lord, her governor, her king' (*MV* III.ii.166), we may be unpleasantly reminded of Katherina kowtowing to Petruchio. But it is she who saves the situation when trouble arises; and on her return from triumph in Venice she is ready for a pretended quarrel, in place of the 'modest stillness and humility' expected by husbands from wives, as by monarchs from their subjects.

Men being what they too often are, it is not easy for women to steer between being either too self-assertive, as Beatrice has been, or too self-effacing. Helena assures Demetrius that she is his 'spaniel', and loves him all the more for his spurning her (*MND* II.i.203 ff., 242–3). This is disgusting, as Katherina would be if we could take her capitulation seriously. A woman who submits to being bridled by an unjust marriage system is, as Adriana says, no better than a donkey (*CE* II.i.13–14); but the alternative may seem an unamiable angularity. She has a deeply felt sense of how husband and wife ought to be 'undividable, incorporate'; she is not too much of a rebel to think of the woman as the more dependent, clinging to the man like the vine twined round the elm (II.ii.110 ff.). Its blank verse makes this long speech all the more impressive, the play's rhyming couplets being nearly all designed for comic effect. We are aware of a sad discrepancy between a high ideal of marriage and the bitter reality of her own.

Women are right to feel mistrustful of what love means to men, and want to make sure of its sincerity. The four French ladies suspect that the four gentlemen of Navarre are playing with them, and resolve on a tit for tat. They are soon able to feel that they have scored a success; and the princess can tax the men with being 'perjured' because by meeting women they have broken their vow (*LLL* V.ii.346). Her underlying meaning is that men are not to be trusted when they talk of love. Berowne protests that they are in earnest, and reproaches his Rosaline, as Benedick does Beatrice, with being too fond of sarcasm, of making 'Wise things seem foolish and rich things but poor' (V.ii.378).

All the same, men are subject to strong temptation, and too often give way to it. There is frank talking about the carnal side of love, like Berowne's unromantic allusion to Cupid as 'King of Codpieces' (III.i.183). In Arden the duke, criticizing Jaques, speaks of 'the brutish sting' he has formerly been enslaved by (*AYLI* II.vii.66). Armado yields reluctantly to his fancy for the country wench Jaquenetta, from snobbish, not moral scruples. 'There is no evil angel but love', he reflects (*LLL* I.ii.165–6), and we soon hear that he has got the girl with child. Another like her, Audrey, looks forward to becoming 'a woman of the world' through the marriage with Touchstone that he has tried to dodge (*AYLI* V.iii). Jaques's comment is realistic as well as cynical: their voyage of love 'Is but for two months victuall'd' (V.iv.188–9).

All men are faithless, according to Juliet's nurse. Julia's confidante Lucetta warns her before she leaves home of how 'deceitful men' delude women with their tears and protestations; Julia rejects this 'base' suspicion and is sure of Proteus's fidelity, the 'infinite' of his devotion to her (*TGV* II.vii) – comic irony, since we already know that he is unfaithful. Proteus has some twinges of conscience, but he satisfies himself in a wordy soliloquy that it is all right for him to discard Julia in favour of his new love, Silvia, and to view his friend Valentine as a rival and an enemy. 'Unheedful vows may heedfully be broken' (II.vi). Poor Julia, coming to join him, has to hear him making love to Silvia. It is the latter who reproves him as 'perjured, false, disloyal' to both his mistress and his friend (IV.ii). Julia's love survives unshaken. 'Because I love him, I must pity him', she sighs (IV.iv.95). Shakespeare almost seems to regard a woman's love, once plighted, as something, like the marriage vow itself, that she cannot honourably withdraw.

The duke is sure his daughter Silvia's love for Valentine will quickly evaporate (III.ii). He is wrong: her love is proof against her ordeal of imprisonment, but she is very poorly rewarded. At some stage in the writing Shakespeare must have intended a serious conclusion; and the theme of love and friendship in competition was one that Elizabethans were fond of. Deploring the decay of friendship in these bad days, Valentine sounds like a stripling Timon; his homily on the virtue of repentance and the duty of forgiveness is in quite solemn language (V.iv). But its writer must have realized that his story was collapsing into absurdity, and decided to put a hasty end to it. In any case the play is a fantasia on constancy and inconstancy, with the two heroines carrying off the palm. Its moral may be read in Proteus's words near the close – 'O heavens, were man/But constant, he were perfect!' (V.iv.110–11). Constancy as a cardinal virtue has a place in many of Shakespeare's later plays, in all sorts of relationships. His influence, over the years, must have contributed heavily to an accepted pattern of romantic love growing into faithful wedded love, and had a deep effect on social – especially middle-class – conduct.

Of family life we are shown scarcely anything below the level of the higher classes, where property, dignity, social calculations, all come in. By comparison with the Histories, the upper-class family of comedy is far less dense and close: the individual is not embedded in it, the group is much less a microcosm of society. Comedy has to treat men and women, mostly young, as individual selves; they must be fairly mobile and manoeuvrable. Older men in these plays, chiefly martinets of the stock type, are widowers; children are motherless; some daughters, and in the later plays sons, have no fathers either. Several of the young women have no visible family connections at all: Julia, Helena, Olivia, and (to all appearances) nearly all those in *Love's Labour's Lost*. Shakespeare must have decided early on that *The Two Gentlemen of Verona* would be better without a father for Julia – one heavy father in a play is enough – but forgot to cross out two allusions to him (I.ii). In the forest Rosalind casually mentions to Celia that yesterday she ran into her exiled father, and they exchanged a few words – but 'what talk we of fathers': she can think only of her Orlando (III.iv). She and her father have been separated since her childhood; still, Shakespeare could have worked up an emotional reunion, if he had wished.

Where fathers and sons are in question, the most deserving parent is old Aegeon in *The Comedy of Errors*, who has brought up one son and gone roaming in search of a lost one. In *The Taming of the Shrew* a hard-headed observer feels sure that Vincentio will not agree to hand over his large property and be content 'in his waning age' to sit at his son's table, a dependant (II.i.39–63). Yet his son Lucentio, after playing an unfilial – not to say criminal – trick on him, gets his pardon more easily than his eloping bride Bianca gets her father's. A more typical autocrat is the Antonio of *The Two Gentlemen of Verona* who orders his son Proteus off to court to seek his fortune at twenty-four hours' notice, and brooks no remonstrance: 'For what I will, I will, and there an end' (I.iii).

Fathers and daughters are more likely than not to be at loggerheads over marriage issues which usually turn on status or wealth. Fathers represent the outlook of a society where revenue comes first. One of Bianca's suitors, Gremio, is 'an old gentleman', but since he has plenty of money he is as eligible in her father Baptista's eyes as anyone else (*TS* I.i). Silvia's father the Duke of Milan is equally materialistic. He is well aware that she loves Valentine and hates Thurio, but he prefers Thurio – 'Only for his possessions are so huge', as Valentine complains. He sounds almost like Lear when he threatens to cast her off, and 'let her beauty be her wedding-dower', for baulking his hope of being 'cherish'd by her child-like duty' in old age (*TGV* III.i). This hope scarcely seems to comport with marriage to Thurio or anyone else; the duke is thinking on two separate lines, so as to make his unreasonableness clear to all who hear him. By drawing such forbidding portraits Shakespeare was taking part in public debate at a time when opinion about family life was aroused, and open to healthy influences.

Hermia's father Egeus is cast in the same mould as Silvia's. Duke Theseus, in other respects a wise and benign ruler, takes the high conservative ground when it comes to parental authority. A father must be looked up to 'as as god', he tells Hermia: 'you are but as a form in wax/By him imprinted' (*MND* I.i.47–50). James I was fond of telling his subjects that kings are like gods; Theseus's adage completes the trio of god, king, father. Shylock would not dissent; he takes as rigid a view of the *patria potestas* as any Gentile, and believes his daughter 'damned' for running away from him (*MV* III.i.30), and with a Christian, and taking his ducats with her. His house has been a 'hell' to live in, Jessica says (II.iii.2). In a Jewish setting Shakespeare is free to paint in even more sombre hues the misery of a life where the daughter hates the father and revenges herself in the same unfeeling spirit as his own.

Beatrice is an orphan, which opens the way for her to grow up as a free spirit and a feminist. Her lively talk to Hero about how a young woman should choose for herself and say 'Father, as it please *me*' (*MAAN* II.i.48 ff.) is meant for our ears, not for her demure cousin. Hero is content to be married off in short order, whether to Don Pedro or to Count Claudio seems to make no difference to her. It does not occur to Leonato that he ought to consult her. He makes amends when he rejects the charge against her, and talks to his prince with blunt anger. But half of this anger, and his brother's, is what they feel as heads of a *family* which has been dishonoured; its honour will be repaired by Claudio agreeing to marry another member of it. From this old-fashioned standpoint, which even Beatrice – in the interests of a happy ending – does not repudiate, Hero is at least as much a family appendage as a person with feelings of her own. Anne Page belongs to a bourgeois circle, moving more quickly than aristocracy could do towards the notion of individual freedom of choice. She dutifully admonishes her lover Fenton to seek her father's approval (*MWW* III.iv); but she is firmly determined against the suitors favoured by her parents. Silvia speaks for all the modern-minded young women: 'heaven and fortune still reward with plagues' an 'unholy match' without love (*TGV* IV.iii).

Apart from Mrs Page, the sole mother in the Comedies is the Abbess of *The Comedy of Errors*, who has been separated from her family since her children's infancy by one of the storms and shipwrecks that Shakespeare, like Prospero, could conjure up at will. His young ladies who look forward so romantically to love and marriage show no eagerness for what was to follow: child-bearing, premature aging, infants dying, their own lives often cut short. Aegeon may talk of 'the pleasing punishment that women bear' for the sin of Eve, but a woman in the same play, Luciana, has remained single from fear of 'troubles of the marriage-bed' (*CE* I.i.46; II.i.27). Thoughts of them may account for some part of Shakespeare's misgivings about the romance of love. His missing mothers have left few offspring behind them. Siblings are hard to find, and in *The Taming of the Shrew, As You Like It*, and *Much Ado about Nothing* they are enemies. Elsewhere in Shakespeare brothers and sisters mean more to each other than any other relatives, but there is little of this in the Comedies (Kiernan, 'Relationships'). The happiest relations are between the two pairs of girl–cousins: Rosalind and Celia, Beatrice and Hero.

The idea of some freedom of choice in marriage, at least a right of refusal, was gaining ground in England. Spread of education fostered it. Some strands even of religious thinking were favourable. Luther had considered a couple's consent, not parental sanction, the essential condition for marriage (305). Shakespeare was helping to quicken the trend, by presenting it more persuasively than anyone else could. In two of the more 'bourgeois' plays the principle is admitted, at least in the abstract. When Petruchio and Baptista have exchanged information about their resources and agreed on dowry and settlement, the older man unexpectedly adds that Petruchio must secure Katherina's love – 'for that is all in all' (*TS* II.i.129). Possibly he fears an explosion if she is not humoured. In *The Merry Wives of Windsor* the numskull Master Slender, sponsored by Mr Page as a son-in-law, is asked whether he feels he can love Anne and, as his cousin Shallow puts it bluntly, 'upon good dowry, marry her'. He finds it ludicrously hard to grasp Shallow's meaning (I.i.206 ff.).

The Comedy of Errors is another urban, mercantile play, but the discontented Adriana was married in feudal style: as a ward of court, with a fortune, she was bestowed by the ruler on a man who saved his life in battle. Her grievance is that, having got her estate, he has neglected her and spent her money on other women. All the comfort she gets is advice to submit patiently. But 'Love will not be spurr'd to what it loathes', as Julia says near the end of *The Two Gentlemen of Verona* (V.ii). Silvia is the most eloquent of all on the repulsiveness of a forced marriage, and the evils it must bring in its train. Her 'very soul abhors' the boorish Thurio, and she feels that it is her duty as well as desire to escape him (IV.iii). Hermia chooses life imprisonment rather than submit to an 'unwished yoke' (*MND* I.i.79 ff.). In an exalted poetical fashion, watching Bassanio about to choose his casket, Portia dramatizes him into Hercules slaying the sea-monster and rescuing the Trojan maiden, its destined sacrifice (III.ii.53 ff.). She herself, in this fantasy, is the maiden; the monster is the unwelcome suitor who will get her if Bassanio fails.

Good old Sir Eglamour helps Silvia to run away because he knows her to be 'virtuously' inclined (*TGV* IV. iii). So are all Shakespeare's brave young paladins of their sex and its rights, and this adds weight to their cause. Their protests are repeated by one of their sweethearts, Fenton of Windsor (*MWW* V.v.231 ff.). Otherwise a nonentity, he is speaking for Shakespeare in his rebuke to Anne's parents, in language deeply serious, even solemn; of all the play's lessons this is the one that Shakespeare is most concerned to underscore. It is indeed safe to say that on this text, this negative truth about marriage, he always preaches with complete conviction; on the positive side, reliance on romantic love to bring the right partners together, he is far from equally certain. On both counts experience has borne him out.

Beatrice has been growing up into the most determined independent of all: she objects not to one man or another as a husband, but to the thought of being married to any man, 'overmastered with a piece of valiant dust' (*MAAN* II.i.55–6). She changes her mind in favour of

Benedick, who has himself been an objector to the matrimonial chain. He is an observant and thinking man (we actually find him reading a book) as well as a wit; like many in Shakespeare he is ready to talk about the badness of the times. 'The time of good neighbours' – of community feeling, fellowship – has gone by, he says: men are quickly forgotten nowadays, by their widows as well (V.ii).

Bachelors like him have their own reasons for fearing to be pushed or trapped into marriage. It will deprive them of some carefree enjoyments; it may coop them up, shut them off from a career. Valentine, setting out from home, thinks of love as cutting short youthful 'wit' and development (*TGV* I.i.45 ff.). It can be a folly, a Circe altering men from their proper shapes. 'Julia, thou has metamorphosed me', Proteus laments, and made me 'lose my time' (I.i.66–7); this resentful feeling may be taken as helping to explain why his love for her cools so swiftly. 'You are metamorphosed with a mistress', Valentine's servant is soon telling him (II.i.28–9), as if he too has been reading Ovid.

Shakespeare's happy endings sometimes demand hasty marriages, against his presumable better judgement, but he always disapproves of any anticipation of marriage by loving couples. When Lysander in the forest wants to lie down to sleep close beside Hermia, she insists on their keeping apart, and he at once assents (*MND* II.ii.45 ff.). When Hero is accused of having been seduced, her fiancé self-righteously declares that *he* was not to blame for her 'sin' (*MANN* IV.i.46 ff.). Apart from his own feelings, as father of two girls left at Stratford with a mother who had herself been imprudent, Shakespeare had to think of forestalling criticism from the strait-laced. 'Young blood doth not obey an old decree' (*LLL* IV.iii.214): Berowne's words are another pointer to un-easinesses that might beset the older generation, as they did Polonius.

In the absence of actresses, any Elizabethan play was likely to have many more male than female characters; here is one reason why Shakespeare has few married couples to show us. Matrimony has a prominent place in the farces, but then retreats to fairyland and to Windsor. Most of what we see of it is unprepossessing, above all because it is permeated by the male desire for domination, the man's conviction of a right and duty to assert his superiority. In the Induction to *The Taming of the Shrew* the keynote is struck when the lord instructs his page, dressed up as Sly's lady, to show loving and humble service, as a well-bred wife should. At the end of the play Petruchio can boast of the 'awful rule, and right supremacy' that he has established over his wife; her father is delighted to hear of it (V.ii.108). Ford of Windsor holds that a 'revolted' wife incurs damnation (*MWW* III.ii), just as kings thought of rebellious subjects. Oberon accosts Titania as 'rash wanton', and reminds her that he is her 'lord' (*MND* II.i.63).

In *The Comedy of Errors* marital relations supply the one serious theme running through the slapstick. Adriana's wretchedness is a good illustration of the evils that a loveless marriage must bring with it. She is embittered by her husband's conduct, and her sour tongue has made him even worse. He must be older than she is; to her sister she calls him 'deformed, crooked, old, and sere' (IV.ii). He is overfond of the landlady of the Porpentine inn, 'a wench of excellent discourse,/Pretty and witty' (III.i.109–10). Adriana understands how indignant a husband must be at the thought of his wife's body being 'contaminate' by another man's lust: she argues that he should have equal regard for *her* feelings (III.ii.130 ff.). Her unmarried sister Luciana tells her sententiously that throughout Nature, as well as in the human sphere, the female is and must be subject to the male (II.i.18 ff.). Still, Luciana addresses a long appeal to her brother-in-law (or rather to his twin brother, by error) to treat her sister better, or at least make a decent pretence of fondness, and conceal his misconduct. Women are easily fooled, she ends (III.i.124 ff.). The Abbess shows even scantier sympathy with the wronged wife when Adriana tells her that she has reproached her husband for his loose conduct day and night, in private and public, and to no avail. 'The venom clamours of a jealous woman' do more harm than good, the Abbess rejoins sternly (V.i.58 ff.).

In the Comedies as in the Histories, there is a pervasive mistrust of conjugal fidelity. Leonato is only joking about his wife's assurances to him that Hero is really his daughter (*MAAN* I.i.99 ff.); but it is a joke that no modern father would make, publicly and with his daughter listening; and the frequency with which something of the same kind is said must point to a prevalent insecurity among Elizabethan husbands. According to Beatrice, even the Devil's traditional horns give him the look of 'an old cuckold' (II.i.40). Don John the Bastard shares Benedick's conviction that a man who marries 'betroths himself to unquietness' (I.iii). His own irregular birth may give him a better title to carp at holy wedlock.

So in other plays too. One of the concluding songs of *Love's Labour's Lost*, supposed to be sung by a cuckoo, has an obvious allusion to cuckolds. *As You Like It* overflows with the idea that all women are born unfaithful. Touchstone is ready with badinage about matrimony and its penalty, horns, awaiting men of every class. 'Poor men alone? No, no; the noblest deer hath them as huge as the rascal' (III.iii). From a sharp-eyed court jester the words are telling, and the comment on aristocracy is disrespectful. A song after the killing of a deer inevitably has a chorus about the horns destined to all mankind (IV.ii). Rosalind herself, in love and descanting on love, amuses herself by talking about these appendages as the natural consequences of marriage (IV.i.50 ff.). Advocates of freedom of choice could, of course, maintain that they were consequences of forced wedlock, or legal rape.

Masculine jealousies were fanned by the often fiercely anti-feminine jeremiads of the pulpit. General distrust could too readily sharpen into suspicion of a particular woman. Claudio is very easily taken in, like Othello after him, by a clumsy deception – a trick perhaps deliberately meant by Shakespeare to strike us as unconvincing. Master Ford throws dust in his own eyes with spontaneous folly and, like Posthumus in a later play, sets out to test his wife. All Shakespeare's jealous men are suffering from quite groundless fears, and show themselves in a foolish or an odious light; their creator is warning husbands in his audience against stumbling into the same quicksand. His repeated lessons must have gone some way towards making such behaviour less common, and convincing his public that, in Mrs Page's words, 'Wives may be merry, and yet honest too' (*MWW* IV.ii.98).

Lovers

Individualism, voluntarily embraced or not, had an isolating effect which prompted a search for new ties in place of old. They could be looked for in practical partnerships, or more emotionally in warm friendship or ideal love as ways of reunion with a world grown strange. It was the tidal force of this social need that lent energy to relationships otherwise as lacking in substance as sceptics took them to be. Friendship and love had the same animating spirit, and their names could be interchanged. Berowne addresses the woman he is in love with as his 'friend'; Maria uses the word of her probationary lover (*LLL* V.ii.404, 830). Men never hesitate to speak of their 'love' for other men.

In *The Two Gentlemen of Verona*, and temporarily in *Much Ado about Nothing*, we see a male friendship disrupted. In the Comedies close ties seem more natural between women – usually young, but at Windsor middle-aged and more matter-of-fact; and strongest when the pair are close relatives. Less intimate are the cordial relations of Julia and Portia with their 'maids'. But feminine friendships as well as masculine can capsize, when jealousy comes in. Helena has been Hermia's 'sweet playfellow', but is ready to betray her and foil her escape. Their girlhood affection is as touchingly recalled (*MND* I.i.214 ff.; III.ii.198 ff.) as that of Rosalind and Celia. Memories are not all sentimental. Helena remembers that her schoolmate could be a 'vixen', and 'fierce' when angered (*MND* III.ii.323–5), and it looks as if this may be true enough.

Love is the wellspring of poetry in these plays, but its meaning is enigmatic. It may be a firm lifelong bond, or a shimmering illusion. A lover, Shakespeare seems often to have felt, is condemned 'To worship shadows and adore false shapes' (*TGV* IV.ii.126). Love can appear illusory because it was too often an aristocratic pastime – the occupation of the idle, as Napoleon said – and because it was in a way a novelty. Romantic love has helped to inspire poetry and legend even in the veiled East; but now sober men and women found themselves stepping or being pushed into story-land. Lucentio is astonished to discover that he has fallen in love with Bianca at first sight (*TS* I.i.147 ff.). Instantaneous love, of course, saves time, and theatre time is precious. It also saves Shakespeare from having to explain *why* A has fallen in love with B; but he cannot conceal some uncertainty about what it means.

One distress seldom undergone by Shakespeare's lovers, except the undeservers, is that chronic bane of sonneteers, love unrequited. Orsino is a rare sufferer, and we are not meant to take his self-pityings seriously. Another rarity is for a lover to find that he has a rival for his lady's affections, as with other writers he nearly always does. Shakespeare treats such situations as comical, or one-sided; a woman who hesitates between two suitors cannot be capable of real love, he seems to feel. Touchstone and William are rivals for Audrey's hand; Orsino threatening to kill 'Cesario', as his rival for Olivia, is threatening a girl, whom he will soon be marrying (*TN* V.i.124 ff.). Claudio momentarily, foolishly, suspects a rival in Don Pedro (*MAAN* II.i). Thurio has no chance of Silvia, or Demetrius of Hermia, or Dr Caius of Anne, except by enlisting parental authority on his side. For a real tug of war Valentine and Proteus are the only candidates, and Shakespeare chooses to throw away his opportunity for a Palamon and Arcite tussle.

In the opening colloquy of *The Two Gentlemen of Verona* Valentine speaks feelingly of the pangs of love, and how they outweigh its joys, as if Shakespeare were living again through some moods of the Sonnets. Valentine feels superior to his infatuated friend; but by the time the two meet again he has to confess his own surrender to love's 'high imperious thoughts', and his having to do 'penance' with tears and sleepless nights (II.iv.128 ff.). It is now Proteus's turn to be amused by his friend's discomfiture. As very often, Shakespeare is seeing love in a humorous rather than romantic light. Berowne is another who, having been a mocker of Cupid, to his disgust finds himself succumbing (*LLL* III.i.172 ff.). Real emotion can be felt in his long-drawn-out self-communing about Rosaline, which reminds every reader of the Dark Lady. On his lower level, Armado is another reluctant victim. It is 'base for a soldier to love', he laments (I.ii.57).

Shakespeare was not fond of showing comedy lovers together, and having to think of things for them to say to each other. Celia compares a lover's vows and verses to the antics of a clumsy rider in the tilt-yard (*AYLI* III.iv), a spectacle that Shakespeare must have witnessed. Valentine gives the duke, who is pretending to be in love, a lecture on the art of lovemaking, with gifts and flattery for staple (*TGV* III.i.93 ff.); a mechanical set of tricks that Shakespeare must also have seen at work. He gives us scarcely any courting between any of the three couples in *The Merchant of Venice*, and we hear hardly any billing and cooing. Claudio leaves it to Don Pedro to plead his suit for him; Orsino employs 'Cesario' as his proxy. Julia falls in love with a letter from Proteus (*TGV* I.ii); when we see them together they are already confessed lovers, and about to be parted. Separation may be more poetically inspiring than an encounter. Valentine is talking not to Silvia, but about her, when he declares that he is 'as rich in having such a jewel/As twenty seas' (II.iv.167–8).

It was the more extravagant cult of love that struck sensible people as irrational, and likely to have dubious effects on its acolytes. Theseus associates it with poetic flights, and with lunacy (*MND* V.i.7 ff.). The tragic love of Pyramus and Thisbe was a much-admired tale in Shakespeare's time (Frye, *Shakespeare* 30); he guys it in a very offhanded style. In *A Midsummer Night's Dream* the inconstancies and uncertainties of human emotion are accelerated by the magic drops, the shifting moods of a year condensed into an hour. In the first scene Lysander talks, as if prophetically, of love vanishing like a lightning flash in a dark sky: 'So quick bright things come to confusion' (149). It is ironic that after the potion has been put in his eyes he should wake up and tell himself that 'reason' must have made him realize the truth: it is Helena he likes best, not Hermia (II.ii.117 ff.). Bottom might be commenting on this when he remarks that 'reason and love keep little company together nowadays' (III.i.136–7).

Orsino opens *Twelfth Night* with reflections on love in a highly poetical – or musical – if somewhat vacuous style; he winds up by calling his sensations only 'fancy'. When we find him at the end of the play in love with a different woman, we can agree with him. Earlier he has told this other woman that a wife should be younger than her husband, because men are more giddy and inconstant, and women's beauty does not last long. A few minutes later he says the opposite: that women are the more inconstant, their attachment being only sensuality, 'appetite', an affair of the 'palate' (II.iv.29 ff., 93 ff.). He is, therefore, pining for a woman he knows to be, like all women, unworthy of him.

Of all the comedies *As You Like It* is the one where everything 'romantic' is held up to the sharpest questioning and mockery, and new points of view on men's and women's relations are aired. Rosalind, herself passionately in love, is the leading spirit in this raillery. When she meets Orlando in the forest, and with no bashful hesitation pretends to be 'a saucy lackey', she laughs at his confession of being in love – 'Love is merely a madness' – and undertakes to cure him; he is to pay court to

her, as if to his mistress, and she will snub him and bring him to his
senses (III.ii.293 ff.). It is a neat comic invention. Celia can be just as witty,
and teases her in the same fashion when she has a fit of doubt about
Orlando's love: 'The oath of a lover is no stronger than the word of a
tapster' (III.iv). Neither of these young princesses is likely to know much
about tapsters and their tricks – Shakespeare is often careless about
choosing imagery appropriate to its user –, but Rosalind understands well
enough.

At this point we have just seen Touchstone trying to snare Audrey
into a false marriage. It is a maxim of his that 'the truest poetry is the
most feigning', especially on the subject of love (III.iii); a hit at the sham
throbbings of Elizabethan amorous verse. Phebe brushes aside Silvius's
complaint that her cruelty is killing him (III.v.83 ff.); Rosalind assures
Orlando that the notion of men dying for love is mere literary fable: a
mistress's frown 'will not kill a fly' (IV.i.105). A song at a woodland
banquet in Arden is about ingratitude, hollow friendship, and foolish
love (II.vii.173 ff.). And even men and women who truly love, Rosalind
warns Orlando, both alter quickly once they are married (IV.i.138 ff.).
How does she know? Shakespeare is again lending his eager young folk a
fund of wisdom out of his own store. When Rosalind is ready for her
final denouement, the lovers, each in turn, profess a true passion.
Amusingly tart even now, she cuts short the amorous chorus – ''tis like
the howling of Irish wolves against the moon' (V.ii).

One of Shakespeare's devices for creating a sceptical detachment is to
let old men recall, as something incomprehensible, the calf love of their
early years, which to their juniors can only sound laughable. Old Corin
the shepherd of Arden was once in love, and ran into pranks as wild as
Silvius's now; so did Touchstone (II.iv); so did even Polonius. Another
way of bringing high-flown romance down to earth is to transpose it
from an aristocratic to a plebeian key. It is at home only on the heights;
to see men who work with their hands fall frantically in love is to make
it ridiculous. Silvius has enough resources to buy a farm, but as a lovelorn swain talking in pastoral verse he is a joke. Touchstone's 'love' for
Audrey parodies the more refined emotions of Arden (Bethell 93). Lower
down still, Launce's very earthy description of the milkmaid he is
growing fond of is more disgusting than diverting (TGV III.i.261 ff.).
Dromio of Syracuse is horrified at being claimed as her own by the
kitchen wench his twin brother has been dallying with, a 'very beastly
creature' (CE III.i.194 ff.). At Venice we hear casually that Lancelot has
got a 'negro' or 'Moor' woman with child (MV III.v.35 ff.).

A light but astringent appraisal of love pervades the Comedies. It can
be a medium for a critical estimate of upper-class society, whose prime
ostensible value is often love. Similarly the critique of Honour in the

later Histories is a sapping and mining of the same castle from a different angle. Courtier-style love is a pastime, a relief from boredom. By contrast, for the advancing citizen or Puritan class, with a meaningful life to live, it was within this life that a place had to be found for love. It became less declamatory, more sober and also firmer.

Apart from a scatterbrain like Audrey, women do not seek wealth or status by catching the right man. Behind the male lover's smile may lurk the fortune-hunter, though this too is rare; it shows chiefly in the commercial atmosphere of Padua and Venice. Gentlemen were not expected to wear their purses on their sleeves; on the other hand, it was no discredit to them to take an intelligent interest in dowries and legacies; rather, it was their family duty to 'marry well'. Lorenzo wants Jessica's – or rather Shylock's – money, but like Bassanio he plays the lover's part convincingly. Although Claudio is careful to begin by making sure that Hero is an heiress, he does not hesitate to reject her when he thinks her unworthy to be his countess. No question arises of whether Bassanio and Portia would have been willing to marry on a crust, if destiny had not taken them by the hand. For the well-born to descend to beggary for the sake of love might have struck Shakespeare's audience, as it would have struck Jane Austen's, as more eccentric than admirable. Orsino's love is too 'noble' to be affected by wordly gear: he is not interested in Olivia's 'dirty lands' (*TN* II.iv.80 ff.) – but of course he has no need of them.

Romance and humour are woven together. They are interacting aspects of the world Shakespeare is contemplating. His gospel is very much what Carlyle was fond of calling 'veracity': delusion and deception must be stripped away, and truth, genuineness, brought to the front. These plays leave us with a conviction that true love does exist, but a suspicion that pinchbeck imitations are more numerous.

Advances in any epoch bring into sight fresh vistas, tantalizing visions not yet realizable. These attach themselves most readily to private spheres of life, less intractable in appearance than the collective. In early modern Europe, as again two centuries after Shakespeare in the Romantic age, an ideal of perfect love between man and woman offered itself as symbol. It illuminated women in particular, as redeemers. Shakespeare's parallel study of history was showing him how little its great men could be trusted to lead mankind out of the wilderness. As little could be expected from women in great places who competed with men and had to behave like men. In a sphere of their own they might be very different; at any rate, it was easier for a poet to invest them with such a glow of promise. As always until quite lately they have been, for men, exotic and strange. Women have been compelled to learn more about men, chiefly on their worse sides, than men have needed to know about women (which may explain why most of our novelists nowadays are women). In a time of unfolding horizons imagination could find in them embodiments of its idealizings. Berowne's rhapsody about them is a panegyric on Love, which fills the gods with 'harmony', and on the poetry of love, able to 'ravish savage ears' and soften tyrants (*LLL* IV.iii.341 ff.). The Shakespeare who wrote this was as yet more poet than dramatist or thinker. And it might be objected that any woman quite so transcendental would be, as Beatrice said of a royal husband, 'too costly to wear every day' (*MAAN* II.i.307).

Aristocratic sonneteers were flattering women in order to seduce or simply entertain them. More sincere appreciation of their qualities was more likely to emerge in the middling social levels, among those who were rising in the scale, aspiring to further success, and conscious of a need for reinforcement by feminine abilities. Shakespeare can be reckoned among their teachers and spokesmen. This elevation of women was not something that could be undertaken yet in any direct fashion, though more freedom and education for them were already being advocated. Beyond lay a still nebulous dream of the future, sharing with all history's highly charged fantasies an element of real meaning. Shakespeare took stories that were half folk-tales, where heroines in adversity were most at home; in such settings romantic love could be brought down to earth without soiling its wings. His eyes were on a future that could be guessed at; naturalistic writing concentrates its interest on the here and now. To keep romance free of mawkish sentimentality he gave each heroine enough wit, as well as charm, to be able to look at and sometimes laugh at themselves and their loves.

'How many fathom deep I am in love', Rosalind exclaims (*AYLI* IV.i.201). It is by such chance touches, very different from the convulsive embraces of the modern stage or screen, that Shakespeare transports us into a state where ordinary inertias of the mind are cast off. It is not love fulfilled that he likes to conjure up, but the condition of being in love and looking hopefully and happily forward. Rosalind is its most bewitching expression. This ardent love of hers is for a man she knows little of, as is the case with most of the Comedy lovers. Romantic love can be fired only by the unknown; it owes more to a wish to believe than to any reason for believing. Still, Rosalind and Orlando are getting to know each other after a fashion; and even if there is no common purpose, no quest, for them to share, they are undergoing together in exile a kind of ordeal, a test such as love demands. We can hope well for their future, as even the gloomy Jaques manages to do (V.iv.185).

A painter, Shakespeare seems to have thought, should strive to outdo Nature and show us a true horse, for example, but a more flawless one than we have ever seen (*Venus and Adonis* 289 ff.). He may well have felt similarly about his own art. He was drawing his heroines from his own creative imagination, or sense of possibilities, more than from living reality. He was trying (not in a deliberate, schematic manner) to take over, to transfuse into middle-class veins, the essences of the old order, improved and refined; he was faring better with women, if only because women and their capacities were in many ways still untried.

To love gracefully was an accomplishment he prized, but to love sincerely is more fundamental. No honest, simple affection is to be spurned. Rosalind interrupts Phebe with an indignant rebuke: Silvius has more to recommend him than she has; she ought to learn to 'thank heaven, fasting, for a good man's love' (*AYLI* III.v.35 ff.). That love can be thought of as a leveller has always been part of the attraction of folk-tale romance to mankind imprisoned in its civilized zoo, with separate cages for each species. Olivia is stung by the indignity of being rejected by a youth who, though well-bred, is no more than the duke's 'servant', but she cannot bring herself to abandon her efforts to win him (*TN* III.i). In the forest of Arden something of the equality of the golden age is restored. 'My pride fell with my fortunes' (*AYLI* I.ii.240): Rosalind, like her father, has had lessons to learn, and must owe to them some part of her friendly ease of manner with all and sundry. Nearly all the heroines are well-born, but not all are pampered by fortune, and some are unfortunates, cast down by fate to our own humble level or worse. Depriving them of external advantages allows their inbred qualities to shine out.

Men have never died for love, Rosalind assures her hearers; some women may have done so, Shakespeare seems prepared to think. In *Love's Labour's Lost* the princess refers, as Viola does, to a sister who died of disappointed love and melancholy (V.ii.13 ff.): a good reason for her now to be looking at love cautiously. It is always (except in 'happy endings') something to be taken very seriously. *Love's Labour's Lost* is an outlawing of all insincerity or trifling between men and women. If they are to benefit by the growing freedom that society allows them, women must make use of it wisely. Moreover, love should not be egotistic, self-isolating; it should have a social as well as a private character. Rosalind bestirs herself to straighten out the affairs of other forest-dwellers. (Shaw called her, for her pains, 'a fantastic sugar doll' [26]). When Portia saves the life of her husband's friend, and Beatrice finds Benedick ready to risk his own life in defence of the innocent, the same principle takes a graver form. As in all romantic fiction it is implied – if, as a rule, not stated – that the trials and tribulations undergone by lovers are, like those in the *Magic Flute*, the guarantee of their future happiness.

The princess in *Love's Labour's Lost* is spared such ordeals, except in token form, but she combines romantic gifts with practical abilities. She has been sent to Navarre by her father, the king of France, on an important diplomatic mission, centuries before the appointment of any real women to ambassadorial posts. (True, we are soon allowed to forget that there is any business to be conducted.) There is a feminist note in her lightly spoken words: 'praise we may afford/To any lady that subdues a lord', or husband (IV.i.39–40). Out of consideration for the amateur actors she overrules the king of Navarre's reluctance to let them perform and bore his guests (V.ii.513 ff.). She has the humane feeling so strong later in the Marina of *Pericles*, and puts deer-shooting in the same category as the 'crimes' of 'glory' committed by rulers in their wars (IV.i.24 ff.). She typifies the ideal of womanhood, virtuous and intelligent and cultivated, that makes Berowne think of love as the originator of all inspiration, valour, art, and of women as the source of 'the true Promethean fire' (IV.iii.286 ff.). The whole play is a summons to women to show their sex worthy of such praise and such expectations.

Both Julia and Silvia fully deserve the gems of poetry allotted to them as rewards. Julia sets out alone in quest of her lover, 'a true-hearted pilgrim' of love (*TGV* II.vii.9). Silvia has won praise on all sides. She is 'too fair, too true, too holy' or chaste, to be seduced by his incense, Proteus soon discovers (IV.ii.5–6). Julia adds her tribute of praise to Silvia as 'A virtuous gentlewoman, mild and beautiful', even if she does herself the justice of considering her own beauty no whit inferior (IV.iv.178 ff.). When things go wrong, however, through the baseness or brutality of men, there is nothing they can do to set them right. Beatrice can take action through her influence over Benedick. These two are equals in both good qualities and failings, and she is one of the few heroines who get a husband really worthy of them. Portia has been called 'the vision of … a humanity not yet in being' (Sinsheimer 91; cf. 13) – a title she deserves in her inspired moments, at least, but one which might be conferred on Shakespeare's heroines collectively.

In some of the early plays women have not acquired the faculty of guiding their fellows and directing events; at the end they are losing it. In between they have won some triumphs, yet their success has been limited. This comedy world is one where accident reigns, or has a wide sway, and individuals good or bad splash through the waves as best they can. What the shining lights can do is to draw round them charmed circles of goodwill, sunshine, hopefulness. Rosalind does this in the forest. She has nothing to do with the overthrow of wickedness: Shakespeare unfrocks his pair of villains, and makes good men of them, by a couple of stage tricks. A society so badly warped as his was not to be redeemed by any magic juice that even he could drop into men's and women's eyes; its deep-seated discords had to be left unresolved. Shadows hover over the sunlit – or moonlit – scene. There is the rustling of a tragic future in Lysander's lament about 'War, death, or sickness', ready to destroy (*MND* I.i.142) – as they are already doing in the Histories.

In all times and places where it has been cherished, love has had more meanings than those simply of relations between two human beings; it has been in some degree – but very seldom as distinctly as with Shakespeare – part of a glimmering hope of a better future for mankind, of progress towards liberation and harmony. It could not glow with any steady light. None of the three unions at the end of the last Comedy is edifying. Olivia has hurriedly wedded a stranger, mistaking Sebastian for his twin sister 'Cesario', and impelled by a 'most jealous and too doubtful soul' (*TN* IV.iii.22 ff.). As Puck said of those under the spell of Oberon's magic, the destinies of lovers may turn out 'preposterously' (*MND* III.ii.121).

Social Currents

Shakespeare as a social critic can be seen trying – more by instinct than by design, no doubt – to sketch a pattern of truly 'aristocratic' behaviour. In the Histories he was concerned with conduct in high places, in great affairs; in the Comedies, in more private settings. In the former he began with traditional types, and sought by degrees to invest some of them with a newer consciousness. In the latter he began with men and women often really of a well-off middle-class sort, whatever their nominal standing, and bestowed on some of them the finer traits of a higher rank.

At the outset he had, as Byrne says, to learn something of how the high and mighty lived, as well as to ruminate on how they ought to live. The elaborate Induction to *The Taming of the Shrew* may suggest that he had thought of a full-length English play, but felt unequal to this and retreated to Padua. As he went on learning, he has been accused of flattering aristocracy by his evident preference for it, at least as a theme, compared with anything his gallery of middle-class life can show. What he was doing, however, was not 'idealizing' the upper class, but offering it ideals to form itself on: 'We must educate our masters.' And his earlier portraits were not, in fact, always very attractive.

The task of welding together the better qualities and principles of an older and a newer class could not be simple. One early outline of a model gentleman, not a young one, is Sir Eglamour, as described by Silvia. He is 'valiant', 'wise', 'well accomplish'd', and so faithful a husband that when his lady died he vowed himself to 'pure chastity' (*TGV* IV.iii). A more mature prescription is Olivia's, when she reproves Malvolio for his self-centred quickness to take offence. It is better to be 'generous, guiltless, and of free disposition' (*TN* I.v.88 f.) – free, that is, from petty suspicions and rancours. In *As You Like It*, as years later in the Romances, men and women have to go out into the wilderness to recover the fine freedom of mind and temper that conventional living cramps or poisons, as it has done in Frederick and Oliver.

An indication of how little was needed to impress the common mind is the Windsor innkeeper's encomium on Fenton: 'He capers; he dances …' (*MWW* III.ii); what more can be asked of a young gentleman? More in Shakespeare's line is the importance attached in the plays to good manners, not for self-display but as an index of respect for self and for others. Even disguised, Viola has a propriety of bearing that at once impresses Olivia; it confirms Viola's claim to gentle birth. It impresses the duke equally; when Olivia marries Viola's brother, Orsino assures her that she has not done amiss: 'right noble in his blood' (TN V.i.263). His only evidence is Viola's good manners, more and more in Shakespeare's time the certificate of gentility.

Conversely, though less convincingly, good blood makes for good manners, as in the case of Orlando. Blue blood is indelibly blue; a folktale motif useful – not here alone – to Shakespeare as a story-teller, but blending with the retrograde idea of an upper class as a superior caste. Feudalism encouraged this. Primogeniture reserved estates to eldest sons alone, but gentility extended to all the offspring; and the multitude of younger sons sent out into the world, many of them to London as apprentices, made the most of a claim to good birth that might be their sole asset. So also did the many landowners with shrinking estates, fearful of sinking down into the common herd.

Their point of view finds an unexpected mouthpiece in Portia's suitor the prince of Arragon. Gentility may be pushed off its perch by winds of change, but it cannot lose its 'merit', or intrinsic virtue, only waiting to be restored to its rightful place. He is a legitimist, upholding 'the true seed of honour', or old landed elite, against the 'barbarous multitudes' of upstarts from the mass of 'low peasantry' (*MV* II.ix.31 f.). All this was a familiar Tudor jeremiad, stoked by the unprecedented revolution in landed property of the second half of the century: a complaint about the rise of nobodies, the decay of old families, the confusion of social ranks. Fallen dignity can always look well by contrast with upstart impudence. But we are not called on to agree with Arragon. He is about to choose the wrong casket, and his speech is meant to tell us why. Bassanio makes no such divine-right pretensions, though he is an obvious case of a man of high birth deep in debt, and in danger of being swept away.

Shakespeare's much more modern standpoint is that of the duty of every man to make the most of his gifts and his chances, as he himself was doing. His era was a very jumbled one in English social history, but at all levels above the humblest a time of opportunity and competition.

Each individual must push himself to the front, or be elbowed aside. Achilles must go on fighting, and William Shakespeare must go on writing plays, or their laurels will quickly fade. Royal favourites jockeyed for position at court; in every parish neighbours squabbled about who was entitled to style himself 'Gent.', or 'Esquire'.

Even young men with an apparently secure future must understand that to cut any figure in the world, or even to make sure of survival, they must find an occupation. This was a lesson that all the old landed classes of Europe had to learn, often painfully. The new standing armies were their great recourse, but there was less and less room in them for illiterate backwoodsmen such as Prussian Junkers were until compelled to submit to education; it was men like Benedick who were wanted for officers. Success in any walk of life required preparation. Orlando himself realizes how much he has been deprived of, in the first words of *As You Like It*. A gentleman, as Valentine says, needed study and education to be 'complete in features and in mind' (*TGV* II.iv.60 ff.), and for this he must go out into the world. 'Home-keeping youth have ever homely wits': he pities his friend Proteus, chained by love to 'shapeless idleness' (I.i.2, 63). Panthino points out to his employer, Proteus's father, some of the varied professions beckoning to young men: army, university, exploration of 'islands far away'; his own suggestion is a more old-fashioned one, that Proteus should repair to the emperor's court, 'practise tilts and tournaments', and 'converse with noblemen' (I.iii).

At Stratford Shakespeare must have known country gentlemen of the muddy-witted sort: the comedies contain a choice selection of such oafs – Thurio, Slender, Sir Andrew Aguecheek. Thurio's great possessions deserve pity, for being owned by such an ass (*TGV* V.ii). He turns out to be a craven as well, like Sir Andrew. In such figures Shakespeare is satirizing a large section of the more backward and boorish of the English gentry, much of it sliding downhill because it did not know how to manage its property in this new era. It furnished many of the easily cheated 'gulls' who abounded in Elizabethan social satire.

From the Squire Westerns it was no great distance to an unpleasant type that Shakespeare has much to say about, though it is characteristic of him not to bring it on to the stage. It consisted of the offscourings or hangers-on of gentility, or men pretending to some status, or plain ruffians; they were the 'swashbucklers' who often set London streets in an uproar. Rosalind and, quite unnecessarily, Portia, setting off in disguise, are each resolved to outface these 'mannish cowards' (*AYLI* I.iii.121; *MV* III.iv.63 ff.). Another testimony is the indignant speech of Hero's old uncle about the young men of the day, of whom he considers Claudio one – 'Scambling, out-facing, fashion-monging boys', who 'lie and cog and flout, deprave and slander' (*MAAN* V.i.94–5). There was much in the swirling life around him that Shakespeare disliked. He may himself, on occasion, have been molested in the streets.

Armado is a more harmless specimen of the decaying layers of an old order: a caricature of aristocratic affectation, an embodiment of what is absurd in courtly culture. His inability to count is a joke not at his poor arithmetic, as is sometimes supposed, but at his pseudo-refinement: he cannot tell what three times one makes, because such calculations are beneath him – 'I am ill at reckoning: it fitteth the spirit of a tapster.' He is no less ill at paying his attendants. Gambling, on the other hand, is a gentlemanly accomplishment, part of 'the varnish of a complete man' (*LLL* I.ii.39–42). Berowne's caustic comments on Boyet, as a *cavalier servente* who 'knows the trick/To make my lady laugh', may be taken as Shakespeare's opinion of such parasites in great households. In Arden the banished duke and his friends look back on their court life with mixed feelings; it is left to the snobbish jester to pine for it as the earthly paradise. Anyone who has not been at court, he assures the bucolic Corin, must have clumsy manners, and must therefore be damned (*AYLI* III.ii.11 ff.).

Jaques asks the good-looking Orlando whether he has not cajoled goldsmiths' wives out of rings (*AYLI* III.ii.268 ff.). Needy courtiers preying on foolish citizenesses were a standard butt. Shortage of cash compels Falstaff to join their ranks, and try to turn his knighthood to account. His defeat by women of the despised trading class makes his failure the more resounding. To Sir John a bourgeois husband, however prosperous, is a mere 'peasant', and fair game. He tries to catch Mrs Ford, as Touchstone does Audrey, with the idea that under his wing she will soon be shining at court (*MWW* II.ii.261; III.iii). He fails. Yet between the classes they stand for there was always a blurring at the edges. Mrs Page wants to give her daughter to Dr Caius because he is not only well off but has 'friends potent at court' (IV.iv.88–9).

We are shown the gentry, good and bad, a good deal through the eyes of their servants, or through interplay between the two. At the top of the ladder of service were the gentlemen-servitors and ladies' maids, often drawn from the great pool of younger sons and unmarried daughters. Shakespeare is getting things mixed up when he makes Lucentio's lackey in *The Taming of the Shrew* call Tranio his 'fellow', after Tranio has been talking with Lucentio like a tutor and friend, and quoting Latin (I.i). Panthino in *The Two Gentlemen of Verona* can be reckoned a major-domo. Julia discusses her suitors with her intelligent and well-spoken woman Lucetta, and when leaving home puts her in charge of the house and all its contents (II.vii). Nerissa is Portia's 'maid', but entitled to marry Bassanio's gentleman Gratiano. Hero has two gentlewomen, who take part in the social life of the household.

A ready tongue, a turn for bandying jokes with an easy-going master, might be a recommendation in a servant of humbler station. In this role he was a successor to the jester, and ancestor to a long line of attendants of the race of Sam Weller. Speed is joking with his master's friend Proteus in the first scene of *The Two Gentlemen of Verona.* He can use quite fine language, and even talk in rhymed fourteen-syllable lines whose use, he says, he has learned from something he has been reading (II.i). Jocular exchanges have most point when they reflect contrasting social viewpoints. Speed remonstrates with the lovelorn Valentine about his indifference to their dinner-time: love may feed on air, but 'I am one that am nourished by my victuals' (II.i).

Antonio of Syracuse commends his Dromio as 'A trusty villain' whose 'merry jests' have often dispelled his cares (*CE* I.ii.19 ff.). A term of abuse can soften into an endearment. Berowne uses the word 'slave' twice, in casual talk to the clown Costard (*LLL* III.i.149, 160), good-humouredly instead of in the haughty style of the Histories. Plebeians could use it among themselves; Launce calls his fellow-servant 'an unmannerly slave' (*TGV* III.2). He himself is a blundering simpleton whom Proteus, when irritated, abuses as a 'whoreson peasant' and 'foolish lout' (IV.iv). We may take such dullards for newcomers from the countryside, or from small-town life, by contrast with the native Cockney wits. They are on the stage to be laughed at, though also sometimes to raise laughs against others. Sly's tipsy talk of his ancestors who 'came in with Richard the Conqueror' (*TS* Induction.i) derides a snobbish pretension familiar in England then as in later times. Lancelot Gobbo, as a native of Venice, must have been at the theatre and picked up scraps of the bombast beloved by the ruffling youth. 'These foolish drops do something drown my manly spirit', he exclaims, to cover his tearful leave-taking from Jessica (*MV* II.iii.13–14). Pistol is given to more impassioned flights of nonsense, all that is left to him and his companions to keep up their spirits with. Such threadbare retainers of decayed gentlemen have no future; like much else in Shakespeare's world, they are moribund survivals from the past.

Touchstone the jester accosts Corin in the forest as 'you clown' (*AYLI* II.iv). Rosalind and Celia, who are with him, are much more civil; and this is generally true of the Comedy heroines. There is a charming air of camaraderie in the joking between princess and gamekeeper in *Love's Labour's Lost*, in rhymed couplets (IV.i.10 ff.). But as time goes on, there is a moving apart. The gentry learn to practise wit among themselves. An older, easy-going coexistence between classes was fading, or being broken off unceremoniously. Shakespeare must often have known 'unregarded age in corners thrown', like his Adam in *As You Like It*, brutally dismissed by Oliver; he gives Orlando the small savings of a lifetime and accompanies him to the forest. Adam is the most truly religious person in the Comedies (except, perhaps, Shylock), with a deeply held trust in heaven. In his way, he is a Puritan who has always practised thrift and kept his health by leading a wholesome, abstemious life (II.iii.42, 47 ff.).

In the Histories middle-class life is virtually a blank. Italy had never been so thoroughly feudalized as France and England, and this left differences that must have been visible to Shakespeare in the sources he drew on. Even so, middle-class modes of living show only here and there in the Comedies; on the other hand, what may loosely be called middle-class ideas and qualities are fairly steadily enlarging their influence. Where the middle point of the social scale was to be fixed had hitherto depended on the old markers of birth and rank; now there was an alternative measuring-rod, money. Here too it seems as if Shakespeare's preference was for the halfway mark. Contentment with a modest competence was an ancient doctrine often repeated by Elizabethan writers. Nerissa laughs at her mistress's sighs, and praises the golden mean: 'for aught I see, they are as sick that surfeit with too much as they that starve with nothing' (*MV* I.ii.5 ff.).

A malaise seems to hang over the heaped-up treasures of wealthy Venice. The two rich men both come to grief, and the rich lady suffers painful suspense over her father's eccentric will. Antonio's first speech, the first of the play, begins: 'In sooth I know not why I am so sad'. Portia's first words are 'By my troth, Nerissa, my little body is aweary of this great world' (I.ii.1–2). Antonio's unexplained melancholy seems a presentiment of sorrows to come; wealth appears as an unnatural, ill-omened thing, a burden to the possessor like the crown to a king, and a perverter of society. His profits are wafted to him over far oceans; he has only to wait and receive them. To such a man life may well feel unreal, a mirage, or 'A stage', as he says, 'where every man must play a part' (I.i.78).

The 'lower orders' figure more distinctly than the middle classes, but not collectively. There is scarcely any allusion, except by the alien Shylock in the courtroom, to the suffering poor as a class. Bottom and his friends are the only flesh-and-blood group of hand-workers. Untutored they may be, but not altogether ignorant – of theatrical matters, for instance. Bottom knows what roles are in fashion; Quince has some understanding of a producer's job, and wants a prologue 'written in eight and six' (*MND* III.i). These 'rude mechanicals' (III.ii.9) have more common sense than the gentlefolk chasing one another through the woods, and their company gives us a welcome change. Once more we hear plebeians struggling with novel words: Flute has to correct Quince's 'paramour' to 'paragon' (IV.ii).

We are reminded in all kinds of ways that the Comedy world belongs to a late, decadent stage of feudalism. This is very clear in *Love's Labour's Lost*. Armado's letter to the king begins with a string of compliments to his 'soul's earth's God' (I.i.218–19) such as the sonneteers addressed to their mistresses or patrons. With more than a touch of irony, the princess sends word to the king that she and her party are awaiting 'Like humble-visaged suitors, his high will' (II.ii.34) – i.e. waiting to know when he will be ready to see them. Shakespeare probably had such experiences in unpleasant earnest; Sonnet 57 hints at them:

> Being your slave, what should I do but tend
> Upon the hours and times of your desire?

Rosaline threatens to torment Berowne by making him 'fawn, and beg, and seek,/And wait the season, and observe the times' (V.ii.61 ff.): the proud mistress was the feminine replica of the haughty aristocrat making his clients dance attendance on him. Courtship and courtiership were much the same thing. Silvia addresses both her admirer Valentine and his nearly arrived friend as 'servant' (*TGV* II.iv).

Just as Shakespeare makes us see the loud-mouthed street bully indirectly, by vivid description and with a few comic imitators like Pistol, he does not show us much of the bourgeois class, but in subtler ways lets us know a great deal about how society is being *bourgeoisified*, or permeated by money and money-making. Summer's beauty can be called 'costly' only in a society where everything has to be paid for. The impatient heir is 'gaping' for his patrimony; Theseus compares the moon, whose slow waning delays his wedding, to an old woman 'Long withering out a young man's revenue' (*MND* I.i.5–6). Images and odd phrases in *Love's Labour's Lost* show that remote Navarre is breathing the same air as Athens. The obnoxious Boyet is 'wit's pedler', whereas Berowne and his friends 'sell by gross' (V.ii.317 ff.): one of many comparisons all the more illuminating because so incongruous to the speakers. In Padua a father is anxious to marry off an elder daughter and so, like a shopkeeper, get rid of a 'commodity' which has long lain 'fretting' by him (*TS* II.i.321).

In Venice, Antonio undergoes the humiliation of having to follow the Jew he has spat on through the streets and beg for mercy. In the money-making jungle there is no pity for the distressed, as we see again, metaphorically, in *As You Like It* (II.i.45 ff.) when Jaques is pitying a wounded stag and finding a 'thousand similes' to moralize on. They turn on money, property, sordid greed. One of them may suggest that the poet is thinking of his father's business troubles: the sufferer is abandoned by its 'velvet friends', who have no sympathy to spare for 'the poor and broken bankrupt'. They are compared to 'fat and greasy citizens': words full of aristocratic distaste for the bourgeoisie, like Jaques's talk a little later about the luxurious apparel of rich citizens' wives (II.vii 75–6).

The Taming of the Shrew abounds in what Trollope, in *The Kellys and the O'Kellys* (ch. 1), called the 'particulars always interesting to gentlemen who seek money and love at the same time'. Petruchio's father has just died, leaving him an estate, but he wants more, and is prepared to marry any woman for money (I.ii.48 ff.). Hortensio predicts that Katherina will find a husband in spite of her temper, because her father Baptista is offering a good dowry, and 'there be good fellows in the world' who will snap up such a bargain (I.i.127–9). Baptista offers his younger daughter Bianca to the highest bidder, and we learn all about the applicants' resources. Lucentio, or Tranio as his proxy, carries the day by boasting of his great wealth (II.i). Hortensio gives up hope of Bianca, and promptly transfers himself to a rich widow whom he has long had the refusal of. He can boast himself a 'gentleman', which may be his attraction for her (IV.ii).

Fenton at Windsor confesses, like Bassanio at Belmont, that he has been a spendthrift; worse, he has been given to 'riots' and 'wild societies'; his interest in Anne Page began with thoughts of her father's money (he and Shakespeare may both have forgotten that she has a young brother), but he assures her it is now quite different (*MWW* III.iv.5 ff.). Fenton is 'too great of birth' for Mr Page's liking, though probably not for Miss Page's. Bassanio admits to Portia that all his wealth runs in his veins (*MV* III.ii.255–6). In return she does not forget to tell him that with her ring she is giving him her possessions as well as herself (III.ii.168 ff.). He has won the golden fleece that floated in his mind in Venice (I.i.170–1), and that his companion Gratiano rather tactlessly recurs to now in Portia's presence.

Overseas trade is lucrative, but hazardous, for political as well as other reasons. At the opening of *The Comedy of Errors* old Aegeon of Syracuse is being condemned to death for venturing into Ephesus, because of a quarrel between the two states. In *The Taming of the Shrew* a Mantuan is tricked by a tale that Mantuan ships at Venice are being seized, and all Mantuans in Padua, a Venetian city, are to be executed (IV.iii). Antonio of Venice is very sorry for the loss of his ships, but neither he nor anyone else has a tear to spare for the luckless seamen who must have lost their lives, or been cast away like some who are seen at Genoa by Shylock's friend Tubal (*MV* III.i.97–8). Capitalism dehumanizes; it is the merchandise that matters, not the men. As very often, one longs to know whether Shakespeare means us to notice this, or has noticed it himself. But a habitual chord of his social commentary is touched by Dogberry's saying that 'men grow hard-hearted and will lend nothing for God's sake' (*MAAN* V.i.314–15). A debtor is not to be envied, even without a Shylock at his heels. We hear of one debtor under arrest, and his dolorous condition in jail, kept in 'durance worse than Hell' by a pitiless warder – 'A fiend, a fury' (*CE* IV.ii.32 ff.).

You take my life, Shylock protests to the Doge, if you take away the capital I live by (*MV* IV.i.371–3). Many a small English cultivator ejected from his rented patch of land, or his share in the use of a village common, might have voiced the same complaint. In *As You Like It*, that golden comedy, there are scattered references to social evils: they are needed to explain why the rigours of life in the woods – the duke, unlike his daughter, seems to have no roof over his head – can seem more bearable than those of 'civilization'. Shakespeare is romanticizing the past when he contrasts the virtues of an 'antique world' with a mercenary present. Orlando has fared as badly as the prodigal son, without deserving it (I.i.35–7). Even in Arden the refugees encounter a 'churlish' master, or rich farmer, who has no thought of earning merit by generosity to others (II.iv.73 ff.). Sidney Lee did not doubt that Shakespeare had in mind the grievances of the peasantry of his native south Warwickshire (*Stratford* 278–9).

In this play we have an antithetical picture of society reminiscent in some ways of the Histories. At the top, among the well-placed, are fraternal hatred and fratricidal plotting; at the bottom, a jester escorts his mistresses into exile, as Adam follows Orlando. Things have been turned upside down; the high become dependent on the low. Silvan companionship and cheerful endurance are not a realistic forecast of the century to follow; they are a daydream of a better time, leading to one when blind Fortune's gifts will be 'bestowed equally' instead of 'mightily misplaced' (*AYLI* I.ii.29 ff.). But there is no dawning of such a time at the end of the Comedies; in *Twelfth Night* the social order is breaking, or fading into a haze.

Affairs of State

An inconsistent picture of government emerges from the Comedies. On the one hand authority is growing impersonal and formal; and where we hear of it (we never see it) as still active, it can be expected to misbehave. On the other hand, though rebellions and civil wars have been stopped, at street level things are still disorderly, because authority lacks strength, as Shakespeare's obsessive talk of noisy bullies and rowdies warns us.

Portia has some conventionally fine words about 'the dread and fear of kings' (*MV* IV.i.189), but such language is out of place in republican Venice, and there is nothing dreadful about the rulers who tread Shakespeare's comic stage. We are living in a post-absolutist era, when the function of government, in peacetime, is little more than to declare and uphold the law. Bound by custom, rulers are constitutional monarchs or

presidents, unable to infringe even the worst law for the best reason. In
Venice the Doge cannot override Shylock's bond to save a good man's
life, and in Athens Theseus cannot set aside a law which enables a father
to have a disobedient daughter executed. In Ephesus the duke pities
Aegeon, but cannot exempt him from the rigour of the law. Absolutism
had not altered the fact that England and Europe were full of musty old
laws, nearly impossible to shake off without revolution.

We may then feel called on to wish for governments to be more
capable of initiative and action, yet chance allusions to unfettered power
point to the dislike and suspicion that 'the court' and its denizens habitually inspired in England. Honeysuckles keeping out sunlight are like
'favourites made proud by princes' (*MAAN* III.i.9 ff.). The good duke in
As You Like It contrasts the free life of Nature, which teaches knowledge
of reality instead of flattering, with the 'painted pomp' of 'the envious
court' (II.i.1 ff.). It is always curious to think of Queen Elizabeth listening
to speeches like these – unless they were toned down for her benefit.

The Comedies are situated in a peaceful present instead of, like the
Histories, in a lawless past. Shakespeare takes for granted the 'Tudor
peace', and sometimes makes it sound more complete than it really was.
He was telling both government and public how they *ought* to behave.
Respect for law and legality was no doubt growing, but there must be
some humorous exaggeration when Sly the tinker, threatened with arrest
for debt by a parish officer, replies that he will 'answer him by law'. The
Capulet servants may want to be sure of having the law on their side, but
it is not long before they are battling with their Montague foes. Law-
enforcement machinery is minimal, as it really was in England. Locally it
is entrusted to worthies like Justice Shallow, or Constable Dogberry,
who considers that the best way to deal with a thief is to have nothing to
do with him (*MAAN* III.iii). Parson Evans is against notifying the Privy
Council of a riot, because 'The Council, look you, shall desire to hear the
fear of Got, and not to hear a riot' (*MWW* I.i.32 ff.).

Even where a prince has an important role to play, it is not as a
wielder of power. Shakespeare makes his duke of Milan a ridiculous
monarch as well as an odious parent; he pursues his runaway daughter
himself, instead of sending his guard, and is captured by a parcel of *banditti*. Don Pedro looks like a member of a jolly house-party. Benedick
refers to him and Claudio as a pair of 'hobby-horses' (*MAAN* III.ii). Only
in *The Taming of the Shrew* and *The Merry Wives of Windsor* is no head of
State visible, but only in *The Comedy of Errors, A Midsummer Night's Dream*
and *The Merchant of Venice*, the three classical or republican polities, is he
an impressive figure. And 'Mighty Theseus', as his court official addresses
him (*MND* V.i.38), has only a small paternalistic state to manage, of the
sort of which Germany had scores or hundreds; despite his conquests, the

laws of his Athens run no more than seven leagues from the city. Navarre is told by the princess that by his retirement, and giving up 'housekeeping', or the duties of hospitality, he is committing a 'deadly sin' (*LLL* II.i.104). She is treating him as a country gentleman. No duties of government come into question; he has none.

Illyria is a similar country. 'Who governs here?' Viola, shipwrecked on the coast, inquires (*TN* I.ii.23). The answer ought to be 'Nobody'. Duke Orsino is perhaps only a governor, and at one point he dwindles to a Count (III.i.37). At the outset he is baring his lovelorn heart to his courtiers, and summoning them to join him in repose on 'sweet beds of flowers'. Clearly he has nothing better to do with his time. He is more his natural self when he hails the jester affably as 'my good fellow', and rewards his wit with a piece of gold (V.i.10–11, 27–8). As in the latter Histories, monarchy is learning the arts of popularity. Theseus insists on watching the workmen's play, despite a warning that it will be poor stuff, and adds an obvious allusion to Elizabeth's progresses, with their speeches of welcome read out by sufferers from stage fright, and so on (*MND* V.i.81 ff.).

Along with its fellow-traveller, kingship, war has receded into the background. Two battles are heard of, both of them events prior to the play. In *Much Ado about Nothing* we hear at once of a cheerful victory, with few losses, and the rebel, Don Pedro's brother, already pardoned. Before *Twelfth Night* begins there has been a sea-fight; booty was carried off by the attackers, but most of it has been handed back, for the sake of restoring trade (III.iii). Imagery may be of warfare far away. Puck travels 'Swifter than arrow from the Tartar's bow' (*MND* III.ii.101). But there are more realistic touches as well, sometimes suggestive of revulsion against the brutalities of war. Browne's simile of a town captured with the aid of fire, but also destroyed by it (*LLL* I.i.146), may be a memory of some recent happening in France or the Netherlands. Glory and crime often go together (*LLL* IV.i.31). Jaques pictures a soldier as quarrelsome, hard-swearing, brave, but for no better motive than pursuit of 'the bubble reputation' (*AYLI* II.vii.148–52).

Yet Shakespeare remains an admirer of the manly courage that can show itself fully only when life itself is staked on the gage. He is never tired of ridiculing pretended courage; it may be doubted whether any other writer of his time returns so often to this theme. Sir Toby, no faint-heart, remarks on how loud oaths and an overbearing manner may have more effect than a bold spirit (*TN* III.iv.180 ff.). Shallow makes no boast of being a fighting man now, but likes it to be understood that he has been 'a great fighter' in his time, and could make 'four tall fellows skip like rats' (*MWW* II.i.202–4).

Valentine, Orlando, Benedick, Sebastian, exhibit courage before our eyes, and thus prove themselves worthy of the fair ladies in Shakespeare's gift. Duke Orsino pays tribute to Antonio's bravery on the enemy side in the naval encounter; he himself took part in it, which gives him a more manly air than he has shown hitherto (*TN* V.i.50 ff.). Petruchio talks of his experiences of sea-tempest and battlefield, with 'great ordnance' firing, as evidence that he will not flinch from a woman's tongue (*TS* I.ii.201 ff.). Shakespeare's own preference is for the courage of more civilized men. His instinctive wish was to refine whatever he touched. He evokes repeatedly the Renaissance association between war and letters. Navarre is a quiet place, but Longaville has earned a right to be extolled as a man 'well fitted in arts, glorious in arms' (*LLL* II.i.45). Bassanio is first mentioned as 'a scholar and a soldier' (*MV* I.ii.108), which we can take on trust even if we never see him with either a book or a sword in his hand.

Mars and Venus were close together in Shakespeare's pantheon. Even 'the stern and direful god of war', she boasts to Adonis, has been her 'captive' and 'slave' (*VA* 97 ff.). Love and war, or rather the capacity to undergo the test of war, are related to each other as two of life's prime values; irreverently enough in the phrase we hear from Toby about 'boarding' a woman, as if a ship to be made prize of. On the other hand, admiration of masculine courage could be expected from women, seeing that they often had to depend on it for protection. According to Proteus, 'Falsehood, cowardice and poor descent' are the three things they despise most in men (*TGV* III.ii.32–3). Before the wrestling match in *As You Like It* Celia and Rosalind try to dissuade Orlando, but once the bout starts they ardently hope for him to win, and it is his defiance of the champion that kindles Rosalind's interest in him. His tongue would scarcely have won it for him, but later on, as a makeweight, Shakespeare gives him a lioness to fight, off-stage. 'There is no love-broker in the world', Sir Toby asserts, more persuasive with women than 'report of valour' (*TN* III.ii.36–7); in pursuit of it Sir Andrew is steered into the business of his challenge to 'Cesario', his fancied rival for Olivia's hand.

In his duelling episodes Shakespeare's ambivalence of feeling about violence and bloodshed shows most clearly. He makes fun of the duel again and again, yet it remains for him the *ultima ratio* of a gentleman, as war is of a king. On this ground a man of honour was above any law except that of honour. Only a poltroon like Sir Andrew would take care, when drawing up a challenge, to 'keep o' th' windy side of the law', as Fabian sarcastically commends him for doing (*TN* III.iv.168–9). As the proposed antagonist is really a girl, the whole affair is nonsensical. So it is, on the surface at least, when the elegant Armado is challenged by Costard the clown. Costard embodies the common sense of the anti-heroic:

'Peace be to me, and every man that dares not fight' (*LLL* I.i.225–6). Yet when a serious occasion arises, it is he who is ready to fight, not the courtier. He is fond of Jaquenetta, and Armado has trifled with her affections. Costard comes to the village girl's defence like a humbly born Benedick.

Challenged by Valentine, Thurio replies, sensibly enough, that he is not going to risk life and limb on account of a girl who cares nothing for him; her father the duke considers this 'degenerate and base' (*TV* V.iv.132 ff.). When Lysander and Demetrius blunder about after each other in the misty woods, crying out on each other's cowardice, it looks as if Shakespeare is having a hit at men who trumpet their love of fighting when there is nobody to fight. Touchstone likes to air his wit on the subject of 'honour' (*AYLI* I.ii.56 ff.), and he backs his claim to gentility with a humorous tale of how he once nearly had to fight a duel for criticizing the cut of a courtier's beard (V.iv.45 ff.). His rigmarole about the 'seven causes' – Quip Modest, Lie Direct, etc. – is scarcely more silly than the pedantic textbooks written in Italy and other countries on the minute niceties of the laws of Honour.

Dr Caius, the fire-eating Frenchman, sends a challenge to Parson Evans, who is backing Slender for Anne Page's hand. To call out a parson, and on such grounds, was hardly proper, but Evans is a martial Welshman, like Fluellen. He asks the landlord of the Garter to measure the weapons; the jolly host arranges for the opponents to be waiting for each other at different places – Caius full of sanguinary threats, Evans not quite so bellicose. When the host confesses his little trick, all are soon friends again (*MWW* III.i). Sir Andrew thinks it smart to challenge a man and then leave him waiting at the rendezvous (*TN* II.iii.132 ff.). He is soon being pushed by officious friends into facing an encounter in earnest, as were a great many men all through the history of duelling. 'He cannot by the duello avoid it', Sir Toby solemnly pronounces (III.iv.305). Later on, when Andrew falls foul of Sebastian and is knocked down, he threatens only 'an action of battery against him, if there be any law in Illyria' (IV.ii.33–5). Toby is so disgusted that he takes the quarrel on himself. A duel follows, and he is injured, but takes it in good part. Sebastian, newly married to Olivia, has to apologize for wounding her kinsman (V.i.208 ff.): a comic parallel to Romeo having to fight his wife's cousin.

In all this buffoonery the duel is shown in its absurder colours; only in *Much Ado about Nothing* is a serious challenge given for a serious reason, and with the worthiest motives. It comes with all the more weight from Benedick because he seems to have a reputation for prudent avoidance of unnecessary quarrels. This is the only sense that can be made of Pedro's bantering words – meant for him to hear – about how he keeps out of danger 'with a most Christian-like fear' (II.iii.188 ff.). Benedick is acknowledged to be a brave soldier. His philosophy is Shakespeare's: 'In a false quarrel there is no true valour' (V.i.120).

Religion is at as low an ebb as its ally, royalty. There is no mention of it as a bar to Portia's marrying the Muslim prince of Morocco. Neither she nor any of the others thinks of offering thanks to heaven for Antonio's deliverance, as Henry V would have done so unctuously. There is a plentiful sprinkling of religious allusions, and one, to a heretic being burned alive, is a reminder that religion was no laughing matter (MAAN I.i.218–20). An ill-judged love, now renounced, is a 'heresy' abandoned (MND II.ii.145–6). Orlando's virtues are 'sanctified and holy traitors' to him, because bad men take advantage of them (AYLI II.iii.13): there is a strong whiff here of Catholic conspiracy, that bugbear of Elizabethan England. There are turns of speech borrowed light-heartedly from sermons or pious tracts, and smiled at in the concluding song of Love's Labour's Lost about how 'coughing drowns the parson's saw'. Most of the scattering of phrases about Providence are as perfunctory as Mrs Quickly's 'all is in His hands above' (MWW I.iv). Human passions are too strong to be curbed except 'by a special grace', or divine aid, Berowne admonishes his friends (LLL I.i.152).

Words that stand out more earnestly are Hero's pathetic appeal to God as the only protector left her against the 'catechizing' or interrogation she is subjected to. She is answered with good advice from a sympathetic priest, a man who can see the truth because, we are told, he has learned from the book of life as well as from reading (MAAN IV.i). Shakespeare finds convenient uses for Catholic priests, as an Italian setting licenses him to do, in The Two Gentlemen of Verona, for instance, when Silvia escapes by going to 'Friar Patrick's cell', ostensibly for confession (IV.iii). These men are always well-meaning and try to be helpful; at any rate, they are better men of God than the proud prelates of the Histories. Some Catholic sentiment descending to him from his family may have helped to make Shakespeare treat them benignly.

'Sir' Nathaniel in Love's Labour's Lost has a very English air, from a time when Anglican clergymen did not command much respect. He seems to be a regular 'curate', yet Berowne alludes to him uncomplimentarily as 'the hedge-priest' (V.ii.540). In Arden a real hedge-priest or impostor plies his trade, 'Sir' Oliver Martext. Feste is ready with jokes about the clergy (TN IV.ii.4 ff.), and has no scruples about masquerading as one of them. In the Church of England beliefs too were debatable. Salvation by faith instead of by good works was the shibboleth of the Reformation, but the Thirty-nine Articles were designed to be ambiguous, and now the issue was hotly argued. Maria, laughing at Malvolio, unwittingly takes the Protestant side when she says that a good Christian 'means to be saved by believing rightly' (III.ii.69).

So does the princess in *Love's Labour's Lost* when she calls it a 'heresy' to think of being 'saved by merit' (IV.i.21–2), but an airy skit on Catholic thinking lurks in the plot of this play. Navarre's ambition of winning fame by austere study is a parody of Catholic hopes of winning heaven by ascetic rigours and self-mortification. A Protestant believed in sober self-control, in the midst of an active, useful life, not in displays of asceticism. His mentors did not favour the taking of private vows like those Navarre gets his friends to join him in. There seems to be a laugh at casuistry, a discipline in which Jesuit skill or oversubtlety was unquestioned, when the other three acolytes call on Berowne to concoct some plausible excuse for them to break their vows, 'some salve for perjury' (IV.iii.286).

Shakespeare has equal enjoyment in making fun of the opposite camp, that of the 'Puritans', often accused of hypocritical austerity. When Bassanio cautions Gratiano against his over-levity and 'skipping spirit', Gratiano promises to be the soul of discretion at Belmont, and always to have a prayer book in his pocket. Martext the bogus priest comforts himself with pious jargon, after being berated by Jaques; no one, he says defiantly, can 'flout me out of my calling' (*AYLI* III.iii). For the Puritan his work, whatever it might be, was laid out for him by his heavenly taskmaster. (Falstaff makes a joke of highway robbery being his 'vocation'.) There is a disparaging reference in *Twelfth Night* to one set of radical Puritans, seceders from the Church of England: the 'Brownists' or followers of Robert Browne (III.ii.31).

Shakespeare has been taxed with being too hard on Malvolio, as a worldly, egotistic 'puritan'. He seems to want to make it clear, through that shrewd person Maria, that Malvolio is not a puritan in any really religious sense (*TN* II.iii.153 ff.); perhaps also that he himself is not anti-Puritan, when he makes the stupid tippler Sir Andrew say that he would like to beat any Puritan like a dog, which even Toby finds surprising (II.iii.147 ff.). Malvolio knows how to be 'a kind of puritan' at times (II.iii.146); there is no contradiction between this and his ambition to be a great man, surrounded by obsequious attendants. He belongs to an 'upwardly mobile' middle class, ready to challenge an unthrifty gentry and step into its shoes. He would like to be 'Count Malvolio', consort of a wealthy heiress; he dislikes loose living like Sir Toby's, but once gentrified he may be expected to behave as foolishly as he does in his yellow stockings and cross-garters. Charles I thought the play ought to have been called *Malvolio*; he may have seen in him some traits of his own Roundhead opponents. Toby accused Malvolio of thinking that because he was virtuous, there should be no more cakes and ale (II.iii.120–2); the Commonwealth was too apt to make outlawing of cakes and ale a substitute for reform of graver evils, those of wealth and poverty.

Though there is little formal piety in these plays, forgiveness and reconciliation are sometimes held up to us as ideals: Valentine is their first advocate. But the message is an awkward one to fit into plays where the villains are the most comical characters, and the happy endings are a joke. Shylock's case is the exception, because here two religions are set up as opposites. It has been noted that it is illogical for Portia to address to a Jew the Christian argument that we should extend to others the forgiveness that we ourselves pray for. If, however, we put the most favourable construction on her words, they are really spoken to her fellow-Christians. It has to be impressed on them early in the trial that when their turn comes to have the whip hand they must show themselves better able than an unbeliever to rise to a moral challenge. Some of them do respond and display, as the Doge says, 'the difference of our spirit' from Shylock's (*MV* IV.i.364). Gratiano's brutal triumphing over the defeated foe is the spirit of everyday 'Christianity'; true Christianity has to transcend it. All this can only remain one-sided; Shylock is foiled, but no more reconciled than Malvolio. His forced conversion is meaningless. It is the nominal Christians whom Shakespeare is converting, by getting them to practise what they preach.

Epilogue

It would be agreeably simple to identify 'serious' drama, historical or tragical, with the crumbling of an old order, and comedy with a new one growing up to replace it. In reality older and newer elements are intermingled in both, and good and bad; though in the case of comedy what we see is gradual decay rather than sudden collapse. The salient contrast is between attitudes to life, or philosophies of life. Watching 'serious' drama 'we look before and after, and pine for what is not', like Shelley. In comedy we are content to make do with the present. Still, the present is not stationary; today is also part of a process of change. The plays themselves, in this series, are altering. As often noticed, they make repeated use of the same devices, in particular the disguising of young women as young men. What is altering all the time is not the materials Shakespeare makes use of, the mechanics of composition, but colouring, atmosphere, outlook, the essence of each text.

Much wit in these comedies is merely playful, but there is a cumulative impression of its working on the side of new, more sensible thinking, escape from a limbo of outworn, meaningless things. A smouldering fire is consuming old rubbish. Shakespeare can often be heard laughing at the faded wisdom of bygone days. 'Divers philosophers hold that the lips is parcel of the mouth' (*MWW* I.i.215–16): the scholastic pedantry that Bacon was sweeping away sounds all the more absurd in the odd English of a Welsh parson. So does the musty Latin lesson he gives to young William; Mrs Quickly's misunderstandings of the words add to the fun (IV.i).

Something of the same kind is happening with the cherished credos of popular superstition, too often sponsored and exploited by the learned, both lay and clerical. Without too hasty an enlisting of Shakespeare on the side of rationalism, we may fairly see his references to the supernatural as pointing that way. Antipholus of Syracuse is soon convinced that Ephesus must be full of 'Dark-working sorcerers', 'Soul-killing witches', and so on (*CE* I.ii.97 ff.), when we know that his bewilderment is simply the result of his being with the wrong Dromio. Shakespeare's simple-minded contemporaries were just as ready to explain everything that turned out badly as caused by magic. Pinch is an emaciated wretch who has taken to fortune-telling and the occult for want of any better livelihood (V.i.238 ff.). With the example of the unlucky Antipholus of Ephesus, Shakespeare points out how easily a citizen could find himself locked up as a lunatic, or one possessed by an evil spirit (V.i).

'White' magic was often resorted to for help in finding missing things or persons (Thomas chs 7–8). Orlando seems only mildly surprised when Rosalind assures him that she will produce his lost mistress for him by secret arts learned from a 'profound' but 'not damnable' magician (*AYLI* V.ii); surely she does not mean him to take her promise seriously. Mr Ford believes an old woman in the house to be a witch (*MWW* IV.ii); surely this is meant to be part of the folly that suspicion of his wife has plunged him into. Illyria's practical jokers pretend to think that Malvolio is possessed by a fiend, and Fabian suggests calling in the 'wise woman' who was to be found in every English village (*TN* III.iv).

A dual process was going on – as in the Histories on another plane – of Shakespeare getting to know more of the realities of his England, and turning over in his mind what parts of them were worth preserving, what ought to be got rid of. His main field of speculation was the area where the lesser aristocracy or gentry, and the cultured middle class, met and in varying degrees mingled. Castiglione, in his book on the model man of the world, complained that among the French only warlike virtues were esteemed (88, 93). Shakespeare rated these very highly, but he looked for others too, and was seeking to bring together courage and honour, sense and education. He had so much success that a good part of all later English – and European – thinking about the 'gentleman', and what he ought to be, must be credited to him.

In the Comedies it is the better and weaker qualities of youth that we see most of. Shakespeare's young gentlemen are not a vicious set. We do not see them gambling, drinking or philandering. A censure that he passes on their class in England – it does not apply to any of his own characters – is that they are too fond of outlandish clothes and manners. 'The young baron of England' who is one of Portia's suitors is ridiculous because his costume is a medley from three countries, yet he knows nothing of any foreign language (*MV* I.ii.64 ff.). Shakespeare may have recognized that resentments against an upper class come out more sharply when it begins to look alien.

He wanted his young men to be doing something with their gifts; in this he did not differ much from a Puritan preacher and writer like Perkins, always indignant at the idle rich and their hangers-on, as mere parasites. Some of Shakespeare's men may be landowners, but this is not emphasized, and the occasional one, like Thurio, whose sole recommendation is the 'dirt' he owns, does not invite esteem. Mostly they have or mean to acquire some occupation; but their existence suffers from a certain emptiness. Towards the end, after Benedick, Shakespeare seems to tire of his young men, and prefer the company of older men from among the undeserving poor of the old order: Falstaff and Sir Toby.

Some grafting of complementary qualities can be seen between men and women, as well as between classes. Women too should have education, intelligence, freedom to speak, and courage, moral if not physical; men should have more of their sensitiveness and sympathy. Women remain attractively different from men – far more than in the Histories, where the sexes are only too close in their ambitions and ruthless egotism. Now that it is their better, instead of worse, qualities that are drawing them together, love can take on true meaning. Something not altogether unlike the later Romantic idea of woman as redeemer shows here and there in the Comedies, as it does more distinctly in Shakespeare's last plays. It is not sustained in the final Comedies, any more than the evolution of the gentleman. Rosalind disguised as a man could be queen of the forest, but Viola discovers that her disguise is making trouble, and has to admit the 'frailty' of her too impressionable sex, of 'women's waxen hearts' (*TN* II.ii.25 ff.). She and Olivia – and Anne Page – have no confidantes, and are the most isolated of the heroines.

A stereotyped pattern of villain against hero is not a favourite with Shakespeare, in either comedy or tragedy. It implies too simple a distribution of evil and good – elements in reality dispersed, whether latent or active, through the social frame. In Venice alone we have what appears to be a clear-cut antithesis between wholesome community and wicked intruder. But Shylock is not a true villain, a human being who chooses evil. Instead the drama shows how badly men of all sorts can act, without feeling bad. Of the daily injustices of social life, overlooked from force of habit, the nearest we come to a revelation is Shylock's charge against the Venetians – which no one answers – of cruel usage of slaves and beasts of burden. Shylock is baffled easily enough, but to exorcize these general discords is far harder. The music of the spheres we hear of in Act V seems to be a harmony of the heavens only, not to be looked for on earth.

A small-town provincial, finding his feet in London and moving between there and Stratford, Shakespeare makes much use in the Comedies of shifts between town and country. Even when the location is urban, a good many scenes are laid in gardens. Both *A Midsummer Night's Dream* and *As You Like It* are mainly rural, though as usual the characters mostly come from the town. We are not yet near to Timon, shaking the dust of Athens off his feet; but there is enough sense of disgust with mankind, or the workings of its social life, to make exile under trees and stars seem a good exchange. Only by withdrawing to a utopian settlement in the wilds, as the young Romantic poets were to dream of doing, can men re-create their lost fellowship.

But it is only in fantasy that Shakespeare can think, now and then, of turning the clock back, or forward, like this. The Comedies end with a play of wonderful charm, but over-romantic, as *Henry V* is overheroic; it needs the hearty earthy strain of Sir Toby and his set as an antidote to artificial refinements. Appropriately, Shakespeare moves his scene further away now than Italy, to a Ruritania of his imagination.

PART V

Life Unfolding

1

Chance and Destiny, Fate and Accident

It would not be surprising if a man devoting as much of his energy as Shakespeare did to writing plays, memorizing parts in other men's plays, performing all kinds of roles, came to be sometimes haunted by a sense of unreality. He would be likely to feel this more in Comedy, pure fiction, than in History, grounded on fact. 'Thou talkst of nothing', exclaims Romeo, interrupting Mercutio's Queen Mab speech; he agrees – 'True, I talk of dreams' (*RJ* I.iv.96). *A Midsummer Night's Dream* is full of questionings about the two realms of being, real and fancied, and the meaning that poetry, in between them, can have. Theseus is a matter-of-fact Anglo-Saxon; he dismisses the lovers' tales as delusion, and goes on to compare them with the poet's pen turning 'airy nothing' into words (V.i.2 ff., 208). The best actors are only shadows, he declares, like the worst, and the Epilogue echoes him: 'If we shadows have offended ...' Force of feeling among spectators, called up by force of language, could turn them into creatures of flesh and blood – for a while, at least.

'Imagination bodies forth/The form of things unknown ...' (*MND* V.i.14–15). 'Imagination' was not a new word, but it was taking on new meanings, as it did for the Romantic poets later, becoming a powerful *daimon* or genie. But what unknown things was it bringing to light? We may venture to think of Shakespeare looking deeper, into recesses of human life from which thoughts and feelings of the future were to emerge. He can be heard pondering on imagination, and on himself as a creative artist, in the imprisoned Richard II's long self-communing, where the soul, standing for instinct or emotion, is the dominant partner, and the brain, or reason, its helper: 'My brain I'll prove the female to my soul ...' (V.v.1 ff.; cf. Knight, *Imperial Theme*, ch. xi).

Things historical, like Richard's crown, were real, but they or their meanings were shifting; familiar shapes were adrift on or being whirled along by an irresistible current. In a long soliloquy while a battle is being fought the hapless Henry VI muses on Time, and how smoothly and tranquilly it ought to flow along; instead it has become for war-torn England a raging flood (*3H.VI* II.v.1 ff.). So it was for Shakespeare's England and Europe. As a result his contemporaries were preoccupied, far more than most of their forefathers, with the processes of change and what they might bring. No mind has been more sensitive to them than Shakespeare's, almost to the point of obsession. 'Time's deformed hand' (*CE* V.i.300) was to him very often destructive. For the individual, aware of life slipping away, Time is a tyrant, as in the Sonnets; from a collective standpoint it may be a fertile, organic dimension of life. 'Time is the nurse and breeder of all good' (*TGV* III.i.243) – even if these words are spoken by a false friend, seeking to deceive.

Shakespeare's skill in 'the manipulation of time' on the stage has been praised (Beckerman 157). Time as a theme for discussion is more than usually audible in *As You Like It*, in those leisurely forest hours where it might be supposed to have fallen asleep. As a pretext for accosting Orlando, the disguised Rosalind asks him the time: what can it matter in Arden? but it gives her an opening for witty talk about how time sometimes goes too slowly, sometimes too fast, as for a thief on his way to the gallows (III.ii): an odd choice of subject for a sprightly creature talking to the man she loves. In another scene she calls Time 'the old justice' who tries and tests everything (IV.i.194–5). Orlando thinks of 'the creeping hours of time' (II.vii.111).

In another forest even the fairies have learned to measure out time, into fractions of a minute (*MND* II.ii.2). For centuries religion, commerce, war, had been helping to give Europe a more urgent sense of time than weighed on any other region. It was Europe that had invented serviceable mechanical clocks, and was now producing watches (see Landes). In Shakespeare clocks and watches have a conspicuous place. Jaques is vastly amused at the sight of Touchstone consulting his watch and talking sententiously of the passage of life and time (*AYLI* II.vii. 12 ff.). In Malvolio's daydream of being married to a countess and sitting in state among his attendants, he takes out his watch and winds it up, doubtless with a self-important air (*TN* II.v.59–60). A watch could be a status symbol. A neighbour who also owns one is the parish priest; it keeps him in mind of his progress towards the grave (V.i.161). Berowne compares a wife to a clock that always goes badly (*LLL* III.i.189–90), as many early timepieces did. In *King John* the Bastard talks of 'Old time the clock-setter, that bald sexton time' (III.i.324).

We may assume that Shakespeare acquired a watch and needed to look at it often. Whatever his own method – or lack of method – of working, he could appreciate a feeling of many busy men of his day, which Puritanism elevated into a religious principle, that any waste of time was culpable. Navarre opens *Love's Labour's Lost* with mixed metaphors about pursuit of fame as the preserver against 'cormorant devouring Time' and 'his scythe's keen edge'. 'The clock upbraids me with the waste of time', says Olivia self-reproachfully when Viola remains deaf to her wooing (*TN* III.i.132). Prince Hal's first words to Falstaff, who wakes up and asks the time, are 'What the devil has thou to do with the time of the day?' – and he ends this scene with an assurance that we shall find him 'Redeeming time when men least think I will' (*1H.IV* I.ii.3 ff., 209). Sure enough, once king he is reported to be husbanding his time with the greatest care. Here is a monarch steeping himself in a very middle-class virtue. Even Hotspur the cavalier is touched at the end by the Puritan recognition that 'the time of life is short', as he says to his friends before the battle (V.ii.83). As he lies dying, his last words are about how 'time that takes survey of all the world/ Must have a stop' (V.iv.82–3) – must end for him, with his death, or for the universe, as Prospero foretells? Only Falstaff keeps his gentlemanly indifference, except at moments when he feels the cold hand freezing him into an old man. 'Let time shape, and there an end' (*2H.IV* III.ii.331–2), he concludes his easy acceptance of the world and all its injustices, among them those he can profit by.

To make good use of time, a man must learn what he can of how things come about, and how they can be anticipated or regulated. Writing so many plays about history, Shakespeare is likely to have done a good deal of thinking about its motive forces. He would have agreed with Henry V's shrewd archbishop that the age of miracles had gone by, and rational explanations must be sought instead (I.i.67–9). Shakespeare seems to have thought of things happening through logical processes of their own, ceaselessly at work; in the long run they will 'fashion the event' (*MAAN* IV.i.234).

Ordinary folk were still thinking in terms of external forces, foreign to man and most clearly manifested by the stars. Traditional notions of a cosmic theatre full of signs and wonders were still upheld by the learned, though common sense was knocking at the door. Shakespeare was ready enough to make use of them, at least as stage props for his own theatre. When Titania and Oberon quarrel, Nature falls into disorder (*MND* II.i.82 ff.). We may laugh, as Hotspur does, at the portents Glendower boasts of having accompanied his birth; less coolly, perhaps, when Henry VI recalls, in his last words before Crookback strikes him down, the 'hideous tempest' that signalled Richard's monstrous birth (*3H.VI* V.vi. 46 ff.). When Henry IV is dying his sons talk of the portents that common people are observing (*2H.IV* IV.iv.120 ff.). Prophecies were ubiquitous in Shakespeare's day and for long after, usually with an astrological

foundation, and never more so than during the Civil Wars and Interregnum, when they were part of the staple of political propaganda
(Thomas, index: 'Interregnum').

It needs no great effort to convince oneself that Shakespeare was
among those who were taking a more rational view of such things. He
employs ghosts, in *Richard III*, and similar paraphernalia, but they are
mere embellishments, standing outside the action; or if the spirit-
conjuring in *Henry VI Part 2* is an exception, it is an early, very crude one.
Such things could be effective, and might be expected by the audience,
but Shakespeare's handling of them is of a kind to undermine credulity.
Clarence is arrested on the strength of prophecies and tales of plotting
and wizardry; we know that these have been put about by Richard to
poison their brother Edward IV's ear; and Edward swallows them
because he has grown 'sickly, weak, and melancholy' (*R.III* I.i.32 ff., 136).
When Richard accuses his opponents of using witchcraft to wither his
arm (*R.III* III.iv.67 ff.) we take it for granted that he is lying, and the
audience must have done the same, knowing that the arm had always
been withered.

Prophecy tells men the future; a curse can determine it. Many curses
are bandied about in the Histories, reaching their climax in *Richard III*,
where women, reduced to helplessness, launch maledictions which are
fulfilled one by one. Some at least of Margaret's opponents feel a chilling
pang of fear, like Buckingham when her warning against Richard makes
his hair stand on end (I.iii.246 ff., 303). In passages like these the stylized
verses seem to import that the speakers are uttering more than their own
thoughts, that they are somehow 'inspired'.

A sense of impending fate is built up. Even Richard, with all his
vibrant energy, can be startled by an Irish bard's prediction (IV.ii.100 ff.).
But there is no need for us to believe that anything is happening otherwise than by natural causes. These men of the Histories are driven by
blind ambitions and hatreds, from which they cannot dream of emanci-
pating themselves; lacking any higher purpose, their lives are so
meaningless that they think instinctively of a blind Fate overruling them.
'The sands are numbered that make up my life', says York, about to be
captured. His impotent struggles remind his foes of a trapped bird or
rabbit, a sight more familiar to Elizabethans than to modern men (*3H.VI*
I.iv). 'What fates impose,' his son Edward tells himself when caught in his
turn, 'that men must needs abide' (IV.iii). A little later we have, close
together, 'Fortune's spite', 'Fortune's malice', 'the stars' (IV.vi). The habitual thought of the world as a 'stage' could help to foster a feeling of the
human being as no more than a puppet.

There is very little in the Histories to suggest faith in a superintending
Providence; it can come naturally only to men and women who are able

to feel worthy of help from above, and these are very few. There are moments when Shakespeare, as poet if not as thinker, comes close to the idea – not of his own inventing – of a hereditary curse hanging over the House of Lancaster, as over the House of Atreus in Sophocles, because of an ancestral crime. Henry wrestles with it before Agincourt, remembering that his father was a usurper. Dramatically it comes in very naturally here. He is putting into religious shape what is really a pagan conception, as he does with his creed of war, conquest, and fame. A wilder sense of destiny or mission makes Crookback feel, as he stabs Henry VI, that this is a task for which he was 'ordained' (*3H.VI* V.vi.58). When he tells Elizabeth later on to blame not him but fate, she answers in religious terms: 'avoided grace makes destiny' (*R.III* IV.iv.218–19) – men can loosen fate's grip by listening to conscience.

Shakespeare was becoming a true historian in aim, if not always in method: he was studying the past in order to understand the present better, and what was needed to make the future better than either. In the Wars of the Roses it was evident to him that the red rose bloomed chiefly in the North of England, the white in the South; it was clearest of all that Hotspur and his northern party were the more feudal and anachronistic, like the rebel earls of 1569. Diana Vernon in *Rob Roy*, whose ancestors were Yorkist, accused the dramatist of being a Lancastrian. Really he did not take sides; manifestly both sides were bad, or far more bad than good. Success *ought* to favour a just cause; this was a conviction of Henry VI (*3H.VI* II.ii.45–6, 62), but his own wretched fate gainsays it. In the end neither side has won; they have both destroyed themselves and made way for a new, better dispensation, with the candidate most useful to his country in command. After so many ups and downs, legitimacy can mean little. 'Time', however it may be personified as a directing spirit, is turning into 'History'; 'prophecy' is becoming recognizable as a change in men's thinking, with power to bring about a changed situation.

Pious literature abounded in stories of 'special judgements', inflicted by heaven on sinners. A bricklayer gets drunk on the Sabbath, and next day falls off his ladder and breaks his neck. Here the Almighty's intention is crystal-clear, but very often it was so opaque that theology had to fall back on the thought of God's inscrutable purposes. These covered everything, but to the vulgar eye they were indistinguishable from the workings of the stars, or the Fortune that might seem the true deity of Renaissance man. Spenser's allegorical figure Mutability, in *The Faerie Queene*, challenges Jove for the mastery of the universe (Part 2 Bk 7).

Before a secular, scientific outlook could form, the old mythic notions had to give way to recognition of the simply accidental, the demystified happening, on the one hand – and, on the other, of broad patterns of change, sweeping chance events along with them. Sonnet 115 speaks of Time's 'millioned accidents' which alter men's minds and 'change decrees of kings'. In comedy, chance is always to be expected. Borachio's mischief-making starts with his happening to overhear a conversation, and ends with his happening to be overheard in turn. In tragedy, accident is more often harmful. Romeo and Juliet perish because a sudden outbreak of plague prevents a message from reaching Mantua. But this does not go against the grain of the drama. It was very unlikely that a secret union like theirs could fail to come to grief. As Lukács said, Shakespeare treats such accidentality 'with sovereign ease': it does not conflict with the play's doom-laden 'atmosphere of necessity' (*Historical Novel* 120–21). In his own day 'Fortune' could be used at times as what would now be termed a 'code word', a cover for mankind's self-inflicted *mis*fortunes. 'Under the fiction of this blind goddess,' wrote Nashe, 'we aim at the folly of princes and great men in dispensing of honours' (136).

Accident cannot be eliminated, but it can be made skilful allowance for. Intelligible designs take shape amid the welter, with causes and consequences that may be confronted. This is most patent in *Henry IV* with its more modern political life and critical outlook. When Henry is gloomily recalling the deposed Richard II's prediction of nationwide confusion, Warwick braces him by urging that such forecasts have no incomprehensible warrant. From knowledge of the past we can prophesy:

> With a near aim, of the main chance of things
> As yet not come to life, which in their seeds
> And weak beginnings lie intreasured,

but go on to become 'the hatch and brood of time'. 'Are these things then necessities?' the king rejoins. 'Then let us meet them like necessities' (*2H.IV* III.i.67 ff.).

Challenges dictate vigilance and energy; problems can be scrutinized and resolved. Men can take a rational view of things or situations when they feel capable of mastering them. In *Henry IV Part 2* 'necessity' hems men in, but the winning side is confident in its resources, while the losers feel increasingly vulnerable. 'We are time's subjects', says Hastings fatalistically, winding up a discussion of their plans by the conspirators (I.iii.110). 'The stream of time', the archbishop feels, is driving him and his friends into a hazardous channel, leaving them no choice.

Shakespeare was developing, not pioneering, a rational approach, which was at the same time a profoundly imaginative one. His characters have behind them 'the whole Renaissance philosophy of history' (L.B. Campbell 225), the belief in it as a useful science. Living when he did, he might well take up such ideas with a fresh and more searching mind, as well as clothing them in more splendid language. Things were changing more and more quickly and drastically now, with the advent of a society where money was to become all-powerful, and old ties were being weakened or disrupted.

Any epoch of deep-seated change is likely to have indistinct presentiments of what is to come, as well as a mixture of relief and regret at what is being left behind. Looking back, in her biography of her husband, a Parliamentary officer who died in prison after the Restoration, on her girlhood towards the end of James I's reign – a few years after Shakespeare's death – Lucy Hutchinson wrote: 'The land was then at peace – if that quietness may be called a peace, which was rather like the calm and smooth surface of the sea, whose dark womb is already impregnated with a horrid tempest' (2). Shakespeare, drawing on More by way of Holinshead, had written something remarkably similar when he made his nervous citizen in *Richard III* observe that at the approach of any great transformation:

> By a divine instinct men's minds mistrust
> Ensuing dangers; as, by proof, we see
> The waters swell before a dangerous storm.
> (II.iii.41 ff.)

The words may have an archaic sound, like those of Sonnet 107 about 'the prophetic soul/Of the wide world, dreaming on things to come'. But this 'soul' is nearing a metamorphosis into something more secular and tangible: public opinion and its guidance by careful observers able to descry in advance the drift of future events. Warwick's admonition to Henry IV is repeated in a later play by Nestor, to the other Greek chieftains outside Troy. Great happenings are preceded by smaller ones, 'indices' in which can be seen

> The baby figure of the giant mass
> Of things to come at large.

In *King John* 'baby eyes' and 'the giant world enraged' are close together (V.ii.56–7). Shakespeare had a liking for the epithet 'giant'; it expressed his always sensitive feeling of a frighteningly huge complex of things over against the puny human being. Yet this is not a power in itself, a monster with a vital strength of its own; it is the image men and women singly have of the social life they collectively build up, or the reverberating changes they bring about or fail to prevent. It is not an external deity, or fate, but something they have not yet learned to cope with sensibly. From this viewpoint, which Shakespeare shared with the more progressive thinkers of his age, he and they were not living through a 'waning age' (*TS* Induction. ii.62), the last chapter of a world running down; they were bound on an adventurous voyage towards a future day when men would know better how to live.

2

Towards the Tragic

Shakespeare's belief in the capacity of the human race to advance must have been strong; but so was his recognition of its failings, and of the barriers they constituted against any betterment of the human lot, the terrible cost of any movement towards a brighter future. In this lay the essence of tragedy. He had from the outset an impulse towards the tragic; his 'tragic period' would be an intensifying of it, an eclipse of the comic spirit, not a new birth. Apart from darkening moods of his own, sombre accents were part of what his audience wanted to hear from him, at first in the shape of melodrama as crude as most of ours of today. Worsening conditions of life for many, while others prospered, deepened spreading moods of resentment and guilt. Stories of towering figures and their fall could give expression to a pervasive sense of instability, of everything being in a melting-pot from which anything might emerge; a state of mind containing tragical and revolutionary elements. Out of these un-digested workings of the mass mind, and his own, Shakespeare was to learn by degrees to distil the spirit of tragedy, in the highest form mankind has known.

Both of his long poems were 'tragical' narratives. Early on he composed (or reworked) two tragic plays. Some of the Histories, like *Richard III*, were entitled 'tragedies', and indeed any weighty matters of state could be thought of as belonging to that sphere. In *Richard III* Buckingham assures his confederate that when it comes to swaying the public he knows how to 'counterfeit the deep tragedian' (III.v.4 ff.). Edward IV's queen, asked the reason for her abrupt entrance and dishevelled hair, replies that she comes 'To mark [make?] an act of tragic violence' (II. ii. 29): her husband is dead, danger is in the air.

In the early Histories long tirades or 'railings' are a stilted attempt to soar into tragic altitudes where one day the earth-shaking denunciations of Lear and Timon will be heard. 'Well could I curse away a winter's night', cries the banished Suffolk – even if he had to stand 'naked on a mountain top' (*2H.VI* III.ii.335–6). From women such outpourings can sound more natural, since they must often suffer without being able to act. 'I prythee, give me leave to curse awhile', says Joan of Arc, now a doomed captive (*1H.VI* V.iii.43). Shakespeare made use also of boys, helpless victims of another kind, Arthur or the princes in the Tower, as a Chorus bewailing the world's evils – as other youngsters, like Moth in *Love's Labour's Lost*, make us laugh at its silliness. Elizabethans found *language* so magical that to clothe troubles in words could itself afford relief. Hamlet was only too ready to 'unpack his heart with words'.

Hazlitt considered historical events too painfully real to be proper themes of tragedy, which requires 'fictitious danger and fictitious distress' (*Shakespeare* 186). This is rather an argument against contemporary themes, as too close to the spectator's eye. The Wars of the Roses were quite remote enough from Shakespeare's theatre, as they are from us; though for his grand historical tragedies he was to move much further away, to medieval Scotland or the ancient world. Feudal lords of the fifteenth century, born to live dangerously and often die painfully, were rich in tragic suggestion, if not fulfilment. They offered a spectacle of feverish energy lavished on a pursuit of supremacy which, when won, turned to ashes in their mouths.

Power-hunger was to be one of Shakespeare's great tragic themes. In the Histories he saw it swelling into a kind of madness, the delirium of a moribund class. In York's long soliloquy about his plans (*2H.VI* III.i. 331–83) he is trying to 'steel' himself against doubt or 'pale-faced fear'; he calls himself a 'madman', his frenzied struggle for power is 'this mad-bred flaw'. This is finally intensified into the nightmarish isolation of his son Richard III, nearing his end; and then translated by Shakespeare, in *Henry V*, into the unbalanced power-greed of a nation seeking conquest. By then the modern State is being built up: the man on the throne, Henry IV and his son, may be more secure, but they are cut off in a new way from their fellows. These two are not 'tragic', but loneliness was to be part of every tragic protagonist's nemesis.

In the plays before *Henry IV*, amid the convulsions of the dying feudal order, every now and then individuals are touched by the tragic Muse. Talbot is meant for one of these, and has moments of eloquence, but most of his rhyming rhetoric makes him sound less a man than a creaking iron war-machine, as the French see him (*1H.VI* I.iv.47 ff.). Henry VI is too pathetic, and too inactive, to be tragic; but even enemies are moved by York's tears over his youngest son, and his last hour and death are clearly designed as tragical (*3H.VI* I.iv). If they scarcely seem so to us, it is because he has done, and said, too little to enlist our sympathy. Warwick shows more authentic grandeur, though, like York, little inwardness. His last long speech – always an acid test of quality, like the last words that London crowds loved to hear from criminals on the scaffold – is good, if over-elaborate. It tells us that all is, in the end, 'earth and dust' (*3H.VI* V.ii.5 ff.).

Richard III is not allowed to address us like this. But having admired his blend of tigerish vitality and sardonic humour, we cannot watch his fall without some softening of our 'surly virtue'. His physical deformity and the embitterment it condemns him to has a share in this. Towards the close of *King John* both the king and the Bastard rise to a quite tragic intensity of speech. But there is no matching situation, only a king with a bad conscience dying of poison; and there is nothing to warrant his nephew's passionate regret for him. Instead there is a descent into absurdity when we are told that John, after his deathbed ravings, is singing like a dying swan (V.vii). With Richard II the tragic spirit flags. He is a hollow man, living on make-believe and self-pity, instead of – like Hamlet – learning self-criticism.

After him a new England is struggling into existence, one inoculated with humour and scepticism, especially as most of this comes from Falstaff. By now the salt of feudal values is losing its savour. What remains of it is left to Hotspur. From one point of view *Henry IV Part 1* is his tragedy, as *Julius Caesar* is that of Brutus. He resembles Macbeth in being a famous warrior of the north, a defender of his country until he is led astray, by others and by his own hasty temper, into treason. He is driven on not so much by ambition as by his anachronistic nature; he is a knight errant in quest of fame, in a commercializing world where there is not room for him outside his own natural habitat, the Borders. In the Histories Shakespeare is surveying a transition from anarchic feudalism to despotic but popular monarchy; it eliminates much evil, but also, as the necessary price, something grand, heroic, which he clearly admires and regrets.

Because Hotspur's qualities have outlived their time, they have grown morbid, excessive. When he talks of war as 'sport', and revels in the thought of Mars 'up to his ears in blood' (I.iii.299; IV.i.116–71), he sounds a mere killer (as Hal burlesques him), like Talbot. The laws of his own archaic mode of life doom him, he feels the hand of destiny on him. 'Whither I must, I must' (II.iii.107). As battle approaches, his cry of 'Doomsday is near' seems to mingle the shadow of a tragic fate with boiling excitement (IV.i.134). He rushes into the fray precipitately, betrayed or deserted by some of his allies, and perishes – a sacrifice to progress. His last words end, like Warwick's, with 'dust': all that he has stood for is fading into nullity. What is left is a symbolic reconciliation between the dead hero and his antagonist. Prince Hal has had to travel far into the past, as well as far from Eastcheap, to meet his foe; briefly, on the stricken field, they can share a common chivalry. Faithful to his mission of preserving and blending, Shakespeare rescues something of the reckless Hotspur by transferring it – not altogether convincingly – to the calculating Henry V.

In Part 2 there is nothing like this; no fighting, to strike the sparks of tragedy, only nervous hesitation on one side, deceit on the other. There are moments when King Henry speaks in tragic tones (e.g. III. i), but he is too busy a man, harassed and fretted, to feel tragical for long, and he dies in his bed, careworn but successful. Hotspur was the great loser, Henry V is the great winner, who promptly claps an extinguisher on that other nonconformist, Falstaff. It is time for a new start, but none is open to Shakespeare except a patriotically aggressive war abroad. He is true to history here, but morally the new start is as anachronistic as anything Hotspur could think of; it leads to nothing better than his pursuit of 'honour', or fame. We have gone round in a circle and got back to where we began with Talbot trying to conquer France; only Henry's rodomontade sometimes reaches a better standard.

There must have been in Shakespeare's make-up a fund of hopeful cheerfulness. It had his personal success, as writer and money-maker, if not in all other respects, to prop it; also an abiding interest in common humanity and sympathy with its flounderings, acquired earlier perhaps by life in a setting like Stratford rather than in London. His favourite image from nature was sunrise, as in the break of day before Bosworth (*R.III* V.iii.86–7), or Don Pedro's welcome to dawn after the nocturnal vigil in *Much Ado about Nothing* (V.iii). Yet Shakespeare has been called 'the great pessimist' (Clark xvi). His Comedies ·show copiously how foolish, and selfish, human beings can be; his Histories show how dreadful, and how dreadfully unfortunate, they can be. There is a strong infusion of barbarity in a comedy like the *Dream*, and even more of folly in a History like *Henry IV*. In the Comedies the deity invoked is Love, but from the first with no wholehearted faith in its *bona fides*; in the Histories, faith in monarchy is under varied strains.

Two opposite pictures of England flit through the Histories: an ideal one of what the country might be, a gloomy one of what it is. They come together in Gaunt's great speech. On the whole England is being weighed in the balance and found wanting. Henry V's predatory spring across the Channel could be no escape; Falstaff's wit could not give comedy a new lease of life, and it was no part of his vocation to set things right in a bad world, except by hastening its disintegration. Historical drama must take the road towards Tragedy; Comedy must move towards the 'problem play'.

Shakespeare was far from being alone in moving into a landscape under louring skies. As L.C. Knights says, 'a particular kind of melancholy' was settling on English literature about 1600, and its root cause lay in social conditions (315, 323); it was no mere *fin de siècle* pose. One of its accompaniments was the increasing stir that religion was making about the turn of the century. With the emotions it fomented, the sometimes agonizing self-examination it demanded, it encouraged moods, and concern with psychological states, that could help to prepare the soil for a new species of drama.

But feudings among rival believers were helping more than ever to foster doubts about religion, in the emancipated minds among which we can count Shakespeare's; and freedom from the crutches of faith, with its easy half-answers to all questions, was a necessary condition for the drama's further advance. Shakespeare might grope towards a tenuous notion of a 'Providence', but his continuing belief was in mankind, in spite of all its sins and imbecilities; a belief without which tragedy would have sunk into nihilism. Spain by contrast teemed with drama, but failed to reach genuine tragedy, because faith, guarded by the dragon of the Inquisition, could never be questioned, at least openly; and because, largely for the same reason, Spain was not moving towards revolution, but drifting into decay. In Shakespeare's world Constance's cry of 'Arm, arm, you heavens!' (*KJ* III.i.107) could be travestied by Pistol's bluster, after his cudgelling by Fluellen: 'All hell shall stir for this!' (*H.V* V.i.68)

Shakespeare was to attain his full tragic vision at a time when England was about to enter on the decades of approach to revolution. These led not to an explosion like that of 1789, swift and sudden, but to a protracted civil war between two minorities. The divided national consciousness revealed by this must have had common roots from much earlier with the flourishing of drama, which by its nature divides its stage-folk into factions. Thanks to this division, and because social and economic development was still very immature, the issues England faced in the 1640s were too heavily wrapped up in and disguised by the ghostly counsels of religion, and substitution of moral for social reform. Hence the conflict was destined to be more fertile of hopes and ideas than of tangible gains. Like the plots of Shakespeare's Comedies, the revolution stopped short and left half its questions hanging in the air.

All the same the 'Great Rebellion' helped to accelerate, and render in large part irreversible, changes in England that taken together deserve to be called revolutionary. In themselves the events of the civil wars may be seen, in one light, as symbolic, or allegorical, like the fall of the Bastille in 1789; or better, as scenes of a drama that gave a human contour to impersonal tides of change. It was a drama in which men fought with passion, but with little clear sense of what they were fighting about, like Matthew Arnold's 'ignorant armies clashing by night'. Perhaps a great extent of what may be called 'visible history', by contrast with the larger, subterranean part, has been of this 'dramatic' or symbolic order.

Bibliography

(This Bibliography includes only names of authors and works cited in the text.)

Adamson, J.S.A., 'The Baronial Context of the English Civil War', *Transactions of the Royal Historical Society*, 1990.

Armstrong, E.A., *Shakespeare's Imagination*, London 1946.

Auden, W.H., 'Introduction' to Signet Classic edn of *Sonnets*, New York and London 1964.

Baldwin, T.W., *The Organization and Personnel of the Shakespearian Company*, Princeton University Press 1927.

Baldwin, T.W., *William Shakespeare Adapts a Hanging*, Princeton University Press 1936.

Barber, C.L., *Shakespeare's Festive Comedy*, Princeton University Press 1959.

Beckerman, B., *Shakespeare at the Globe 1599–1609*, New York 1962.

Bentley, E.R., *The Profession of Dramatist in Shakespeare's Time 1590–1642*, Princeton University Press 1977.

Berry, E., 'The Histories', in Wells (ed.).

Bethell, S.L., *Shakespeare and the Popular Dramatic Tradition*, London 1944.

Boas, F.S., *Marlowe and his Circle*, Oxford 1929.

Boas, F.S., *Queen Elizabeth in Drama and Related Studies*, London 1950.

Booth, Stephen, *Shakespeare's Sonnets*, Yale University Press 1977.

Bradbrook, M.C., *The Growth and Structure of English Comedy*, London 1955.

Bradbrook. M.C., *The Rise of the Common Player*, London 1964.

Bradley, A.C., *Oxford Lectures on Poetry*, London 1909.

Bradshaw, G., *Shakespeare's Scepticism*, Brighton 1987.

Brower, R.A., '*Titus Andronicus*: Villainy and Tragedy', in Heilman (ed.).

Bryant, J.A., *Shakespeare and the Uses of Comedy*, Kentucky University Press 1986.

Burke, P., and R. Porter, eds, *The Social History of Language*, Cambridge 1987.

Burto, W., 'Preface' to Signet Classic edn of *Sonnets*, New York and London 1964.

Bush, D., *English Literature in the Earlier Seventeenth Century 1600–1660*, Oxford 1945.

Butler, M., *Theatre and Crisis 1632–1642*, Cambridge 1984.

Butler, S., *Shakespeare's Sonnets Reconsidered*, 1899; London 1927.

Byrne, M. St C., 'The Social Background', in Granville-Barker and Harrison (eds).

Calvert, H., *Shakespeare's Sonnets and Problems of Autobiography*, Braunton 1987.

Campbell, L.B., *Shakespeare's Histories*, University of California Press 1947.

Campbell, O.J., *A Shakespeare Encyclopaedia*, London 1966.

Castiglione, B., *The Book of the Courtier*, Everyman edn, London 1966.

Chambers, E.K., *The Elizabethan Stage*, 4 vols, Oxford 1923.

Chaplin, C., *My Autobiography*, London 1964.

Clark, K., *Civilisation*, London 1969.

Cohen, W., *Drama of a Nation: Public Theater in Renaissance England and Spain*, Cornell University Press 1985.

Coleridge, S.T., *Essays and Lectures on Shakespeare*, Everyman edn, London n.d.

Collinson, P., *The Religion of Protestants: The Church in English Society 1559–1625*, Oxford 1984.

Conrad, J., *Chance*, author's note, New York 1921.

Cook, A.J., *The Privileged Playgoers of Shakespeare's London, 1576–1642*, Princeton University Press 1981.

Coughlin, P., ed., *Spenser and Ireland*, Cork 1989.

Council, N., *When Honour's at the Stake: Ideas of Honour in Shakespeare's Plays*, London 1973.

Cruickshank, C.G., *Elizabeth's Army*, London 1946.

Daniell, D., 'Shakespeare and the Traditions of Comedy', in Wells (ed).

Dekker, T., *The Guls Hornbooks & The Belman of London*, 1608–9, ed. O. Smeaton, London 1904.

Dobrée, B., 'Shakespeare and the Drama of his Time', in Granville-Barker and Harrison (eds).

Dollimore, J., 'Introduction' to J. Dollimore and A. Sinfield, eds, *Political Shakespeare*, Manchester 1985.

Dryden, J., *Dramatic Essays*, Everyman edn, London n.d.

Ellis-Fermor, U., *The Frontiers of Drama*, 1945, 2nd edn, London, 1946.

Ellrodt, R., 'Shakespeare the Non-Dramatic Poet', in Wells (ed.).

Elton, W.R., 'Shakespeare and the Thought of his Age', in Wells (ed.).

Fiedler, L.A., *The Stranger in Shakespeare*, St Albans 1974.

Ford, B., ed., *The Age of Shakespeare*, Harmondsworth 1955.

French, M., *Shakespeare's Division of Experience*, London 1982.

Fripp, E.I., *Shakespeare Man and Artist*, Oxford 1938.

Frye, N., *Fools of Time: Studies in Shakespearian Tragedy*, Toronto 1967.

Frye, N., *On Shakespeare*, ed. R. Sandler, Yale University Press, 1986.

Fryer, P., *Mrs Grundy: Studies in English Prudery*, London 1965.

Goldstone, J.A., *Revolution and Rebellion in the Early Modern World*, University of California Press 1991.

Gosson, S., *The School of Abuse*, 1579; London 1841.

Granville-Barker, H., and G.B. Harrison, eds, *A Companion to Shakespeare Studies*, Cambridge 1934.

Gray, J.W., *Shakespeare's Marriage*, London 1905.

Gray, T., *Poems, Letters and Essays*, Everyman edn, London 1970.

Greg, W.W., *Henslowe's Diary*, London 1904.

Gurr, A., *The Shakespearean Stage 1574–1642*, Cambridge 1970.

Gurr, A., *Playgoing in Shakespeare's London*, Cambridge 1987.

Hale, J., 'War and Public Opinion in the Fifteenth and Sixteenth Centuries', *Past and Present*, no. 22, 1962.

Hall, Joseph, *Works*, vol. VIII, Oxford 1937.

Harbage, A., *Shakespeare's Audience*, Columbia University Press 1941.

Harbage, A.B., *Annals of English Drama, 975–1700*, rev. by S. Schoenbaum, London 1970; 3rd edn, ed. Sylvia S.Wagonheim, London 1989.

Harrison, G.B., ed., Penguin rev. edn of *Sonnets*, Harmondsworth 1949.

Hart, A., *Shakespeare and the Homilies*, Melbourne 1934.

Hawkins, H., *The Devil's Party: Critical Counter-Interpretations of Shakespearian Drama*, Oxford 1985.

Hazlitt, W., *Characters of Shakespeare's Plays*, 1817; Everyman edn, London 1906.

Hazlitt, W., *Lectures on the English Poets*, 1818; London 1924.

Heilman, R.B., ed., *Shakespeare: The Tragedies. New Perspectives*, Englewood Cliffs, N.J. 1984.

Heinemann, M., 'How Brecht read Shakespeare', in Dollimore and Sinfield (eds).

Heinemann, M., 'Political Drama', in *Cambridge Companion to English Renaissance Drama*, Cambridge 1990.

Heywood, T., *An Apology for Actors*, 1612; London 1841.

Hibbard, G.R., ed., *Three Elizabethan Pamphlets*, London 1951.

Hibbard, G.R., Penguin edn of *The Taming of the Shrew*, Harmondsworth 1968.

Hill, C., *Intellectual Origins of the English Revolution*, Oxford 1965, 1980.

Hill, C., *The World Turned Upside Down*, 1972; Harmondsworth 1975.

Holinshed, Raphael, *Holinshed's Chronicle as Used in Shakespeare's Plays*, ed. A. and J. Nicoll, London 1927 and 1969.

Holland, H.H., *Shakespeare, Oxford and Elizabethan Times*, London 1933.

Holt, J.C., 'The Ballads of Robin Hood', *Past and Present* no. 18, 1960.

Hughes, G., *Swearing: A Social History of Foul Language*, Oxford 1991.

Hutchinson, L., *Memoirs of the Life of Colonel Hutchinson*, Everyman edn, London 1908.

Israel, J.I., *Dutch Primacy in World Trade 1585–1740*, Oxford 1989.

James, M., 'English Politics and the Concept of Honour 1485–1642', *Past and Present*, Supplement no. 3, 1978.

Jonson, B., *Timber: or, Discoveries*, 1641, in *Works*, ed. C.H. Herford *et al.*, vol. 8 Oxford 1947.

Kelly, J.T., *Thorns on the Tudor Rose*, Mississippi University Press 1977.

Kelly, M., *Village Theatre*, London 1939.

Kettle, A., 'Introduction' to A. Kettle, ed., *Shakespeare in a Changing World*, London 1964.

Kiernan, V.G., 'Human Relationships in Shakespeare', in Kettle (ed.).

Kiernan, V.G., *The Duel in European History: Honour and the Reign of Aristocracy*, Oxford 1988.

Kiernan, V.G., 'Why was Early Modern Europe Always at War?', in S.T. Christensen, ed., *Violence and the Absolutist State*, Copenhagen 1990.

Kinghorn, A.M., *Medieval Drama*, London 1968.

Knight, G.W., *The Imperial Theme*, Oxford 1931.

Knight, G.W., *This Sceptred Isle: Shakespeare's Message for England at War*, Oxford 1940.

Knight, G.W., *The Crown of Life*, 2nd edn, London 1948.

Knight, G.W., *The Sovereign Flower: Shakespeare as the Poet of Royalism*, London 1958.

Knights, L.C., *Drama and Society in the Age of Jonson*, London 1937.

Krieger, E., *A Marxist Study of Shakespeare's Comedies*, London 1979.

Lamb, C., *Works*, ed. P. Fitzgerald, vol. IV, London 1876.

Landes, D., *Revolution in Time: Clocks and the Making of the Modern World*, Harvard University Press 1983.

Langsam, G.G., *Martial Books and Tudor Verse*, New York 1951.

Lee, S., *Stratford-on-Avon*, London 1890.

Lee, S., *A Life of William Shakespeare*, 4th edn, London 1925.

Leggatt, A., *Shakespeare's Political Drama*, London 1988.

Levi, P., *The Life and Times of William Shakespeare*, London 1988.

Levin, R., *New Readings vs Old Plays: Recent Trends in the Reinterpretation of English Renaissance Drama*, Chicago University Press 1979.

Levin, R., *Love and Society in Shakespearian Comedy*, Delaware University Press 1985.

Lifshitz, I.M., in *Literature and Marxism: A Controversy by Soviet Critics*, New York 1938.

Lindenberger, H., *Historical Drama: The Relation of Literature and Reality*, Chicago University Press 1985.

Lockhart, J.G., *Life of Sir Walter Scott*, Edinburgh 1936–39.

Lukács, G., *Studies in European Realism*, London 1950.

Lukács, G., *The Historical Novel*, London 1962.

Luther, M., *Table Talk*, London 1857.

McVeagh, J., *Tradefull Merchants: The Portrayal of the Capitalist in Literature*, London 1981.

Markham, G., *The Muster-Master*, ed. C.L. Hamilton, *Camden Miscellany*, 4th series, vol. xxvi, London 1975.

Marshall, F.A., ed., *The Henry Irving Shakespeare*, vol. 2, Toronto and London, 1888.

Maugham, W.S., *A Writer's Notebook*, Harmondsworth 1949.

Melchiori, G., *Shakespeare's Dramatic Meditations: An Experiment in Criticism*, Oxford 1976.

More, Sir T., *The History of Richard III, c.* 1513.

Morgann, M., *Essay on the Dramatic Character of Sir John Falstaff*, 1777.

Morozov, M., 'On the Dynamism of Shakespeare's Characters', in Samarin and Nikolyukin (eds).

Morris, C., *Political Thought in England: Tyndale to Hooker*, London 1953.

Muir, K., 'Shakespeare and Politics', in Kettle (ed.).

Muir, K., 'Changing Interpretations of Shakespeare', in Ford (ed.).

Muir, K., 'Shakespeare the Man', in *A Garland for Shakespeare*, Jalpaiguri 1964.

Muir, K., *The Singularity of Shakespeare*, Liverpool 1977.

Muir, K., and S. O'Loughlin, *The Voyage to Illyria: A Study of Shakespeare*, London 1937.

Murry, J.M., *Shakespeare*, London 1936.

Nashe, T., 'Pierce Penilesse His Supplication to the Devil', 1603, in Hibbard.

Obelkevich, J., 'Proverbs and Social History', in Burke and Porter (eds).

Palmer, J., *Political Characters of Shakespeare*, London 1957.

Perkins, W., *The Whole Treatise of the Questions of Conscience*, 1636.

Phillips, J.E., *The State in Shakespeare's Greek and Roman Plays*, New York 1940.

Prince, E.T., ed., *The Poems*, in The Arden Shakespeare, London 1960, 1969.

Prior, M.E., *The Language of Tragedy*, New York 1947.

Rabkin, N., *Shakespeare and the Problem of Meaning*, Chicago University Press 1981.

Raleigh, W., *Shakespeare*, London 1907.

Rennert, H.A., *The Spanish Drama in the Time of Lope de Vega*, New York 1909.

Ribner, I., *The English History Play in the Age of Shakespeare*, Princeton University Press 1957.

Ronsley, J., *Yeats's Autobiography*, Harvard University Press 1968.

Rossiter, A.P., *English Drama from Early Times to the Elizabethans*, London 1950.

Rowse, A.L., *Shakespeare's Sonnets*, 1964; 3rd edn, London 1984.

Rowse, A.L., *The Elizabethan Renaissance: The Life of the Society*, 1971; London 1974.

Ruskin, J., *Sesame and Lilies*, 1865; Orpington 1889.

Rutherford, Mark, (W.H. White), *More Pages from a Journal*, London n.d.

Rylands, G., 'Shakespeare the Poet', in Granville-Barker and Harrison (eds)

Saccio, P., *Shakespeare's English Kings*, Oxford 1977.

Saintsbury, G., 'Life and Plays', and 'Poems', in *Cambridge History of English Literature*, vol. 5, Part 1, Cambridge 1943.

Salingar, L., *Shakespeare and the Traditions of Comedy*, Cambridge 1974.

Salingar, L., *Dramatic Form in Shakespeare and the Jacobeans*, Cambridge 1986.

Samarin, R., and A. Nikolyukin, eds, *Shakespeare in the Soviet Union*, Moscow 1966.

Sams, E., ed., *Shakespeare's Edmund Ironside: The Lost Play*, Aldershot 1986.

Schoenbaum, S., 'The Life of Shakespeare', in Wells (ed.).

Schopenhauer, A., *Selected Essays*, ed. E.B. Bax, London 1888.

Schücking, L.L., *Character Problems in Shakespeare's Plays*, New York 1922.

Scott, W., *The Monastery*, Edinburgh 1820.

Scott, W., *Anne of Geierstein*, Edinburgh 1829.

Scott, W., *Journal, 1825–32*, Edinburgh 1890.

Shaw, G.B., *Shaw on Shakespeare*, ed. E. Wilson, Harmondsworth 1961.

Sheavyn, Phoebe, *The Literary Profession in the Elizabethan Age*, Manchester 1909.

Sidney, Sir P., *Selected Writings*, ed. R. Dutton, Manchester 1987.

Sinsheimer, H., *Shylock*, London 1947.

Smallwood, R.L., 'Shakespeare's Use of History', in Wells (ed.).

Smirnov, A.A., *Shakespeare: A Marxist Interpretation*, 1934; English edn, New York 1936.

Smith, D.N., *Shakespeare Criticism: A Selection*, Oxford 1916.

Spurgeon, C., *Shakespeare's Imagery*, Cambridge 1935.

Stafford-Clark, D., *Psychiatry To-day*, 2nd edn, Harmondsworth 1963.

Stevens, J., BBC programme, 22 November 1964.

Stevenson, L.C., *Praise and Paradox: Merchants and Craftsmen in Elizabethan Popular Literature*, Cambridge 1984.

Stone, L., 'The Educational Revolution in England, 1560–1640', *Past and Present* no. 28, 1964.

Stribrny, Z., 'Henry V and History', in Kettle (ed.).

Swinburne, A.C., *A Study of Shakespeare* 1874–76; London 1918.

Tawney, R.H., *Social History and Literature*, London 1949.

Thackeray, W.M., *The Memoirs of Barry Lyndon, Esq.*, London 1844.

Thomas, K., *Religion and the Decline of Magic*, London 1971.

Tillyard, E.M.W., *The Elizabethan World Picture*, London 1943.

Tillyard, E.M.W., *Shakespeare's Historical Plays*, London 1944.

Trevor-Roper, H., *The Gentry, 1540–1640*, London 1953.

Trollope, Anthony, *Thackeray*, London 1879.

Tucker, T.G., ed., *The Sonnets of Shakespeare*, Cambridge 1924.

Turgenev, I.S., *Literary Reminiscences*, London 1959.

Underdown, D., *Revel, Riot, and Rebellion … England 1603–1660*, Oxford 1985.

Valbuena Prat, A., *La vida española en la Edad de Oro*, Barcelona 1943.

Van Doren, M., *Shakespeare*, London 1941.

Waddell, H., *The Wandering Scholars*, 7th edn, London 1934.

Wait, R.J.C., *The Background to Shakespeare's Sonnets*, London 1972.

Warner, M., *Joan of Arc*, London 1981.

Weimann, R., 'The Soul of the Age: Towards a Historical Approach to Shakespeare', in Kettle (ed.).

Weimann, R., *Structure and Society in Literary History*, London 1977.

Wells, S., ed., *The Cambridge Companion to Shakespeare Studies*, Cambridge 1986.

Whitman, W., 'What Lurks Behind Shakespeare's Historical Plays', in *Democratic Vistas*, 1871; Everyman edn, London 1939.

Willcock, J., *The Life of Sir Henry Vane the Younger*, London 1913.

Willey, B., *The Seventeenth Century Background*, London 1934.

Wilson, J.D., *The Essential Shakespeare*, Cambridge 1942.

Wilson, J.D., *Life in Shakespeare's England* (anthology), Harmondsworth 1944.

Wilson, J.D., ed., *Shakespeare's Sonnets*, Cambridge 1963.

Winstanley, L., *'Othello' as the Tragedy of Italy*, London 1924.

Wright, L.B., *Middle Class Culture in Elizabethan England*, London 1935.

Wright, L.B., and V.A. LaMar, Folger edn of *Titus Andronicus*, New York 1967.

Index